Butterworths Professional Dictionary Series

DICTIONARY OF
COMPANY LAW

Second Edition

by

E. R. HARDY IVAMY, LL.B., Ph.D., LL.D.

of the Middle Temple, Barrister
Professor of Law in the University of London

LONDON

BUTTERWORTHS

1985

United Kingdom	Butterworth & Co (Publishers) Ltd, 88 Kingsway, LONDON WC2B 6AB and 61A North Castle Street, EDINBURGH EH2 3LJ
Australia	Butterworths Pty Ltd, SYDNEY, MELBOURNE, BRISBANE, ADELAIDE, PERTH, CANBERRA and HOBART
Canada	Butterworth & Co (Canada) Ltd, TORONTO and VANCOUVER
New Zealand	Butterworths of New Zealand Ltd, WELLINGTON and AUCKLAND
Singapore	Butterworth & Co (Asia) Pte Ltd, SINGAPORE
South Africa	Butterworth Publishers (Pty) Ltd, DURBAN and PRETORIA
USA	Butterworth Legal Publishers, ST PAUL, Minnesota, SEATTLE, Washington, BOSTON, Massachusetts, AUSTIN, Texas and D & S Publishers, CLEARWATER, Florida

First Edition 1983
Second Edition 1985

© Butterworth & Co (Publishers) Ltd 1985

British Library Cataloguing in Publication Data

Ivamy, E. R. Hardy
    Dictionary of company law.—2nd ed.
    1. Corporation law—Great Britain
    I. Title
    344.106´66   KD2079

    ISBN Hardcover 0 406 68163 5
    ISBN Softcover 0 406 68164 3

Typeset by Cotswold Typesetting Ltd, Gloucester
Printed by Billings Bookplan, Worcester

Preface

The need for this new edition has been brought about by the consolidation of the Companies Acts by the Companies Act 1985, the Companies Securities (Insider Dealing) Act 1985 and the Business Names Act 1985.

Not only have the section numbers in the earlier Acts been almost entirely altered by the Companies Act 1985 but the wording of so many sections also has been modernised and rephrased.

In addition, Table A and the other Tables are no longer in the Companies Act 1985 itself but are set out in the Companies (Tables A to F) Regulations 1985.

All these changes have been incorporated in the new edition.

University College, London
August 1985   E R HARDY IVAMY

A

'A' list. A list of the present members of the company made out by the liquidator in the course of winding up. (*See* CONTRIBUTORY; LIQUIDATOR).

Allotment of shares. The appropriation to a person of a certain number of shares. There is no binding contract until the allotment has been made by a resolution of the board of directors and notice of allotment has been posted or reached the alottee in some other way: *Dunlop v Higgins* (1849) 1 HL Cas 381; *Household Fire Insurance Co v Grant* (1879) 4 Ex D 216. Allotment remains merely a contract until the allottee's name is registered in the register of members, and he thus becomes a member of the company: *Re Florence Land and Public Works Co, Nicol's Case, Tufnell and Ponsonby's Case* (1885) 29 ChD 421.

Allotment before 'minimum subscription' reached

No allotment must be made of any share capital of a company offered to the public for subscription unless the amount stated in the prospectus as the 'minimum subscription' has been subscribed, and the sum payable on application for the amount so stated has been paid to and received by the company: Companies Act 1985, s. 83 (1). (*See* PROSPECTUS: MINIMUM SUBSCRIPTION). This provision, however, does not apply to any allotment of shares subsequent to the first allotment of shares offered to the public for subscription: ibid., s. 83 (7).

If the minimum subscription has not been subscribed on the expiration of 40 days after the first issue of the prospectus, all money received from applicants for shares must be forthwith repaid to them without interest: ibid., s. 83 (4). If any such money is not repaid within 48 days after the issue of the prospectus, the directors are jointly and severally liable to repay the money with interest at the rate of 5 per cent per annum from the expiration of the 48th day: ibid., s 83 (5). But a director is not liable if he proves that the default in the repayment of the money was not due to any misconduct or negligence on his part: ibid., s. 83 (5).

Any condition requiring or binding an applicant for shares to waive compliance with any of the above provisions is void: ibid., s. 83 (6).

An allotment made by a company to an applicant in contravention of the above provisions is voidable at his instance within 1 month after the date of the allotment, and not later, notwithstanding that the company is in the course of being wound up: ibid., s. 85 (1).

1

If a director of a company knowingly contravenes, or permits or authorises the contravention of any of the above provisions with respect to allotment, he is liable to compensate the company and the allottee respectively for any loss, damages or costs which the company or the allottee may have sustained or incurred: ibid., s. 85 (2). But proceedings to recover any such loss, damages or costs must not be commenced after the expiration of 2 years from the date of the allotment: ibid. s. 85 (3).

Allotment before third day after issue of prospectus

No allotment must be made of any shares of a company in pursuance of a prospectus issued generally until the beginning of the 3rd day after that on which the prospectus is first so issued or such later time (if any) as may be specified in the prospectus: ibid., s. 82 (1). The beginning of the 3rd day or such later time is 'the time of the opening of the subscription lists': ibid., s. 82 (2).

The validity of an allotment is not affected by any contravention of the above provision: ibid., s. 82 (5). But the company and every officer of the company who is in default is liable on conviction on indictment to a fine, and on summary conviction to a fine not exceeding the statutory maximum: ibid., s. 82 (5).

Allotment of shares to be dealt in on stock exchange

Where a prospectus whether issued generally or not states that application has been or will be made for permission for the shares offered by it to be listed on any stock exchange, an allotment made on an application in pursuance of the prospectus is void if

(a) the permission has not been applied for before the 3rd day after the first issue of the prospectus; or

(b) if the permission has been refused before the expiration of 3 weeks from the date of the closing of the subscription lists or such longer period not exceeding 6 weeks as may, within the 3 weeks, be notified to the applicant for permission by or on behalf of the stock exchange: ibid., s. 86 (2).

Where the permission has not been applied for or has been refused, the company must forthwith repay without interest all money received from applicants in pursuance of the prospectus: ibid., s. 86 (4). If any money is not repaid within 8 days after the company becomes liable to repay it, the directors of the company are jointly and severally liable to repay the money with interest at the rate of 5 per cent per annum from the expiration of the 8th day: ibid., s. 86 (5). But a director is not liable if he proves that the default in the repayment of the money was not due to any misconduct or negligence on his part: ibid., s. 86 (5).

All money received must be kept in a separate bank account so long as the company may become liable to repay it: ibid., s. 86 (6). If default

2

is made in complying with this provision, the company and every officer in default is liable on conviction on indictment to a fine, and on summary conviction to a fine not exceeding the statutory maximum: ibid., ss. 86 (6), 730 and Sch. 24.

Any condition requiring or binding an applicant for shares to waive compliance with any of the above requirements is void: ibid., s 86 (7).

Permission is not deemed to be refused if it is intimated that the application for it, though not at present granted, will be given further consideration: ibid., s. 86 (8).

Allotment where issue not fully subscribed

No allotment must be made of any share capital of a public company offered for subscription unless

(a) that capital is subscribed for in full; or

(b) the offer states that, even if the capital is not subscribed for in full, the amount of that capital subscribed for may be allotted in any event or in the event of the conditions specified in the offer being satisfied: ibid., s. 84 (1).

Where conditions are specified, no allotment of the capital must be made unless those conditions are satisfied: ibid., s. 84 (1).

Allotment by private limited company

A private limited company (other than a company limited by guarantee and not having a share capital) is guilty of an offence if it allots or agrees to allot (whether for cash or otherwise) any shares in the company with a view to all or any of those shares being offered for sale to the public: ibid., s. 81 (1). A company guilty of an offence under this provision and any officer who is in default are liable on conviction on indictment to a fine, and on summary conviction to a fine not exceeding the statutory maximum: ibid., ss. 81 (2), 730 and Sch. 24.

Nothing in the above provisions affects the validity of any allotment or of any agreement to allot shares: ibid., s. 81 (3).

Authority of company required for allotment of certain securities

The directors of a company must not exercise any power of the company to allot certain securities unless they are authorised to do so by

(a) the company in general meeting; or

(b) the articles of the company: ibid., s. 80 (1).

Authority may be given for a particular exercise of the power or for its exercise generally, and may be unconditional or subject to conditions: ibid., s. 80 (3).

Any such authority must state the maximum amount of the securities which may be allotted and the date on which the authority will expire: ibid., s. 80 (4). This date must not be more than 5 years from whichever is relevant of the following dates:

3

(a) in the case of an authority contained in the company's articles at the time of its original incorporation, the date of that incorporation; and

(b) in any other case, the date on which the resolution is passed by virtue of which the authority is given: ibid., s. 80 (4).

Any such authority may be previously revoked or varied by the company in general meeting: ibid., s. 80 (4). The authority may be renewed by the company in general meeting for a further period not exceeding 5 years: ibid., s. 80 (4). A resolution of a company to give, vary, revoke or renew such authority may, notwithstanding that it alters the articles of the company, be an ordinary resolution: ibid., s. 80 (8). (*See* ORDINARY RESOLUTION).

Any director who knowingly and wilfully contravenes or permits or authorises a contravention of the above provisions is liable on conviction on indictment to a fine and on summary conviction to a fine not exceeding the statutory maximum: Companies Act 1985, ss. 80 (9), 730 and Sch. 24.

Nothing in the above provisions affects the validity of any allotment: ibid., s. 80 (10).

The securities concerned are:

(a) shares in the company other than shares shown in the memorandum to have been taken by the subscribers to it or shares allotted in pursuance of an employees' share scheme; and

(b) any right to subscribe for, or to convert any security into, shares in the company other than shares so allotted: ibid., s. 80 (2).

Pre-emption rights

Certain restrictions are imposed on the allotment of shares with regard to pre-emption rights: ibid., ss. 89, 90, 91.

Subscription of share capital

Shares allotted by any company and any premium on them may be paid up in money or money's worth (including goodwill and know-how): ibid., s. 99 (1). A public company must not accept at any time, in payment up of its shares or any premium on them, an undertaking given by any person that he or another should do work or perform services for the company or any other person: ibid., s. 99(2).

Prohibition of allotment of shares at a discount

The shares of a company must not be allotted at a discount: ibid., s. 100(1).

Payment for allotted shares

A public company must not allot a share except as paid up at least as to one-quarter of its nominal value and the whole of any premium on it: ibid., s. 101 (1). But this provision does not apply to shares allotted in pursuance of an employees' share scheme: ibid., s. 101 (2). (*See* EMPLOYEES' SHARE SCHEME).

4

Payment for non-cash consideration
A public company must not allot shares as fully or partly paid otherwise than in cash if the consideration for the allotment is or includes an undertaking which is to be, or may be, performed more than 5 years after the date of the allotment: Companies Act 1985, s. 102 (1).

Experts' reports on non-cash consideration
A public company must not allot shares as fully or partly paid otherwise than in cash unless
(a) the consideration for the allotment has been independently valued;
(b) a report with respect to its value has been made to the company by an independent expert appointed by the company during the 6 months immediately preceding the allotment of the shares; and
(c) a copy of the report has been sent to the proposed allottee: ibid., s. 103 (1).

Any person carrying out a valuation or making a report, with respect to any consideration proposed to be accepted or given by a company, is entitled to require from its officers such information and explanation as he thinks necessary to enable him to carry out the valuation or make the report: ibid., s. 110 (1).

Experts' reports on non-cash assets acquired from subscribers
In the case of a public company experts' reports are required where the company enters into an agreement with a subscriber to the memorandum of association for the transfer by him to it, during the period of 2 years from the date on which the company is issued with a certificate entitling it to do business (*see* CERTIFICATE AS TO POWER TO DO BUSINESS); of one or more non-cash assets: ibid., s. 104 (1).

Allotments, return as to. *See* RETURN AS TO ALLOTMENTS.

Allottee. A person to whom shares or debentures are allotted. (*See* ALLOTMENT).

'All round reduction'. *See* REDUCTION OF CAPITAL.

Annual general meeting. A meeting of the members of the company held once a year. Every company must in each year hold a general meeting as its annual general meeting in addition to any other meetings in that year and must specify the meeting as such in the notices calling it: Companies Act 1985, s. 366 (1). Not more than 15 months must elapse between the date of one annual general meeting of a company and that of the next: ibid., s. 366 (3). But so long as a company holds its first annual general meeting within 18 months of its incorporation, it need not hold it in the year of its incorporation or in the following year: ibid., s. 366 (2).

If default is made in holding an annual general meeting, the Secretary of State may, on the application of any member of the company, call, or direct the calling of, a general meeting of the company and give such ancillary or consequential directions as he thinks expedient including directions modifying or supplementing, in relation to the calling, holding and conduct of the meeting, the operation of the company's articles: ibid., s. 367 (1). The directions that may be given include a direction that 1 member of the company present in person or by proxy shall be deemed to constitute a meeting: ibid., s. 367 (2). A general meeting so held, subject to any directions of the Secretary of State, is deemed to be an annual general meeting of the company: ibid., s. 367 (4). But, where a meeting so held is not held in the year in which the default in holding the company's annual general meeting occurred, the meeting so held must not be treated as the annual general meeting for the year in which it is held unless at that meeting the company resolves that it be so treated: ibid., s. 367 (4). Where a company so resolves, a copy of the resolution must, within 15 days after its passing, be forwarded to the Registrar of Companies and recorded by him: ibid., s. 367 (5). (*See* LENGTH OF NOTICE FOR CALLING MEETING; MINUTES).

Annual return. A return to be made by the company every year giving various details relating to e.g. its registered office, registers of members and debenture holders, shares, directors and secretary.

Extent of company's duty

The extent of the company's duty to make the return depends on whether the company has or has not a share capital.

(a) COMPANY HAVING A SHARE CAPITAL: Every company having a share capital must, at least once in every year, make a return containing with respect to the company's registered office, registers of members and debenture holders, shares and debentures, indebtedness, past and present members and directors and secretary, the matters specified in Sch. 15: Companies Act 1985, s. 363 (1).

The annual return must be in the prescribed form: ibid., s. 363 (2).

A company need not make a return either in the year of its incorporation or, if it is not required by the Act to hold an annual general meeting during the following year, in that year: ibid., s. 363 (3). (*See* ANNUAL GENERAL MEETING).

If a company fails to comply with the above provisions, the company and every officer of it is liable, on summary conviction, to a fine not exceeding the statutory maximum, and, for continued contravention, to a daily default fine not exceeding one-tenth of the statutory maximum: Companies Act 1985, ss 363 (7), 730 and Sch. 24.

(b) COMPANY NOT HAVING A SHARE CAPITAL: Every company not having a share capital must once at least in every calendar year make a return in the prescribed form stating:

(a) the address of the company's registered office;

(b) if the register of members is kept elsewhere than at that office, the address of the place where it is kept;

(c) if any register of holders of debentures of the company is kept elsewhere than at the company's registered office, the address of the place where it is kept; and

(d) all such particulars with respect to the persons who at the date of the return are the directors of the company, and any person who at that date is its secretary, as are by the Act required to be contained in the company's register of directors and secretaries: ibid., s. 364 (1). (*See* REGISTER OF DIRECTORS AND SECRETARY).

A company need not make a return either in the year of its incorporation or, if it is not required by the Act to hold an annual general meeting during the following year, in that year: Companies Act 1985, s. 364 (2). (*See* ANNUAL GENERAL MEETING).

There must be included in the return a statement containing particulars of the total amount of the company's indebtedness in respect of all mortgages and charges (whenever created) of any description specified in s. 396 (1); Companies Act 1985, s. 364 (3). (*See* REGISTRATION OF CHARGES).

If a company fails to comply with the above provisions, the company and every officer of it who is in default is liable to a fine not exceeding the statutory maximum, and for continued contravention, to a daily default fine not exceeding one-tenth of the statutory maximum: Companies Act 1985, ss. 364 (4), 730 and Sch. 25.

Time for completion of return

A company's annual return must be completed within 42 days after the annual general meeting for the year, whether or not that meeting is the first or only ordinary general meeting, or the first or only general general meeting of the company in that year: ibid., s. 365 (1).

The company must forthwith forward to the Registrar of Companies a copy of the return signed both by a director and by the secretary of the company: ibid., s. 365 (2).

If a company fails to comply with the above provisions, the company and every officer of it who is in default is liable to a fine not exceeding the statutory maximum and, for continued contravention, to a daily default fine not exceeding one-tenth of the statutory maximum: ibid., s. 365 (3).

Application for shares. A request by a person to a company that shares be allotted to him. (*See* ALLOTMENT OF SHARES).

In general, an application for shares may be revoked at any time.

But an application for shares in a company which is made in pursuance of a prospectus issued generally is not revocable until after the third day after the time of the opening of the subscription lists, or the giving before the expiration of the third day, by some person responsible under the Companies Act 1985, ss. 67 to 69 for the prospectus, of a public notice having effect under that section of excluding or limiting the responsibility of the person giving it:

Companies Act 1985, s. 82 (7). (*See* PROSPECTUS; TIME OF OPENING OF THE SUBSCRIPTION LISTS).

A conditional application for shares may be made: *Re Universal Banking Co, Rogers' Case, Harrison's Case* (1868) 3 Ch App 633.

If there is undue delay in allotment, the application will lapse: *Ramsgate Victoria Hotel Co v Montefiore* (1866) LR 1 Exch 109.

Application of partnership property. The rights of partners and creditors concerning the partnership property in the event of a dissolution of the partnership. (*See* DISSOLUTION OF PARTNERSHIP; PARTNERSHIP PROPERTY).

On the dissolution of a partnership every partner is entitled, as against the other partners in the firm, and all persons claiming through them in respect of their interests as partners, to have the property of the partnership applied in payment of the debts and liabilities of the firm, and to have the surplus assets after such payment applied in payment of what may be due to the partners respectively after deducting what may be due from them as partners to the firm: Partnership Act 1890, s. 39. For that purpose any partner or his representatives may on the termination of the partnership apply to the court to wind up the business and affairs of the firm: ibid., s. 39.

In settling accounts between the partners after a dissolution of partnership, the following rules must, subject to any agreement, be observed:

(a) losses, including losses and deficiencies of capital, must be paid first out of profits, next out of capital, and lastly, if necessary, by the partners individually in the proportion in which they were entitled to share profits;

(b) the assets of the firm, including the sums, if any, contributed by the partners to make up losses or deficiencies of capital, must be applied in the following manner and order:

(1) in paying the debts and liabilities of the firm to persons who are not partners in it:

(2) in paying to each partner rateably what is due from the firm to him for advances as distinguished from capital:

(3) in paying to each partner rateably what is due from the firm to him in respect of capital:

(4) the ultimate residue, if any, must be divided among the partners in the proportions in which profits are divisible: ibid., s. 44.

Appropriate rate, in relation to interest, means 5 per cent per annum or such other rate as may be specified by order made by the Secretary of State by statutory instrument: Companies Act 1985, s. 107.

Articles. *See* ARTICLES OF ASSOCIATION.

Articles of association. The internal regulations of the company.

(a) Form and contents
A company limited by shares may register, with the memorandum, articles of association signed by the subscribers to the memorandum and prescribing regulations for the company: Companies Act 1985, s. 7 (1). Articles of association may adopt all or any of the regulations contained in Table A: ibid. s. 8 (1). If articles are not registered, or, if articles are registered, in so far as they do not exclude or modify the regulations contained in Table A, that Table (so far as applicable) constitutes the company's articles, in the same manner and to the same extent as if articles in the form of that Table had been duly registered: ibid., s. 8 (2).

A company limited by guarantee and an unlimited company must register articles: ibid., s. 7 (1).

A company limited by guarantee and not having a share capital must have articles in the form of Table C or as near to that form as circumstances admit: ibid., s. 8 (4).

A company limited by guarantee and having a share capital must have articles in the form of Table D or as near to that form as circumstances admit: ibid., s. 8 (4).

An unlimited company having a share capital must have articles in the form of Table E or as near to that form as circumstances admit: ibid., s. 8 (4).

In the case of an unlimited company having a share capital, the articles must state the amount of share capital with which the company proposes to be registered: ibid., s. 7 (2).

Articles must be printed, divided into paragraphs numbered consecutively, and signed by each subscriber of the memorandum in the presence of at least one witness who must attest the signature: ibid., s. 7 (3).

Any article, which is the same in substance as any article in Table A, cannot be void on the ground of illegality: *Lock v Queensland Investment & Land Mortgage Co* [1896] AC 461.

In the case of a company limited by guarantee and not having a share capital every provision in the articles purporting to give any person a right to participate in the divisible profits of the company otherwise than as a member is void: Companies Act 1985, s. 15 (1).

(b) Inspection and copies
Any person may inspect a copy of the articles kept by the Registrar of Companies on payment of the prescribed fee: ibid., s. 709 (1) (a).

A company must, on being so required by any member, send him a copy of the articles subject to the payment of 5p or such less sum as the company may prescribe: ibid., s. 19 (1). If a company makes default in complying with this provision, the company and every officer of the company who is in default is liable for each offence, on summary conviction, to a fine not exceeding one-fifth of the statutory maximum: ibid., s. 19 (2).

(c) *Construction of the articles*

The articles are subject to the memorandum, and cannot give powers which are not given by the memorandum. But for the purposes of construction, on matters which need not necessarily be put in the memorandum, the memorandum and the articles are to be read together, and the articles may then explain or amplify the memorandum: *Re Wedgwood Coal & Iron Co, Anderson's Case* (1877) 7 Ch D 75; *Guinness v Land Corporation of Ireland* (1882) 22 Ch D 349. The articles should be regarded as a business document and should be so construed as to give them reasonable business efficacy, where a construction tending to that result is admissible on the language of the article, in preference to a result which would or might prove unworkable: *Holmes v Lord Keyes* [1958] 2 All ER 129 at 138, CA (per Jenkins LJ).

But the articles form a contract between the company and the members only in respect of their ordinary rights as members and not in that of any other capacity, e.g. that of a director (who happens also to be a shareholder): *Beattie v E. & F. Beattie Ltd* [1938] 3 All ER 214, CA.

(d) *Effect of the articles*

(i) THE COMPANY AND THE MEMBERS: When registered, the articles bind the company and the members to the same extent as if they respectively had been signed and sealed by each member, and contained covenants on the part of each member to observe all the provisions of the articles: Companies Act 1985, s. 14 (1). Money payable by a member to the company under the articles is a debt due from him to the company, and is of the nature of a specialty debt: ibid., s. 14 (2).

(ii) THE MEMBERS INTER SE: Each member is bound to the other members: *Borland's Trustee v Steel Brothers & Co Ltd* [1901] 1 Ch 279; *Rayfield v Hands* [1958] 2 All ER 194.

(iii) THE COMPANY AND THIRD PARTIES: Generally the articles do not bind the company to a third party: *Eley v Positive Government Security Life Assurance Co* (1876) 1 Ex D 88. But the company may be liable to the third party on an implied contract in the terms of the articles: *Re New British Iron Co, ex parte Beckwith* [1898] 1 Ch 324 at 326 (per Wright J).

(e) *Alteration of the articles*

Subject to the provisions of the Companies Act 1985 and to the conditions contained in its memorandum, a company may by special resolution alter its articles: Companies Act 1985, s. 9 (1). (*See* SPECIAL RESOLUTION). Any alteration so made in the articles is as valid as if originally contained in them and is subject in like manner to alteration by special resolution: ibid., s. 9 (2).

A company cannot deprive itself of its powers to alter its articles: *Andrews v Gas Meter Co* [1897] 1 Ch 361. But a provision in an article relating to voting rights which has the effect of making a special resolution incapable of being passed if a particular shareholder or group of shareholders exercises their voting rights against a proposed alteration is valid: *Bushell v Faith* [1969] 1 All ER 1002 at 1006, CA (per Russell LJ). An article providing that no alteration shall be made without the consent of a specified person is contrary to the Companies Act 1985, s. 9 (supra) and is ineffective, but a provision as to voting rights is wholly different, and it is immaterial that it can have the same result: ibid., at 1006 (per Russell LJ). An article providing that on a proposed alteration of the articles only the shares of those opposed to the alteration should have a vote would breach s. 9 because it would mean that the articles could never be altered: ibid., at 1006 (per Russell LJ).

The company cannot by altering its articles justify a breach of contract with third parties: *British Equitable Assurance Co Ltd v Baily* [1906] AC 35, HL. In such a case the company cannot be prevented from altering its articles, although this may give rise to a claim by the other party to damages for breach of contract: *Punt v Symons & Co Ltd* [1903] 2 Ch 506; *Southern Foundries (1926) Ltd v Shirlaw* [1940] 2 All ER 445, HL.

A resolution passed by the requisite majority of shareholders will bind the minority provided that it is passed *bona fide* for the benefit of the company as a whole: *Brown v British Abrasive Wheel Co* [1919] 1 Ch 290; *Rights and Issues Investment Trust Ltd v Stylo Shoes Ltd* [1964] 3 All ER 628. The expression '*bona fide* for the benefit of the company as a whole' means that 'the shareholder must proceed on what, in his honest opinion, is for the benefit of the company as a whole': *Greenhalgh v Arderne Cinemas Ltd* [1950] 2 All ER 1120 at 1126 (per Evershed MR). The term 'as a whole' means the corporators as a general body; they are entitled to consider their personal financial interests: ibid., at 1126 (per Evershed MR). An alteration which benefits the company is valid even though it seriously affects the position of an individual shareholder: *Allen v Gold Reefs of West Africa Ltd* [1900] 1 Ch 656 (company's lien on all share 'not fully paid up' extended by alteration of article to cover all shares whether fully paid up or not). An alteration giving a majority power to exclude the minority where it is done for the benefit of the company is valid: *Sidebottom v Kershaw, Leese & Co* [1920] 1 Ch 154. An alteration may be valid even though it alters the whole structure of the company: *Andrews v Gas Motor Co* (supra).

(f) Notification of alteration

Where any alteration is made in a company's articles by any statutory provision, whether contained in an Act of Parliament or in an instrument made under an Act, a printed copy of the Act or instrument must, not later than 15 days after that provision comes into force, be forwarded to the Registrar of Companies and recorded by him: Companies Act 1985, s. 18 (1). Where a company is required by s. 18 or otherwise to send to the Registrar any document making or evidencing an alteration in the company's articles, the company must send with it a printed copy of the articles as altered: ibid., s. 18 (2). If a company fails to comply with the above requirements, the company and any officer of the company who is in default is liable, on summary conviction, to a fine not exceeding one-fifth of the statutory maximum, or, on conviction after continued contravention, to a daily default fine not exceeding one-fiftieth of the statutory maximum: ibid., s. 18 (3).

The Registrar must cause to be published in the *Gazette* notice of the receipt by him of any document making or evidencing an alteration in the articles of a company: ibid., s. 711 (1) (b).

A company is not entitled to rely against other persons on any alteration of the articles if

 (i) the alteration had not been officially notified at the material time and is not shown by the company to have been known at that time to the person concerned; or

(ii) if the material time fell on or before the 15th day after the date of official notification (or, where the 15th day was a non-business day, on or before the next day that was not) and it is shown that the person concerned was unavoidably prevented from knowing of the event at that time: ibid., s. 42 (1). (*See* NON-BUSINESS DAY; OFFICIAL NOTIFICATION).

Asset, non-cash. *See* NON-CASH ASSET.

Assignee of partner's share in partnership. A person to whom a partner has transferred his share in a partnership.

An assignment by any partner of his share in the partnership, either absolute or by way of mortgage, does not, as against the other partners, entitled the assignee, during the continuance of the partnership, to interfere in the management or administration of the partnership business of affairs, or to require any accounts of the partnership transactions, or to inspect the partnership books, but entitles the assignee only to receive the share of profits to which the assigning partner would otherwise be entitled, and the assignee must accept the account of profits agreed to by the partners: Partnership Act 1890, s. 31 (1).

Accordingly, the assignee cannot object to salaries paid in good faith by the firm to individual partners for managing departments of the business although his share of the profits may be considerably reduced in consequence: *Re Garwood's Trusts: Paynter v Paynter* [1903] 1 Ch 236.

In case of a dissolution of the partnership, whether as respects all the partners or as respects the assigning partner, the assignee is entitled to receive the share of the partnership assets to which the assigning partner is entitled as between himself and the other partners, and, for the purpose of ascertaining that share, to an account as from the date of the dissolution: ibid., s. 31 (2). (*See* DISSOLUTION OF PARTNERSHIP).

Where a partnership deed contains an arbitration clause and a partner has mortgaged his share in the partnership, the mortgagee is entitled to an account if the partnership is dissolved, and cannot be compelled to submit to arbitration any dispute which arises: *Bonnin v Neame* [1910] 1 Ch 732.

In the case of a limited partnership a limited partner may, with the consent of the general partners, assign his share in the partnership, and on such an assignment the assignee becomes a limited partner with all the rights of the assignor: Limited Partnerships Act 1907, s. 6 (5) (b). (*See* GENERAL PARTNER: LIMITED PARTNER; LIMITED PARTNERSHIP).

Assignment of partner's share in partnership. The transfer by a partner of his share in the partnership to another person. (*See* ASSIGNEE OF PARTNER'S SHARE IN PARTNERSHIP).

A partnership may, at the option of the other partners, be dissolved if any partner suffers his share of the partnership property to be charged for his separate debt: Partnership Act 1890, s. 33 (2). (*See* DISSOLUTION OF PARTNERSHIP: PARTNERSHIP PROPERTY).

But in the case of a limited partnership the other partners are not entitled to dissolve the partnership by reason of any limited partner suffering his share to be charged for his separate debt: Limited Partnerships Act 1907, s. 6 (5) (c). (*See* LIMITED PARTNER: LIMITED PARTNERSHIP).

Association clause. A clause in the memorandum of association stating:— 'We, the subscribers to this memorandum of association, wish to be formed into a company pursuant to this memorandum; and we agree to take the number of shares shown opposite our respective names.' See e.g. Companies Tables A to F Regulations 1985 (S.I. 1985 No. 805), as amended by the Companies (Tables A to F) (Amendment) Regulations 1985 (S.I. 1985 No. 1052). (*See* MEMORANDUM OF ASSOCIATION; SUBSCRIBER).

Auditor. A person who audits the books of a company.

Qualification

A person is not qualified for appointment as auditor of a company unless

(a) he is a member of a body of accountants established in the United Kingdom and for the time being recognised for this purpose by the Secretary of State; or

(b) he is for the time being authorised by the Secretary of State to be so appointed, either as having similar qualifications obtained outside the United Kingdom or else he retains an authorisation formerly granted by the Board of Trade or the Secretary of State under the Companies Act 1948, s. 161 (1) (b): Companies Act 1985, s. 389 (1).

The bodies of accountants which are recognised by the Secretary of State are

  (i) the Institute of Chartered Accountants in England and Wales;
 (ii) the Institute of Chartered Accountants of Scotland;
(iii) the Chartered Association of Certified Accountants; and
(iv) the Institute of Chartered Accountants in Ireland: ibid., s. 389 (3).

The Secretary of State may by regulations in a statutory instrument amend the above list by adding or deleting any body: ibid., s. 389 (4). But he must not make any regulations

(a) adding any body; or
(b) deleting any body which has not consented in writing to its deletion;

unless he has published notice of his intention to do so in the *London* and *Edinburgh Gazettes* at least 4 months before making the regulations: ibid., s. 389 (4).

The Secretary of State may refuse an authorisation to a person as having qualifications obtained outside the United Kingdom if it appears to him that the country in which the qualifications were obtained does not confer on persons qualified in the United Kingdom corresponding privileges: ibid., s. 389 (5).

None of the following persons is qualified for appointment as an auditor

(a) an officer or servant of the company;
(b) a person who is a partner of or in the employment of an officer or servant of the company;
(c) a body corporate: ibid., s. 389 (6).

No person must act as auditor at a time when he knows that he is disqualified for appointment to that office: ibid., s. 389 (9). If an auditor to his knowledge becomes so disqualified during his term of office, he must thereupon vacate his office and give notice in writing to the company that he has vacated it by reason of that disqualification: ibid., s. 389 (9).

Any person who acts as auditor in contravention of the above provision or fails without reasonable excuse to give notice of vacating his office is guilty of an offence, and is liable on conviction on indictment to a fine, and on summary conviction to a fine not exceeding the statutory maximum or, on conviction after continued contravention, to a default fine not exceeding one-tenth of the statutory maximum: ibid., s. 13 (6); ibid., ss. 389 (10), 730 and Sch. 24.

Appointment and removal
The first auditors of a company may be appointed by the directors at

any time before the first general meeting at which accounts are laid: ibid., s. 384 (2). The auditors so appointed hold office until the conclusion of that meeting: ibid., s. 384 (2). If the directors fail to exercise their powers of appointment under the above provision, the powers may be exercised by the company in general meeting: ibid., s. 389 (3).

Every company must, at each general meeting at which accounts are laid, appoint an auditor or auditors to hold office from the conclusion of that meeting until the conclusion of the next general meeting at which accounts are laid: ibid., s. 384 (1).

Where at any general meeting no auditors are appointed or re-appointed, the Secretary of State may appoint a person to fill the vacancy: ibid., s. 384 (5). The company must within one week of the Secretary of State's power becoming exercisable, give him notice of that fact: ibid., s. 384 (5). If a company fails to give such notice, the company and every officer who is in default are guilty of an offence and liable on summary conviction to a fine not exceeding one-fifth of the statutory maximum or on conviction after continued contravention to a daily default fine not exceeding one-fiftieth of the statutory maximum: ibid., ss. 384 (5), 730 and Sch. 24.

The directors or the company in general meeting may fill any casual vacancy in the office of an auditor: ibid., s. 384 (4). But while any such vacancy continues, the surviving or continuing auditor or auditors, if any, may act: ibid., s. 384 (4).

A company may by ordinary resolution remove an auditor before the expiration of his term of office, notwithstanding anything in any agreement between it and him: ibid., s. 386 (1). (*See* ORDINARY RESOLUTION). Nothing in this provision is to be taken as depriving a person removed under it of compensation or damages payable to him in respect of his appointment as auditor or of any appointment terminating with that as auditor: ibid., s. 386 (3). Where a resolution removing an auditor is passed at a general meeting of a company, the company must within 14 days give notice of that fact in the prescribed form to the Registrar of Companies: ibid., s. 386 (2). If a company fails to give notice, the company and every officer of the company who is in default are guilty of an offence and are liable on summary conviction to a fine not exceeding the statutory maximum or, on conviction after continued contravention, to a default fine not exceeding one-fiftieth of the statutory maximum: ibid., ss. 386 (2), 730 and Sch. 24.

Special notice is required for a resolution at a general meeting of a company

(a) appointing as auditor a person other than a retiring auditor; or

(b) filling a casual vacancy in the office of auditor; or

(c) reappointing as auditor a retiring auditor who was appointed by the directors to fill a casual vacancy; or

(d) removing an auditor before the expiration of his term of office: ibid., s. 388 (1). (*See* SPECIAL NOTICE).

On receipt of notice of such an intended resolution the company must forthwith send a copy of it

(i) to the person to be appointed or removed, as the case may be;

(ii) in a case where it is proposed to appoint a person other than the retiring auditor, to the retiring auditor; and

(iii) in the case of the filling of a casual vacancy caused by the resignation of an auditor, to the auditor who resigned: ibid., s. 388 (2).

Where the retiring auditor, or the auditor proposed to be removed, as the case may be, makes with respect to the intended resolution representations in writing to the company (not exceeding a reasonable length) and requests their notification to members of the company, the company must, unless the representations are received by it too late for it to do so,

(a) in any notice of the resolution given to members of the company state the fact of the representations having been made; and

(b) send a copy of the representations to every member of the company to whom notice of the meeting is or has been sent: ibid., s. 388 (3).

If a copy of such representations is not sent out because they are received too late or because of the company's default, the auditor may (without prejudice to his right to be heard orally) require that the representations be read out at the meeting: ibid., s. 388 (4).

Copies of the representations need not be sent out and the representations need not be read out at the meeting if, on the application either of the company or of any other person claiming to be aggrieved, the court is satisfied that the rights conferred on the auditor are being abused to secure needless publicity for defamatory matter: ibid., s. 388 (5). The court may order the company's costs on the application to be paid in whole or in part by the auditor, notwithstanding that he is not a party to the application: ibid., s. 388 (5).

An auditor, who has been removed, is entitled to attend

(a) the general meeting at which his term of office would otherwise have expired; and

(b) any general meeting at which it is proposed to fill the vacancy caused by his removal: ibid., s. 387 (2).

He is also entitled to receive all notices of, and other communications relating to, any such meeting which any member of the company is entitled to receive, and to be heard at any such meeting which he attends on any part of the business of the meeting which concerns him as former auditor: ibid., s. 387 (2).

Resignation

An auditor of a company may resign his office by depositing a notice in writing to that effect at the registered office of the company: ibid., s. 390 (1). Any such notice operates to bring his term of office to an end on the date on which the notice is deposited or on such later date as may be specified in it: ibid., s. 390 (1).

A notice of resignation is not effective unless it contains

(a) a statement to the effect that there are no circumstances connected with his resignation which he considers should be brought to the notice of the members or creditors of the company; or

(b) a statement of any such circumstances: ibid., s. 390 (2).

Where a notice of resignation is deposited at a company's registered office, the company must within 14 days send a copy of the notice to

(a) the Registrar of Companies; and

(b) if the notice contains a statement that there are circumstances connected with his resignation which the auditor considers should be brought to the notice of the members or creditors of the company, to every member of the company, every holder of debentures of the company and all persons entitled to receive notices of general meetings of the company: ibid., s. 390 (3).

If default is made in complying with the above provision, the company and every officer of the company who is in default are guilty of an offence and liable on conviction on indictment to a fine, and on summary conviction to a fine not exceeding the statutory maximum or, on conviction after continued contravention, to a default fine not exceeding one-tenth of the statutory maximum: ibid., ss. 390 (7), 730 and Sch. 24.

The company or any person claiming to be aggrieved may, within 14 days of the receipt by the company of a notice containing a statement that there are circumstances connected with his resignation which the auditor considers should be brought to the notice of the members of the company or the creditors of the company, apply to the court: ibid., s. 390 (4). If the court is satisfied that the auditor is using the notice to secure needless publicity for defamatory matter, it may by order direct that copies of the notice need not be sent out: ibid., s. 390 (5). The court may further order that the company's costs on the application are to be paid in whole or in part by the auditor, notwithstanding that he is not a party to the application: ibid., s. 390 (5).

The company must within 14 days of the court's decision send to the Registrar of Companies, every member of the company, every holder of debentures of the company and all persons entitled to receive notices of general meetings of the company

(i) if the court makes an order under the above provisions, a statement setting out the effect of the order;

(ii) if the court does not make an order, a copy of the notice containing the statment that there are circumstances connected with his resignation which the auditor considers should be brought to the notice of the members of the company or the creditors of the company: ibid., s. 390 (6).

If default is made in complying with the above provision, the company and every officer of the company who is in default are guilty of an offence and liable on conviction on indictment to a fine, and on summary conviction to a fine not exceeding the statutory maximum or, on conviction after continued contravention, to a default fine not exceeding one-tenth of the statutory maximum: ibid., ss. 390 (7), 730 and Sch. 24.

Where an auditor's notice of resignation contains a statement that there are circumstances connected with his resignation which he considers should be brought to the notice of the members of the company or the creditors of the company, there may be deposited with the notice a requisition signed by the auditor calling on the directors forthwith duly to convene an extraordinary general meeting of the company for the purpose of receiving and considering such explanation of the circumstances connected with his resignation as he may wish to place before the meeting: ibid., s. 391 (1). (*See* EXTRAORDINARY GENERAL MEETING).

Where an auditor's notice of resignation contains a statement that there are circumstances connected with his resignation which he considers should be brought to the notice of the members of the company or the creditors of the company, he may request the company to circulate to its members

(a) before the general meeting at which his term of office would otherwise have expired; or

(b) before any general meeting at which it is proposed to fill the vacancy caused by his resignation or convened on his requisition;

a statement in writing (not exceeding a reasonable length) of the circumstances connected with his resignation: ibid., s. 391 (2). The company must in that case (unless the statement is received too late for it do so)

 (i) in any notice of the meeting given to members of the company state the fact of the statement having been made, and

(ii) send a copy of the statement to every member of the company to whom notice of the meeting is or has been sent: ibid., s. 391 (3).

If the directors do not within 21 days from the date of the deposit of the requisition proceed duly to convene a meeting for a day not more than 28 days after the date on which the notice convening the meeting is given, every director who failed to take all reasonable steps to secure that a meeting was convened is guilty of an offence and liable on conviction on indictment to a fine, and on summary conviction to a fine not exceeding the statutory maximum: ibid., ss. 391 (4), 730 and Sch. 24.

If a copy of any such statement is not sent out because received too late or because of the company's default, the auditor may (without prejudice to his right to be heard orally) require that the statement be read out at the meeting: ibid., s. 391 (5).

Copies of a statement need not be sent out and the statement need not be read out at the meeting if, on the application either of the company or of any other person who claims to be aggrieved, the court is satisfied that the rights conferred are being abused to secure needless publicity for defamatory matter: ibid., s. 391 (6). The court may order the company's costs on such an application to be paid in whole or in part by the auditor, notwithstanding that he is not a party to the application: ibid., s. 391 (6).

An auditor who has resigned his office is entitled to attend the general meeting at which his term of office would otherwise have expired or attend any general meeting at which it is proposed to fill the vacancy caused by his resignation or convened on his requisition: ibid., s. 391 (7). He is also entitled to receive all notices of, and other communications relating to, any such meeting which any member of the company is entitled to receive, and to be heard at any such meeting which he attends on any part of the business of the meeting which concerns him as former auditor: ibid., s. 391 (7).

Remuneration

In the case of an auditor appointed by the directors or by the Secretary of State, his remuneration may be fixed by the directors or by the Secretary of State, as the case may be: ibid., s. 385 (2). In any other case it must be fixed by the company in general meeting or in such manner as the company in general meeting may determine ibid., s. 385 (1).

'Remuneration' includes any sums paid by the company in respect of the auditor's expenses: ibid., s. 385 (3).

General position

Auditors are agents for the shareholders, but the shareholders are not necessarily bound by notice of everything of which notice is given to the auditors: *Spackman v Evans* (1868) LR 3 HL 171.

The relationship between an auditor and a company is normally that of professional man and client rather than that of employee and employer, so the notes made by an auditor in auditing the company's accounts are his own property: *Chantrey Martin & Co v Martin* [1953] 2 All ER 691. Although the notes are confidential, they are not privileged against an order for discovery in proceedings by a third party: ibid.

The auditors are not agents of the company and their certificate on the balance sheet is not an acknowledgement of the company's indebtedness for the purpose of the Statutes of Limitation: *Re Transplanters (Holding Company) Ltd* [1958] 2 All ER 711.

Right of Access to Books

Every auditor has a right of access at all times to the company's books, accounts and vouchers, and is entitled to require from the company's officers such information and explanation as he thinks necessary for the performance of the auditor's duties: Companies Act 1985, s. 237 (3). If the auditors fail to obtain all the information and explanations which, to the best of their knowledge and belief, are necessary for the purposes of their audit, they must state that fact in their report: ibid., s. 237 (4). (*See* AUDITOR'S REPORT).

Where a holding company has a subsidiary, then if the subsidiary is a body corporate incorporated in Great Britain, it is the duty of the subsidiary and its auditors to give to the auditors of the holding company such information and explanation as those auditors may reasonably require for the purposes of their duties as auditors of the holding company: ibid., s. 392 (1) (a). In any other case it is the duty of the holding company, if required by its auditors to do so, to take all such steps as are reasonably open to it to obtain from the subsidiary the required information and explanation: ibid., s. 392 (1) (b). (*See* HOLDING COMPANY; SUBSIDIARY COMPANY).

If a subsidiary or holding company fails to comply with the above provisions, the subsidiary company or holding company and every officer of it who is in default is guilty of an offence: ibid., s. 392 (2). If an auditor fails without reasonable cause to give the required information and explanation, he is guilty of an offence: ibid., s. 392 (2). A person guilty of an offence is liable on summary conviction to a fine not exceeding one-fifth of the statutory maximum: ibid., ss. 392 (2), 730 and Sch. 24.

An officer of a company who knowingly or recklessly makes to the auditors a statement conveying any information or explanation which they are entitled to require, which is misleading, false or deceptive in a material particular, is guilty of an offence: ibid., s 393. He is liable on conviction on indictment to imprisonment for a term not exceeding 2 years or to a fine or to both, or on summary conviction to imprisonment for a term not exceeding the statutory maximum: ibid., s. 393.

Right to attend and be heard at meetings

The auditors are entitled to attend any general meeting of the company and to receive all notices of, and other communications relating to, any general meeting which a member of the company is entitled to receive and to be heard at any general meeting which they attend on any part of the business of the meeting which concerns them as auditors: ibid., s. 387 (1).

Duties

The duties of the auditors are (i) to make a report to the members; (ii) to make themselves acquainted with their duties under the articles and the Companies Acts; and (iii) to exercise reasonable care.

(i) REPORT: The auditors must make a report to the members on the accounts examined by them and on every balance sheet, and profit and loss account and on all group accounts, copies of which are to be laid before the company in general meeting during their tenure of office: ibid., s. 236 (1). (*See* AUDITOR'S REPORT).

(ii) ACQUAINTANCE WITH ARTICLES AND COMPANIES ACTS: The auditors are under a duty to make themselves acquainted with the company's articles and the Companies Acts: *Re Republic of Bolivia Exploration Syndicate Ltd* [1914] 1 Ch 139. But an auditor is not bound to be a legal expert: ibid.

(iii) PROPER CARE: An auditor must be honest and use reasonable care, but it is not his duty to give advice and he has nothing to do with the way in which the company's business is carried on: *Re London & General Bank (No. 2)* [1895] 2 Ch 673. He is not bound to be a detective, but is justified in believing tried employees of the company and in assuming that they are honest provided he takes reasonable care: *Re Kingston Cotton Mill Co. (No. 2)* [1896] 2 Ch 279; *Re Thomas Gerrard & Son Ltd* [1967] 2 All ER 525.

But if there is anything calculated to excite suspicion, he should probe it to the bottom: *Re Kingston Cotton Mill Co (No. 2)* (supra). He must not confine himself merely to the task of verifying the arithmetical accuracy of the balance sheet, but should ascertain by comparison with the books of the company that it was properly drawn up so as to show the correct financial position: *Leeds Estate Building and Investment Co v Shepherd* (1887) 36 Ch D 787; *Re Thomas Gerrard & Son Ltd* (supra). He should see that the moneys and securities of the company are actually in the possession of the company, or have been deposited for safe custody with a bank or in other proper custody: custody: *Re City Equitable Fire Insurance Co* [1925] Ch 407.

An auditor, if formally appointed by the articles or under the Companies Act 1985, s. 384, is an 'officer' of the company and liable to be proceeded against for misfeasance: *R v Shacter* [1960] 1 All ER 61. But an auditor who is informally appointed is not such an 'officer': *Re Western Counties Steam Bakeries & Milling Co* [1897] 1 Ch 617.

Any provision, whether contained in a company's articles or in any contract with the company or otherwise, exempting any person employed by the company as auditor from, or indemnifying him against, any liability which would attach to him in respect of any negligence, default, breach of duty or breach of trust of which he may be guilty in relation to the company is void: Companies Act 1985, s. 310 (1), (2).

21

The court may relieve the auditors (whether they are officers of the company or not) from liability if they have acted honestly and reasonably, and ought, in all the circumstances, fairly to be excused: ibid., s. 727 (1).

Auditors' report. A report prepared by the auditors relating to the financial state of the company.

The auditors of a company must make a report to the members on the accounts examined by them and on every balance sheet and every profit and loss account and on all group accounts copies of which are to be laid before the company in general meeting during their tenure of office: ibid., s. 236 (1).

The auditors' report must be read before the company in general meeting and must be open to inspection by any member: ibid., s. 241 (2).

Contents of report

The report must state whether in the auditors' opinion the company's balance sheet and profit and loss account and (if it is a holding company submitting group accounts) the group accounts have been properly prepared in accordance with the Act: ibid., s. 236 (2) (a).

The report must also state, whether in their opinion a true and fair view is given

  (i) in the balance sheet, of the state of the company's affairs at the end of the financial year;

 (ii) in the profit and loss account (if not framed as a consolidated account), of the company's profit or loss for the financial year;

(iii) in the case of group accounts, of the state of affairs and profit or loss of the company and its subsidiaries dealt with by those accounts, so far as concerns members of the company: ibid., s. 236 (2) (b). (*See* GROUP ACCOUNTS; HOLDING COMPANY; SUBSIDIARY COMPANY).

But where a company which is entitled to avail itself and has availed itself of the benefit of any of the provisions of Part III of Sch. 9 e.g. a discount company, the report must state whether in the auditors' opinion the company's balance sheet and profit and loss account and (if it is a holding company) the group accounts have been properly prepared in accordance with the provisions of the Act: ibid., s. 262 (1), (2).

It is the duty of the auditors of a company, in preparing their report, to carry out such investigations as will enable them to form an opinion as to

(a) whether proper accounting records have been kept by the company and proper returns adequate for their audit have been received from branches not visited by them; and

(b) whether the company's balance sheet and (if not consolidated) its profit and loss account are in agreement with the accounting records and returns: ibid., s. 237 (1).

If the auditors are of the opinion that proper accounting records have not been kept or that proper returns adequate for their audit have not been received from branches not visited by them, or if the balance sheet and (if not consolidated) the profit and loss account are not in agreement with the accounting records and returns, the auditors must state that fact in their report: ibid., s. 237 (2).

If the auditors fail to obtain all the information and explanations which, to the best of their knowledge and belief, are necessary for the purposes of their audit, they must state that fact in the report: ibid., s. 237 (4).

Attachment of report to balance sheet
The auditors' report must be attached to the balance sheet: Companies Act 1985, ss. 238, 239.

Right to receive copy of report
A copy of the auditors' report must be sent to every member of the company, every holder of debentures of the company (whether or not he is entitled to receive notices of general meetings of the company) and all persons who are so entitled: ibid., s. 240 (1).

Any member of a company and any holder of debentures of a company is entitled to be furnished on demand with a copy of the auditors' report on the last balance sheet of the company: ibid., s. 246 (1).

'Authorised minimum' capital of a company means £50,000, or such other sum as the Secretary of State may by order made by statutory instrument specify instead: Companies Act 1985, s. 118 (1). An order made under this section which increases the authorised minimum may (a) require any public company having an allotted share capital of which the nominal value is less than the amount specified in the order as the authorised minimum to increase that value to not less than that amount or make an application to be re-registered as a private company; (b) make, in connection with any such requirement, provision for any of the matters for which provision is made by the Act relating to a company's registration, re-registration or change of name, to payment for any share comprised in a company's capital and to offers of shares in or debentures of a company to the public, including provision as to the consequences (whether in criminal law or otherwise) of a failure to comply with any requirement of the order; and (c) contain such supplemental and transitional provisions as the Secretary of State thinks appropriate, make different provision for different cases and, in particular, provide for any provision of the order to come into operation on different days for different purposes: ibid., s. 118 (2). An order must not be made under this section unless a draft of the order has been laid before Parliament and approved by resolution of each House: ibid., s. 118 (3).

B

Balance sheet date, in relation to a balance sheet, means the date as at which the balance sheet was prepared: Companies Act 1985, s. 742 (1) (c).

Bank holiday. A day which is a holiday under the Banking and Financial Dealings Act 1971: Companies Act 1985, s. 744.

Blank transfer. A transfer form relating to shares without the name of the transferee being inserted. (*See* MORTGAGE OF SHARE; TRANSFER OF SHARE).

'B' list. A list of the past members of the company made out by the liquidator in the course of a winding up. (*See* CONTRIBUTORY).

Bona vacantia. Property belonging to no one. Where a company is dissolved, all property and rights whatsoever vested in or held on trust for the company immediately before its dissolution (including leasehold property but not including property held by the company on trust for any other person) are deemed to be *bona vacantia* and belong to the Crown, or to the Duchy of Lancaster or to the Duke of Cornwall for the time being, as the case may be: Companies Act 1985, s. 654 (1).

Bonus share. A share given by the company to a member free, usually in proportion to his present shareholding, e.g. one bonus share for every share at present held by him.

Business, special. *See* SPECIAL BUSINESS.

Business name. A name used by a company which is different from that under which it is incorporated, or the name used by a firm which is different from that of persons carrying on a partnership.

(*a*) *Criminal liability*

Where any person who has a place of business in Great Britain and who carries on business in Great Britain under a name which

(a) in the case of a partnership does not consist of the surnames of all partners who are individuals and the corporate names of all partners who are bodies corporate without any addition;

(b) in the case of a company does not consist of its corporate name without any addition,

he must not without the written approval of the Sectretary of State carry on business in Great Britain under a name which

(a) would be likely to give the impression that the business is connected with Her Majesty's Government or any local authority; or

24

(b) includes any word or expression for the time being specified in regulations made by the Secretary of State: Business Names Act 1985, ss. 1, 2 (1).

But the following additions are permitted:— (i) in the case of a partnership, the forenames of individual partners or their initials, or where 2 or more individual partners have the same surname, the addition of 's' at the end of that surname; and (ii) in any case, any addition merely indicating that the business is carried on in succession to a former owner of the business: ibid., s. 1 (2).

Any person to whom the above provisions apply and who contravenes the above provisions is guilty of an offence, and is liable on summary conviction to a fine not exceeding one-fifth of the statutory maximum or, on conviction after continued contravention, to a daily default fine not exceeding one-fiftieth of the statutory maximum: ibid., s. 7 (1), (2), (3). Where an offence committed by a body corporate is proved to have been committed with the consent or connivance of, or to be attributable to any neglect on the part of, any director, manager, secretary or other similar officer of the body corporate, or any person who was purporting to act in any such capacity, he as well as the body corporate is guilty of that offence and is liable to be proceeded against and punished accordingly: ibid., s. 7 (4).

Any person to whom the above provisions apply must state in legible characters on all business letters, written orders for goods or services to be supplied to the business, invoices and receipts issued in the course of the business and written demands for payment of debts arising in the course of the business

  (i) in the case of a partnership, the name of each partner;

 (ii) in the case of a company, its corporate name; and

(iii) in relation to each person so named, an address within Great Britain at which service of any document relating in any way to the business will be effective: ibid., s. 4 (1) (a).

Further, in any premises where the business is carried on and to which the customers of the business or suppliers of any goods or services to the business have access, he must display in a prominent position so that it may easily be read by such customers or suppliers a notice containing such names and addresses: ibid., s. 4 (1) (b).

Any person to whom the above provisions apply must secure that the names and addresses required to be stated on his business letters are immediately given, by written notice, to any person with whom anything is done or discussed in the course of the business and who asks for such names and addresses: ibid., s. 4 (2).

Any person who without reasonable excuse contravenes the above provisions or any regulations made by the Secretary of State is guilty of an offence and is liable on summary conviction to a fine not exceeding one-fifth of the statutory maximum or, on conviction after continued contravention, to a daily default fine not exceeding one-fiftieth of the statutory maximum: ibid., ss. 4 (6), 7.

The above provisions relating to the statement of the name on all business letters, etc., do not apply to any document issued by a partnership of more than 20 persons which maintains at its principal place of business a list of the names of all the partners if

(a) none of the names of the partners appears in the document otherwise than in the text or as a signatory; and

(b) the document states in legible characters the partnership's principal place of business and that the list of the partners' names is open to inspection at that place: ibid., s. 4 (3).

Where a partnership maintains a list of the partners' names for the above purposes, any person may inspect the list during office hours: ibid., s. 4 (4). Where an inspection is refused, any partner of the partnership concerned who without reasonable excuse refused the inspection or permitted that inspection to be refused is guilty of an offence and is liable on summary conviction to a fine not exceeding one-fifth of the statutory maximum: ibid., ss. 4 (7), 7.

The Secretary of State may by regulations

(a) specify words or expressions for the use of which as or as part of a business name his approval is required; and

(b) in relation to any such word or expression, specify a Government department or other body as the relevant body to indicate whether it has any objections to the proposed use of the business name: ibid., s. 3 (1).

Where a person proposes to carry on a business under a name which is or includes any such word or expression, he must

 (i) request (in writing) the relevant body to indicate whether (and if so why) it has any objections to the proposal; and

(ii) submit to the Secretary of State a statement that such a request has been made and a copy of any response received from the relevant body: ibid., s. 3 (2).

(b) Civil liability

Any legal proceedings brought by any person to enforce any rights arising out of a contract made in the course of a business in respect of which he was in breach of s. 4 (1) or (2) above must be dismissed if the defendant to the proceedings shows

(a) that he has a claim against the plaintiff arising out of that contract which he has been unable to pursue by reason of the plaintiff's breach of s. 4 (1) or (2); or

(b) that he has suffered some financial loss in connection with the contract by reason of the plaintiff's breach of s. 4 (1) or (2);

unless the court before which the proceedings are brought is satisfied that it is just and equitable to permit the proceedings to continue: ibid., s. 5 (1).

C

Call. A demand made on a member by a company that he should pay the amount in whole or in part remaining due on a share which is not fully paid up.

The call must be made in the manner specified in the articles; otherwise it is invalid: *Re Cowley & Co* (1889) 42 Ch D 209. A call is in the nature of a trust to be exercised by the directors for the benefit of the company: *Alexander v Automatic Telephone Co* [1900] 2 Ch 56. On a transfer of shares the transferee is under an implied contract to indemnify the transferor against subsequent calls: *Levi v Ayers* (1878) 3 App Cas 842.

Table A art. 12 states: 'Subject to the terms of allotment, the directors may make calls upon the members in respect of any moneys unpaid on their shares (whether in respect of nominal value or premium) and each member shall (subject to receiving at least 14 clear days' notice specifying when and where payment is to be made) pay to the company as required by the notice the amount called on his shares. A call may be required to be paid by instalments. A call may, before receipt by the company of any sum due thereunder, be revoked in whole or in part and payment of a call may be postponed in whole or in part. A person upon whom a call is made shall remain liable for calls made upon him notwithstanding the subsequent transfer of, the shares in respect whereof the call was made.' A call is deemed to have been made at the time when the resolution of the directors authorising it was passed: Table A, art. 13. If a call remains unpaid after it has become due and payable the person from whom it is due and payable shall pay interest on the amount unpaid from the date it became due until it is paid at the rate fixed by the terms of allotment of the share or in the notice of the call or, if no rate is fixed, at the appropriate rate (as defined by the Act) but the directors may waive payment of the interest wholly or in part: ibid., art. 15 (*see* APPROPRIATE RATE). Subject to the terms of allotment, the directors may make arrangements on the issue of shares for a difference between the holders in the amounts and times of payment on calls on their shares: Table A, art. 17.

In a compulsory winding up the liquidator can make a call with the special leave of the court or the sanction of the committee of inspection: Companies Act 1985, s. 567. In a voluntary winding up he may exercise the power of the court of making calls: ibid., s. 598 (3).

Called-up share capital, in relation to a company, means, unless the contrary intention appears, so much of its share capital as equals the aggregate amount of the calls made on its shares, (whether or not those calls have been paid), together with any share capital paid up without being called and any share capital to be paid on a specified future date under the articles, the terms of allotment of the relevant shares or any other arrangements for payment of those shares: Companies Act 1985, s. 737 (1), (3). 'Uncalled share capital' is to be construed accordingly: ibid., 737 (2).

Capital, authorised. *See* NOMINAL (OR AUTHORISED) SHARE CAPITAL.

Capital, called-up share. *See* CALLED-UP SHARE CAPITAL.

Capital, issued share. *See* ISSUED SHARE CAPITAL.

Capital, maintenance of. *See* MAINTENANCE OF CAPITAL.

Capital, nominal. *See* NOMINAL (OR AUTHORISED) SHARE CAPITAL.

Capital, uncalled share. *See* UNCALLED SHARE CAPITAL.

Capital clause. A clause in a company's memorandum of association stating the amount of share capital with which the company proposes to be registered and the division of it into shares of a fixed amount. (*See* MEMORANDUM OF ASSOCIATION).

Capital redemption reserve. A reserve to which the amount by which the company's issued share capital is diminished on the cancellation of shares redeemed or purchased by a company is transferred: Companies Act 1985, s. 170 (1). In general, where any shares of a company are redeemed or purchased wholly or partly out of the proceeds of a fresh issue and the aggregate amount of those proceeds is less than the aggregate nominal value of the shares redeemed or purchased, the amount of the difference must be transferred to the capital redemption reserve: ibid. s. 170 (2). (*See* PURCHASE BY COMPANY OF OWN SHARES: REDEEMABLE SHARES).

Capitalisation. In Part VIII of the Companies Act 1985, in relation to any profits of a company, means applying the profits in wholly or partly paying up unissued shares in the company to be allotted to members of the company as fully or partly paid bonus shares or transferring the profits to capital redemption reserve: Companies Act 1985, s. 280 (1).

Certificate as to power to do business. A certificate issued by the Registrar of Companies entitling a public company to do business.

A company registered as a public company on its original incorporation must not do business or exercise any borrowing powers unless the Registrar of Companies has issued a certificate or the company is re-registered as a private company: Companies Act 1985, s. 117 (1). The Registrar must issue a company with a certificate if, on application made to him in the prescribed form by the company, he is satisfied that the nominal value of the company's allotted share capital is not less than the authorised minimum, and there is delivered to him a statutory declaration containing certain statements specified below: ibid., s. 117(2). (*See* AUTHORISED MINIMUM; PUBLIC COMPANY).

The statutory declaration must be in the prescribed form and be signed by a director or secretary of the company, and must

(a) state that the nominal value of the company's allotted share capital is not less than the authorised minimum;

(b) specify the amount paid up, at the time of the application, on the allotted share capital of the company;

(c) specify the amount or estimated amount, of the preliminary expenses of the company and the persons by whom any of those expenses have been paid or are payable; and

(d) specify any amount or benefit paid or given, or intended to be paid or given, to any promoter of the company, and the consideration for the payment or benefit: ibid., s. 117 (3). (*See* PROMOTER).

A certificate is conclusive evidence that the company is entitled to do business and exercise any borrowing powers: ibid., s. 117 (6).

If a company does business or exercises borrowing powers in contravention of the above provisions, the company and any officer of the company who is in default are liable on conviction on indictment to a fine and on summary conviction to a fine not exceeding the statutory maximum: ibid., ss. 117 (7), 730 and Sch. 24. If a company enters into a transaction in contravention of the above provisions and fails to comply with its obligations in connection with them within 21 days from being called on to do so, the directors of the company are jointly and severally liable to indemnify the other party to the transaction in respect of any loss or damage suffered by him by reason of the company's failure to comply with those obligations: ibid., s. 117 (8).

Certificate of incorporation. A document signed by the Registrar of Companies showing that the company to which it relates has been formed.

On the registration of a company's memorandum, the Registrar must give a certificate signed by him or authenticated by his official seal that the company is incorporated and, in the case of a limited company, that it is limited: Companies Act 1985, s. 13 (1), (2).

Where the Registrar registers a company's memorandum which states that the company is to be a public company, the certificate of incorporation must contain a statement that the company is a public company: ibid., s. 13 (6). (*See* PUBLIC COMPANY).

From the date of incorporation mentioned in the certificate, the subscribers of the memorandum, together with such other persons as may from time to time become members of the company, are a body corporate by the name contained in the memorandum, capable forthwith of exercising all the functions of an incorporated company but with such liability on the part of its members to contribute to its assets in the event of its being wound up: ibid., s. 13 (3), (4). (*See* CONTRIBUTORY).

A certificate of incorporation in respect of a company is conclusive evidence (a) that all the requirements of the Companies Act 1985 in respect of registration and of matters precedent and incidental to it have been complied with and that the company is a company authorised to be registered and is duly registered under the Act, and (b) if the certificate contains a statement that the company is a public company, that the company is such a company: ibid., s. 13 (7).

Any person may require a certificate of the incorporation of any company on payment of the prescribed fee: ibid., 709 (1) (b).

The Registrar of Companies must cause to be published in the *London Gazette* notice of the issue by him of a certificate of incorporation of a company: ibid., s. 711 (1) (a).

Where an unlimited company is re-registered as a limited company, the Registrar must issue to the company a certificate of incorporation appropriate to the status to be assumed by the company, and on the issue of the certificate the status of the company is changed from unlimited to limited: ibid., s. 52 (1), (2). A certificate of incorporation so issued is conclusive evidence that the requirements as to re-registration and matters precedent and incidental thereto have been complied with and that the company was authorised to be re-registered under s. 51 and was duly so re-registered: ibid., s. 52 (3). A similar certificate of incorporation is issued where a limited company is registered as an unlimited company: ibid., s. 50. (*See* RE-REGISTRATION OF COMPANIES).

Certification of transfer. A certification indorsed on a transfer form showing that a share certificate has been lodged with a company representing more shares than the transferor wants to transfer e.g. where the share certificate represents 500 shares and the shareholder wants to transfer only 250 of them, the company will indorse the transfer form with the words 'Certificate for 500 shares has been lodged' before handling it to the transferee. On the registration of the transfer, the company hands a new certificate for 250 shares each to the transferor and the transferee. (*See* SHARE CERTIFICATE; TRANSFER OF SHARE).

The certification by a company of any instrument of transfer of shares in the company is to be taken as a representation by the company to any person acting on the faith of the certification that there have been produced to the company such documents as on their face show a *prima facie* title to the shares in the transferor named in the instrument, but is not to be taken as a representation that the transferor has any title to the shares: Companies Act 1985, s. 184 (1).

Where any person acts on the faith of a false certification by a company made negligently, the company is under the same liability to him as if the certification had been made fraudulently: ibid., s. 184 (2).

An instrument of transfer is deemed certificated if it bears the words 'certificate lodged' or words to the like effect: ibid., s. 184 (3) (a). The certification of an instrument of transfer is deemed made by a company if (i) the person issuing the instrument is a person authorised to issue certificated instruments of transfer on the company's behalf; and (ii) the certification is signed by a person authorised to certificate transfers on the company's behalf or by an officer or servant either of the company or of a body corporate so authorised: ibid., s. 184 (3) (b). A certification is deemed signed by a person if (i) it purports to be authenticated by his signature or initials (whether handwritten or not); and (ii) it is not shown that the signature or initials was or were placed there neither by himself nor by a person authorised to use the signature or initials for the purpose of certificating transfers on the company's behalf: ibid., s. 184 (3) (c).

If the company parts with the original certificate which has been sent to it by the transferor, and enables him to commit a fraud, it is liable to the transferee if he is damaged thereby, but not to anyone else: *Longman v Bath Electric Tramways Ltd* [1905] 1 Ch 646, CA.

Change of name. The alteration of the name of the company from that in which it has been registered originally.

A company may by special resolution change its name: Companies Act 1985, s. 28 (1). (*See* CERTIFICATE OF INCORPORATION; SPECIAL RESOLUTION). Where a company changes its name, the Registrar of Companies must enter the new name on the register in place of the former name and issue a certificate of incorporation altered to meet the circumstances of the case: ibid., s. 28 (6).

Where a company has been registered by a name which
(a) is the same as or, in the opinion of the Secretary of State, too like a name appearing at the time of the registration in the index of names kept by the Registrar; or
(b) is the same as or, in the opinion of the Secretary of State, too like a name which should have appeared in that index at that time,
the Secretary of State may within 12 months of that time, in writing, direct the company to change its name within such period as he may specify: ibid., s. 28 (2). (*See* INDEX OF NAMES).

If it appears to the Secretary of State that misleading information has been given for the purpose of a company's registration with a particular name or that undertakings or assurances have been given for that purpose and have not been fulfilled, the Secretary of State may within 5 years of the date of its registration with that name in writing direct the company to change its name within such period as he may specify: ibid., s. 28 (3). Where a direction has been given, the Secretary of State may by a further direction in writing extend the period within which the company is to change its name, at any time before the end of that period: ibid., s. 28 (4).

A company which fails to comply with a direction and any officer who is in default are liable on summary conviction to a fine not exceeding one-fifth of the statutory maximum, or, on conviction after continued contravention, to a daily default fine not exceeding one-fiftieth of the statutory maximum: ibid., ss. 28 (5), 730 and Sch. 24.

A change of name by a company does not affect any rights or obligations of the company or render defective any legal proceedings by or against it, and any legal proceedings that might have been continued or commenced against it by its former name may be continued or commenced against it by its new name: ibid., s. 28 (7).

Charge. An incumbrance on the subject-matter over which it is created.

Charge, floating. *See* FLOATING CHARGE.

Charge, registration of. *See* REGISTRATION OF CHARGES.

Circulation of members' resolutions. A resolution by the members required by them to be circulated by a company.

Members representing one-twentieth of the total voting rights of all the members having the right to vote at the meeting, or not less than 100 members holding shares on which there has been paid up an average sum per member of not less than £100, can claim, by requisition at their own expense, to have notice given of any resolution which is intended to be moved at the next annual general meeting, and to have circulated to members any statement of not more than 1,000 words with respect to the business to be dealt with at the meeting: Companies Act 1985, s. 376 (1), (2).

Notice of any such resolution must be given, and any such statement must be circulated, to members of the company entitled to have notice of the meeting sent to them by serving a copy of the resolution or statement on each such member in any manner permitted for service of notice of the meeting: ibid., s. 376 (3). Notice of any such resolution must be given to any other member of the company by giving notice of the general effect of the resolution in any manner permitted for giving him notice of meetings of the company: ibid., s. 376 (4). The copy must be served or notice of the effect of the resolution must be given in the same manner and so far as practicable at the same time as notice of the meeting; and, where it is not practicable for it to be served or given at that time, it must be served or given as soon as practicable thereafter: ibid., s. 376 (5).

A company is not bound to give notice of any resolution or circulate any statement unless

(a) a copy of the requisition signed by the requisitionists (or two or more copies which between them contain the signatures of all the

requisitionists) is deposited at the registered office of the company
  (i) in the case of a requisition requiring notice of a resolution, not less than 6 weeks before the meeting; and
  (ii) in the case of any other requisition, not less than 1 week before the meeting; and
(b) there is deposited or tendered with the requisition a sum reasonably sufficient to meet the company's expenses in giving effect to it: ibid., s. 377 (1).

If, after a copy of a requisition requiring notice of a resolution has been deposited at the company's registered office, an annual general meeting is called for a date 6 weeks or less after the copy has been deposited, the copy (though not deposited within the time required) is deemed properly deposited: ibid., s. 377 (2).

The company is not bound to circulate any statement if, on the application either of the company or of any other person who claims to be aggrieved, the court is satisfied that the rights conferred by s. 376 are being abused to secure needless publicity for defamatory matter: ibid., s. 377 (3). The court may order the company's costs on such an application to be paid in whole or in part by the requisionists, even though they are not parties to the application: ibid., s. 377 (3).

Notwithstanding anything in the company's articles, the business which may be dealt with at the annual general meeting includes any resolution of which notice is given in accordance with s. 376, and notice is deemed to have been so given notwithstanding the accidental omission, in giving it, of one or more members: ibid., s. 376 (6).

City Code on Take-overs and Mergers. A code operated by the Stock Exchange relating to the take-overs and mergers of listed companies. It is not a code of law but of business practice. A Panel on Take-overs and Mergers is responsible for its operation.

Commencement of winding up. The moment when a winding up is deemed to have started.

Where, before the presentation of a petition for the winding up of a company by the court, a resolution has been passed by the company for voluntary winding up, the winding up of the company is deemed to have commenced at the time of the passing of the resolution: Companies Act 1985, s. 524 (1). In any other case the winding up of a company by the court is deemed to commence at the time of the presentation of the petition for winding up: ibid., s. 524 (2).

Commission, underwriting. *See* UNDERWRITING COMMISSION.

Committee of inspection. A committee consisting of creditors and members appointed for the purpose of assisting a liquidator in the winding up of a company.

Appointment
When a winding-up order has been made by the court, it is the business

of the separate meetings of creditors and contributories summoned for the purpose of determining whether or not an application should be made to the court for appointing a liquidator in place of the Official Receiver, to determine further whether an application is to be made to the court for the appointment of a committee of inspection to act with the liquidator, and who are to be the members of the committee if appointed: Companies Act 1985, s. 546 (1). (*See* OFFICIAL RECEIVER). The court may make the appointment and order required to give effect to such determination; and if there is a difference between the determinations of the meetings of the creditors and contributories in respect of the above matters, the court must decide the difference and make such order as it thinks fit: Companies Act 1985, s. 546 (3).

In the case of a creditors' voluntary winding up the creditors may, if they think fit, appoint a committee of inspection consisting of not more than 5 persons: ibid., s. 590 (1). If such committee is appointed, the company may appoint such number of persons as they think fit to act as members of the committee not exceeding 5: ibid., s. 590 (2). But the creditors may, if they think fit, resolve that all or any of the persons so appointed by the company ought not to be members of the committee of inspection: ibid., s. 590 (3). If the creditors so resolve, the persons mentioned in the resolution are not then qualified to act as members of the committee unless the court so directs: ibid., s. 590 (3). On any application to the court it may, if it thinks fit, appoint other persons to act as such members in place of the persons mentioned in the resolution: ibid., s. 590 (3). (*See* CREDITORS' VOLUNTARY WINDING UP).

Constitution and proceedings of committee

The committee of inspection consists of creditors and contributories of the company or persons holding general powers of attorney from creditors or contributories in such proportions as may be agreed on by the meetings of creditors and contributories or as, in case of difference, may be determined by the court: ibid., s. 547 (1).

The committee must meet at such times as it may from time to time appoint, and failing such appointment, at least once a month; and the liquidator or any member of the committee may also call a meeting of the committee as and when he thinks it necessary: ibid., Sch. 17, para. 1. The committee may act by a majority of its members present at a meeting, but must not act unless a majority of the committee are present: ibid., Sch. 17, para. 2. A member of the committee may resign by notice in writing signed by him and delivered to the liquidator: ibid., Sch. 17, para. 3. If a member of the committee becomes bankrupt or compounds or arranges with his creditors or is absent from 5 consecutive meetings of the committee without leave of those members who together with himself represent the creditors or contributories, as the case may be, his office becomes vacant: ibid., Sch. 17, para. 4. A member of the committee may be removed by an ordinary resolution at a meeting of creditors, if he represents creditors, or of contributories, if he represents contributories, of which 7 days' notice has been given, stating the object of the meeting: ibid., Sch. 17, para. 5. On a vacancy occurring in the committee the liquidator must forthwith summon a meeting of creditors or of contributories, as the case may require, to fill the vacancy, and the meeting may, by resolution, reappoint the same or appoint another creditor or contributory to fill the vacancy: ibid., Sch. 17, para. 6 (1). But if the liquidator, having regard to the position in the winding up, is of the opinion that it is unnecessary for the vacancy to be filled, he may apply to the court; and the court may make an order that the vacancy must not be filled, or must not be filled except in circumstances specified in the order: ibid., Sch. 17, para. 6 (2). The continuing members of the committee, if not less than 2, may act notwithstanding any vacancy in the committee: ibid., Sch. 17, para. 6 (3).

No member of the committee of inspection is, except under and with the sanction of the court directly or indirectly, by himself, or any employer, partner, clerk, agent or servant, entitled to derive any profit from any transaction arising out of the winding-up or to receive out of the assets any payment for services rendered by him in connection with the administration of the assets, or for any goods supplied by him to the liquidator or on account of the company: Companies (Winding-up) Rules 1949 (S.I. 1949 No. 330), r. 163. In a winding-up by the court if it appears to the Department of Trade, or in a voluntary winding-up if it appears to the committee of inspection or to any meeting of creditors or contributories that any profit or payment has been made contrary to the above provisions, they may disallow such payment or recover such profit, as the case may be, on the audit of the liquidator's accounts or otherwise: ibid., r. 163.

Companies Acts mean the Companies Act 1985, the Company Securities (Insider Dealing) Act 1985 and the Companies Consolidation (Consequential Provisions) Act 1985: Companies Act 1985, s. 744.

Companies (Winding-up) Rules 1949 (SI 1949 No. 330). The Rules made by the Lord Chancellor under the Companies Act 1985, s. 663 for carrying into effect the objects of that Act so far as relates to the winding-up of companies.

The rules concern (i) preliminary (rr. 1 to 3); (ii) court and chambers (rr. 4 to 10); (iii) proceedings (rr. 11 to 21); (iv) service of process and enforcement of orders (rr. 22 to 25); (v) petition (rr. 26 to 32); (vi) hearing of petitions and orders made on them (rr. 33 to 37); (vii) order to wind up a company under the Companies Act 1985, s. 461

(rr. 38 to 43); (viii) transfers of actions and proceedings (rr. 44 to 49); (ix) special manager (rr. 50 and 51); (x) statement of affairs (rr. 52 to 57); (xi) appointment of liquidator in winding-up by the court (r. 58); (xii) security by liquidator or special manager in a winding-up by the court (rr. 59 and 60); (xiii) public examination (rr. 61 to 67); (xiv) proceedings by or against directors, promoters and officers (rr. 68 to 71); (xv) witnesses and depositions (rr. 72 to 74); (xvi) disclaimer (r. 75); (xvii) vesting of disclaimed property (r. 76); (xviii) arrangements with creditors and contributories in a winding-up by the court (r. 77); (xix) collection and distribution of assets in a winding-up by the court (rr. 78 and 79); (xx) list of contributories in a winding-up by the court (rr. 80 to 85); (xxi) calls (rr. 86 to 90); (xxii) proofs (rr. 91 to 105); (xxiii) admission and rejection of proofs and preferential claims and appeal to the court (rr. 106 to 108); (xxiv) dividends in a winding-up by the court (rr. 119 and 120); (xxv) general meetings of creditors and contributories in relation to a winding-up by the court (rr. 121 to 126); (xxvi) general meetings of creditors and contributories in relation to a winding-up by the court and of creditors in relation to a creditors' voluntary winding-up (rr. 127 to 145); (xxvii) proxies in relation to a winding-up by the court and to meetings of creditors in a creditors' voluntary winding-up (rr. 146 to 156); (xxviii) attendance and appearance of parties (rr. 157 and 158); (xxix) liquidator and committee of inspection (rr. 159 to 168); (xxx) payments into and out of a bank (rr. 169 and 170); (xxxi) books (rr. 171 and 172); (xxxii) investment of funds (r. 173); (xxxiii) accounts and audit in a winding-up by the court (rr. 174 to 181); (xxxiv) final account in voluntary winding-up (r. 182); (xxxv) taxation of costs (rr. 183 to 193); (xxxvi) costs and expenses payable out of the assets of the company (rr. 194 and 195); (xxxvii) statements by liquidator to the Registrar of Companies (rr. 196 to 198); (xxxviii) unclaimed funds and undistributed assets in the hands of a liquidator (rr. 199 to 204); (xxxix) release of a liquidator in a winding-up by the court (rr. 205 and 206); (xl) Official Receivers and Department of Trade (rr. 207 to 216); (xli) books to be kept, and returns made, by officers of courts (r. 217); (xlii) Gazetting in a winding-up by the court (rr. 218 and 219); (xliii) assets and commitments (rr. 220 to 223); (xliv) miscellaneous matters (rr. 224 to 230).

Company, holding. *See* HOLDING COMPANY.

Company limited by guarantee. A company having the liability of its members limited by the memorandum to such amount as the members may respectively thereby undertake to contribute to the assets of the company in the event of its being wound up: Companies Act 1985, s. 1 (2) (b).

Company limited by shares. A company having the liability of its members limited by the memorandum to the amount, if any, unpaid on the shares respectively held by them: Companies Act 1985, s. 1 (2) (a).

Company, oversea. *See* OVERSEA COMPANY.

Company, private. *See* PRIVATE COMPANY.

Company, public. *See* PUBLIC COMPANY.

Company, registration of. *See* REGISTRATION OF COMPANY.

Company, re-registration of. *See* RE-REGISTRATION OF COMPANY.

Company, subsidiary. *See* SUBSIDIARY COMPANY.

Company, unlimited. *See* UNLIMITED COMPANY.

Compensation for loss of office. A sum paid to a director on his ceasing to hold office.

Approval by company

It is unlawful for a company to make to a director of the company any payment by way of compensation for loss of office, or as consideration for or in connection with his retirement from office, without particulars of the proposed payment (including its amount) being disclosed to members of the company and the proposal being approved by the company: Companies Act 1985, s. 312.

Further, it is unlawful in connection with the transfer of the whole or any part of the undertaking or property of a company for any payment to be made to any director of the company by way of compensation for loss of office, or as consideration for or in connection with his retirement from office, unless particulars of the proposed payment (including its amount) have been disclosed to members of the company and the proposal approved by the company: ibid., s. 313 (1). Where an unlawful payment is made to a director of the company, the amount received is deemed to be received by him in trust for the company: ibid., s. 313 (2).

The disclosure must be made while the payment is still a proposed payment i.e. before payment is made: *Re Duomatic Ltd* [1969] 1 All ER 161 at 169 (per Buckley J). The words 'approved by the company' mean 'approved by the company in general meeting': ibid., at 169 (per Buckley J). Disclosure must be made to all the members of the company: ibid., at 169 (per Buckley J).

Where an illegal payment has been made, the court has power under the Companies Act 1985, s. 727 to relieve from liability those responsible for making it: *Re Duomatic Ltd* (supra).

No disclosure of a lump sum, which is payable under a service contract to a director on the date of his employment ceases, is needed. Disclosure is necessary only in the case of uncovenanted payments in respect of loss of office or on retirement: *Taupo Taura Timber Co Ltd v Rowe* [1977] 3 All ER 123, PC.

Payment to be made on transfer of shares

Where in connection with the transfer to any persons of all or any of the shares in a company, being a transfer resulting from

(a) an offer made to the general body of shareholders; or
(b) an offer made by or on behalf of some other body corporate with a view to the company becoming its subsidiary or a subsidiary of its holding company; or
(c) an offer made by or on behalf of an individual with a view to his obtaining the right to exercise or control the exercise of not less than one-third of the voting power at any general meeting of the company; or
(d) any other offer which is conditional on acceptance to a given extent;

a payment is to be made to a director of the company by way of compensation for loss of office, or as consideration for or in connection with his retirement from office, it is the duty of that director to take all reasonable steps to secure that particulars of the proposed payment (including the amount) are included or sent with the notice of the offer made for their shares which is given to any shareholders: Companies Act 1985, s. 314 (1), (2).

If (a) any such director fails to take reasonable steps; or (b) any person who has been properly required by any such director to include the particulars or send them with any such notice fails to do so, he is liable on summary conviction to a fine not exceeding one-fifth of the statutory maximum: ibid., ss. 314 (3), 730 and Sch. 24.

Inclusion in accounts

A note to the accounts of a company must show, so far as the information is contained in the company's books and papers or the company has the right to obtain it from the persons concerned, the aggregate amount of any compensation to directors or past directors in respect of loss of office: ibid., s. 231 (1), Sch. 5, Part V, para. 29.

It is the duty of any director of a company to give notice to the company of such matters relating to himself as may be necessary for the purposes of Part V of Sch. 5: ibid., s. 231 (4). If he makes default in complying with this provision, he is liable on summary conviction to a fine not exceeding one-fifth of the statutory maximum: ibid., ss. 231 (4), 730 and Sch. 24.

Compulsory winding up. *See* WINDING UP BY THE COURT.

Conditional sale agreement. In the Companies Act 1985 has the same meaning as in the Consumer Credit Act 1974: Companies Act 1985, s. 331 (10), i.e. 'an agreement for the sale of goods or land under which the purchase price or part of it is payable by instalments, and the property in the goods or land is to remain in the seller (notwithstanding that the buyer is to be in possession of the goods or land) until such conditions as to the payment of instalments or otherwise as may be specified in the agreement are fulfilled'; Consumer Credit Act 1974, s. 189 (1).

Conservancy authority. For the purposes of the Forged Transfers Act 1891 includes 'all persons entrusted with the duty or invested with the power of conserving, maintaining or improving the navigation of any tidal water otherwise than for profit, and not being a joint stock company': Forged Transfers Act 1891, s. 4 (3).

Consolidation of shares. A conversion of a number of shares of a certain nominal value into a smaller number of shares of a larger nominal value, e.g. the conversion of twenty 5p shares into one £1 share. (Cf. SUB-DIVISION OF SHARES).

Contingent purchase contract. For the purpose of the Companies Act 1985, s. 165, means a contract entered into by a company relating to any of its shares (a) which does not amount to a contract to purchase those shares; but (b) under which the company may (subject to any conditions) become entitled to or obliged to purchase those shares: Companies Act 1985, s. 165 (1).

Continuing guarantee. A guarantee of unspecified duration.

A continuing guarantee given either to a firm or to a third person in respect of the transactions of a firm is, in the absence of agreement to the contrary, revoked as to future transactions by an change in the constitution of the firm to which, or of the firm in respect of the transactions of which, the guarantee was given: Partnership Act 1890, s. 18. (*See* FIRM).

Continuing partners. Partners remaining and carrying on a partnership after the retirement of one or more of their fellow partners.

Where continuing partners carry on the business of the firm with its capital or assets without any final settlement of accounts as between the firm and a retiring partner, they are liable to him. (*See* RETIRING PARTNER).

Contract, pre-incorporation. *See* PRE-INCORPORATION CONTRACT.

Contributories, settlement of list of. *See* CONTRIBUTORY; LIQUIDATOR.

Contributory. Every person liable to contribute to the assets of a company in the event of its being wound up: Companies Act 1985, s. 507 (1). The term 'contributory', for the purposes of all proceedings for determining, and all proceedings prior to the final determination of, the persons who are deemed to be contributories, includes any person alleged to be a contributory: ibid., s. 507 (1). The liability of a contributory creates a debt in the nature of a specialty accruing due from him at the time when his liability commenced, but payable at the times when calls are made for enforcing the liability: ibid., s. 508. (*See* CALL).

If a contributory dies before or after he has been placed on the list of contributories, his personal representatives are liable in a due course of administration to contribute to the assets of the company in discharge of his liability and are contributories accordingly: ibid., s. 509 (1). If the personal representatives make default in paying any money ordered to be paid by them, proceedings may be taken for administering the estate of the deceased contributory and for compelling payment out of it of the money due: ibid., s. 509 (3). If a contributory becomes bankrupt either before or after he has been placed on the list of contributories,

(a) his trustee in bankruptcy represents him for all the purposes of the winding up, and is a contributory accordingly, and may be called on to admit to proof against the bankrupt's estate, or otherwise to allow to be paid out of his assets in due course of law, any money due from the bankrupt in respect of his liability to contribute to the company's assets; and

(b) there may be proved against the bankrupt's estate the estimated value of his liability to future calls as well as calls already made: ibid., s. 510.

In the event of a company being wound up, every present and past member is liable to contribute to its assets to any amount sufficient for payment of its debts and liabilities, and the costs, charges and expenses of the winding up, and for the adjustment of the rights of the contributories among themselves, subject to the following qualifications:—

(a) a past member is not liable to contribute if he has ceased to be a member for 1 year or upwards before the commencement of the winding up (*see* COMMENCEMENT OF WINDING UP);

(b) a past member is not liable to contribute in respect of any debt or liability of the company contracted after he ceased to be a member;

(c) a past member is not liable to contribute unless it appears to the court that the existing members are unable to satisfy the contributions required to be made by them;

(d) in the case of a company limited by shares, no contributions can be required from any member exceeding the amount, if any, unpaid on the shares in respect of which he is liable as a present or past member;

(e) in the case of a company limited by guarantee, no contribution can generally be required from any member exceeding the amount undertaken to be contributed by him to the assets of the company in the event of its being wound up;

(f) a sum due to any member of a company (in his character of a member) by way of dividends, profits or otherwise is not deemed to be a debt of the company, payable to that member in a case of competition between himself and any other creditor not a member of the company, but any such sum may be taken into account for the purpose of the final adjustment of the rights of the contributories among themselves: ibid., s. 502 (1), (2).

41

Nothing in the Companies Act 1985 invalidates any provision contained in a policy of insurance or other contract whereby the liability of individual members on the policy or contract is restricted, or whereby the funds of the company are alone made liable in respect of the policy or contract: ibid., s. 502 (2) (e).

In the case of a company limited by guarantee with a share capital, every member of it is liable (in addition to the amount so undertaken to be contributed to the assets), to contribute to the extent of any sums unpaid on shares held by him: ibid., s. 502 (3).

Corporate personality, principle of. A principle that a company is in law a different person altogether from its members, e.g. (i) a member of a 'one-man company' can lend money to it on the security of its assets and gain priority over the unsecured creditors, for he and the company are separate persons: *Salomon v Salomon & Co Ltd* [1897] AC 22, HL; (ii) a member has no insurable interest in the property of the company: *Macaura v Northern Assurance Co* [1925] AC 619; (iii) the nationality of a company does not depend on that of its members; *Janson v Driefontein Consolidated Mines Ltd* [1902] AC 484.

Exceptions

In certain cases the court will 'lift the veil' of corporate personality, and look at the economic reality of the situation, e.g. (i) where the membership of the company falls below the statutory number of 2 members, as required by the Companies Act 1985, s. 1 (1) (*see* MINIMUM NUMBER OF MEMBERS); (ii) where an officer of the company signs a bill of exchange, cheque, etc., on behalf of the company without any mention of the company's name on it, contrary to the Companies Act 1985, s. 349 (4); (iii) where group accounts are necessary under the Companies Act 1985, s. 229 (*see* GROUP ACCOUNTS); (iv) where there has been fraudulent trading (*see* FRAUDULENT TRADING); (v) where the Secretary of State makes an investigation into the affairs of related companies (*see* INSPECTION AND INVESTIGATION OF COMPANY); (vi) where the company is a sham or mere puppet, e.g. (a) a company formed to get round a covenant in restraint of trade: *Gilford Motor Co Ltd v Horne* [1933] All ER Rep 109; (b) a company formed to prevent the operation of an order for specific performance of a contract of sale: *Jones v Lipman* [1962] 1 All ER 442; and (c) where a person was in sole control of a company and created other companies which he used as a facade so that each could be treated as his 'alter ego': *Wallersteiner v Moir* [1974] 3 All ER 217, CA; (vii) where the company is acting as agent of the shareholders: *Smith, Stone and Knight Ltd v Birmingham Corporation* [1939] 4 All ER 116; (viii) where it is believed that in time of war the company is controlled by enemy aliens: *Daimler Co Ltd v Continental Tyre & Rubber Co Ltd* [1916] 2 AC 307, HL; (ix) where it is desired to establish for tax purposes in what country a company is resident: *Unit Construction Co Ltd v Bullock (Inspector of Taxes)* [1959] 3 All ER 831, HL; and (x) where a subsidiary company is wholly owned by a holding company: *DHN Food Distributors Ltd v London Borough of Tower Hamlets Ltd* [1976] 3 All ER 462, CA. (*See* HOLDING COMPANY; SUBSIDIARY COMPANY).

Credit transaction. For the purpose of Part X of the Companies Act 1985 is a transaction under which one party ('the creditor') (a) supplies any goods or sells any land under a hire-purchase agreement or conditional sale agreement (*see* HIRE-PURCHASE AGREEMENT; CONDITIONAL SALE AGREEMENT); (b) leases or hires any land or goods in return for periodical payments; (c) otherwise disposes of land or supplies goods or services on the understanding that payment (whether in a lump sum or instalments or by way of periodical payments or otherwise) is to be deferred: Companies Act 1985, s. 331 (7).

Creditors' voluntary winding up. A winding up in the case of which a declaration of solvency has not been made in accordance with the Companies Act 1985, s. 577: Companies Act 1985, s. 578 (*See* DECLARATION OF SOLVENCY).

Cum dividend. With the dividend. A term used in connection with the purchase of shares resulting in the buyer having a right to the dividend in respect of them. (*See* DIVIDEND; SHARE).

Cum rights. With the rights. A term used to denote the fact that a buyer of shares is entitled to subscribe for further shares in proportion to the number bought. (*See* RIGHTS ISSUE; SHARE).

Cumulative preference share. *See* PREFERENCE SHARE.

D

Debenture. A document given by a company as evidence of a debt to the holder arising out of a loan and usually secured by a charge. A debenture may be a single one or it may be one of a series.

Types of debentures

Debentures may be (a) payable to the registered holder (see register of debenture-holders, p. 48, post); or (b) payable to bearer.

(a) DEBENTURES PAYABLE TO REGISTERED HOLDER: The principal contents of a debenture payable to a registered holder are (i) the date when the principal is to be repaid by the company; (ii) the rate of interest; (iii) the dates on which the interest is to be payable; (iv) a statement that the undertaking of the company is charged with such payments; and (v) a statement that the debenture is issued subject to 'conditions'.

(b) DEBENTURES PAYABLE TO BEARER: The object of making a debenture payable to bearer is that it may become a negotiable instrument, i.e. (i) it is transferable by delivery; (ii) a transferee in due course gets a title independent of any defects in the title of the transferor; (iii) no notice of transfers need be given to the company; and (iv) no stamp duty is payable on a transfer.

Bearer debentures are recognised as negotiable without the necessity of proving a custom of merchants to treat them as such: *Edelstein v Schuler & Co* [1902] 2 KB 144.

The form of a debenture is much the same as the form of debenture payable to the registered holder except that the agreement is to pay 'to the bearer on presentation of this debenture' and to pay interest 'in accordance with the coupons annexed hereto'.

'Conditions'

The 'conditions' in debentures payable to a registered holder usually state (i) that the debenture is one of a series of debentures issued to secure a specified sum and that they are all to rank *pari passu* and that it is secured by a floating charge. (*See* FLOATING CHARGE); (ii) the right of the company to redeem the whole or any part of the money owing; (iii) that a register of debenture holders will be kept (see p. 48, post); (iv) that the registered holder is to be exclusively entitled to the benefit of the debenture; (v) that every transfer of the debenture must be in writing and must be delivered to the registered office of the company (see p. 208, post); (vi) that no transfer can be registered during the 7 days preceding the days fixed for the payment of interest; (vii) that in the case of joint holders the sums owing to them are deemed to be owing to them on joint account; (viii) that the principal and interest are to be paid without regard to any equities between the company and the original or any intermediate holder; (ix) the circumstances in which the principal becomes immediately payable, e.g. (a) if the company makes default for a period of 14 days in the payment of interest; (b) if a receiver is appointed. (*See* RECEIVER); (x) that the money owing will be paid at the company's bankers or at its registered office; (xi) how notices are to be sent to the registered holder; (xii) the power of the debenture holder to appoint a receiver and manager of the property charged (*See* RECEIVER; MANAGER); and (xiii) that the company will keep insured the property subject to the charge.

The 'conditions' in a debenture payable to bearer contain some of the above clauses, but omit all reference to a register or registered holder. They usually contain clauses stating that (i) interest shall be payable only to the person producing the coupon attached to the debenture; (ii) when the principal sum is paid off, the debenture and the coupons must be surrendered; (iii) the company may safely pay interest to the bearer of the coupon; (iv) notice affecting the holders (e.g. of intention to pay off the principal) may be given by advertisement; (v) the debenture is to be treated as negotiable; and (vi) on the request of the holder, the company will register his name as the holder of the debenture.

Analysis of some of the 'conditions'

(a) 'PARI PASSU': When the debentures are to rank *pari passu*, all the debentures of the series are to be paid rateably so that if there is not enough money to go round to pay off the whole of the principal and interest in full, they are to abate proportionally: *Re Midland Express Ltd, Pearson v Midland Express Ltd* [1913] 1 Ch 499, CA. If the words *pari passu* are not inserted, the debentures are payable according to the date of issue or, if they were all issued on the same day, then according to the numerical order: *Gartside v Silkstone and Dodworth Coal and Iron Co* (1882) 21 Ch D 762. If the words *pari passu* are put in, a debenture-holder who seeks to enforce his security must sue on behalf of himself and all other debenture-holders of the same series. But he may take other steps against the company to get his own debt paid without consulting the interests of the other debenture-holders, provided that he does not attack any specific asset of the company.

The company cannot create a new series to rank *pari passu* with the old series unless a power to do so is expressly reserved: *Gartside v Silkstone and Dodworth Coal and Iron Co* (supra).

(b) FLOATING CHARGE: Unless otherwise agreed, a company is free to make specific mortgages of its property having priority over the floating charge: *Governments Stock and Other Securities Investment Co v*

Manila Railway Co [1897] AC 81, HL. It may assign the rent of land which is subject to a floating charge: *Re Ind Coope & Co Ltd, Fisher v Ind Coope & Co Ltd* [1911] 2 Ch 223.

A floating charge is also liable to be postponed to the rights of (i) a landlord who distrains for rent (*Re Roundwood Colliery Co, Lee v Roundwood Colliery Co* [1897] 1 Ch 373, CA); (ii) a creditor who obtains a garnishee order absolute (*Robson v Smith* [1895] 2 Ch 118); or (iii) a judgment creditor if the goods are seized and sold by the sheriff or the debt is paid to the sheriff to avoid a sale (*Davey & Co v Williamson & Sons* [1898] 2 QB 194).

Where either a receiver is appointed on behalf of the holders of any debentures of a company secured by a floating charge or possession is taken by or on behalf of the debenture holders of any property comprised in or subject to the charge, then, if the company is not at the time in the course of being wound up, the persons entitled to preferential payments in the event of a winding up must be paid out of any assets coming to the hands of the receiver or other person taking possession in priority to any claims for principal or interest in respect of the debentures: Companies Act 1985, s. 196 (1), (2). (*See* PREFERENTIAL PAYMENTS).

Where a debenture creates a floating charge and contains a provision that the company is not to create any prior charge, a person who takes a mortgage without notice of the debenture gets priority, e.g. even an equitable mortgage of title deeds if he has no notice of the provision: *Re Valletort Sanitary Steam Laundry Co Ltd, Ward v Valletort Sanitary Steam Laundry Co Ltd* [1903] 2 Ch 654.

An express power to create mortgages ranking in priority to a floating charge does not authorise the issue of a new floating charge in priority to the first: *Re Benjamin Cope & Sons Ltd, Marshall v Benjamin Cope & Sons Ltd* [1914] 1 Ch 800.

(c) DISREGARD OF EQUITIES: Where a 'condition' of a debenture states that the principal and interest are to be paid without any regard to any equities between the company and the original or any intermediate holder, the company is entitled to disregard notice of any equitable interest or trust: *Société Générale de Paris v Walker* (1885) 11 App Cas 20, HL. If a 'condition' to this effect is not inserted, a debenture, being a chose in action, is assignable subject to all equities: *Athenaeum Life Assurance Society v Pooley* (1858) 3 De G & J 294.

(d) PLACE OF PAYMENT: If no place of payment is stated, the company must find the debenture-holder and pay him: *Fowler v Midland Electric Corporation for Power Distribution Ltd* [1917] 1 Ch 127, CA. A demand for payment at the place specified in the 'conditions' is not necessary before proceedings are commenced: *Re Harris Calculating Machine Co, Summer v Harris Calculating Machine Co* [1914] 1 Ch 920. The proper method of payment and the currency in which the capital and interest are payable depend on the law of the place where payment is to be made: *Adelaide Electrical Supply Co Ltd v Prudential Assurance Co Ltd* [1934] AC 122, HL.

Issue of debentures

The power to issue debentures is usually set out expressly in the memorandum. The company can allot the rest of a series of debentures already issued at any time before winding up even after an action has been commenced by the debenture-holders to enforce their security: *Re Hubbard & Co Ltd, Hubbard v Hubbard & Co Ltd* (1898) 68 LJ Ch 54. On winding up the power to issue debentures ceases.

Debentures may be issued at a discount: *Re Regent's Canal Ironworks Co* (1876) 3 Ch D 43; *Mosely v Koffyfontein Mines Ltd* [1904] 2 Ch 108, CA.

If money is advanced to the company under an agreement that debentures will be issued, the lender becomes in equity the holder of the debentures: *Pegge v Neath and District Tramways Co Ltd* [1898] 1 Ch 183. An agreement to issue debentures usually creates an equitable charge requiring registration: *Re Fireproof Doors Ltd, Umney v Fireproof Doors Ltd* [1916] 2 Ch 142.

A contract with a company to take up and pay for any debentures of the company may be enforced by an order for specific performance: Companies Act 1985, s. 195.

The provisions of the Companies Act 1985 relating to prospectuses inviting the public to subscribe for shares also apply in the case of an invitation to subscribe for debentures. (*See* PROSPECTUS).

Transfer of debentures

Debentures payable to a registered holder are transferred in the manner specified in the 'conditions'.

The company cannot register a transfer unless a proper instrument of transfer has been delivered to it, or the transfer is an exempt transfer within the Stock Transfer Act 1982: Companies Act 1985, s. 183 (1), (2). The form is generally similar to that used in a transfer of shares.

Debentures payable to bearer are transferred by delivery.

A company can become a transferee of its own debentures: *Re George Routledge & Sons Ltd, Hummel v George Routledge & Sons Ltd* [1904] 2 Ch 474.

Debentures are transferable, unless the contrary is agreed, subject to all equities, e.g. after a resolution to wind up the company a shareholder can only transfer his debentures subject to his liability for calls due on his shares: *Re China Steamship Co, ex parte Mackenzie* (1869) LR 7 Eq 240. (*See* CALL). But this is not so if the debentures are bearer debentures or if the company has precluded itself from setting up such equities: *Re Goy & Co Ltd, Farmer & Co Ltd* [1900] 2 Ch 149.

But where the transferee is only a trustee for the transferor or his creditors, the company can enforce the equities against the transferee: *Re Brown and Gregory Ltd, Shepheard v Brown and Gregory Ltd* [1904] 1 Ch 627, CA.

Re-issue of debentures
Where a company has redeemed debentures previously issued, then
(a) unless provision to the contrary, whether express or implied, is contained in the articles or in any contract entered into by the company; or
(b) unless the company has, by passing a resolution to that effect or by some other act, manifested its intention that the debentures shall be cancelled,
the company has power to re-issue the debentures, either by re-issuing the same debentures or by issuing other debentures in their place: Companies Act 1985, s. 194 (1). On a re-issue of redeemed debentures the person entitled to the debentures has the same priorities as if the debentures had never been redeemed: ibid., s. 194 (2). Where a company has deposited any of its debentures to secure advances from time to time on current account or otherwise, the debentures are not deemed to have been redeemed by reason only of the company's account having ceased to be in debit while the debentures remained so deposited: ibid., s. 194 (3).

Register of debenture-holders
The company usually keeps a register of debenture holders, but it is not bound to do so.

A register of debenture-holders must not be kept elsewhere than at the registered office of the company, at any other office of the company at which the work of making it up is done, or if the company arranges with some other person for the making up of the register to be undertaken on behalf of the company by that other person, at the office of that other person at which the work is done: Companies Act 1985, s. 190 (3). Every company which keeps a register must send a notice in the prescribed form to the Registrar of Companies of the place where the register is kept and of any change in that place: ibid., s. 190 (5).

Every register must (except when duly closed) (but subject to such reasonable restrictions as the company may impose in general meeting, so that not less than 2 hours in each day are allowed for inspection) be open to the inspection of the registered holder of any debentures or any holder of shares in the company without fee, and of any other person on payment of a fee of 5p or such less sum as may be prescribed by the company: ibid., s. 191 (1). Any registered holder of debentures or holder of shares may require a copy of the register or any part of it on payment of 10p or such less sum as may be prescribed by the company, for every 100 words or fractional part of 100 words required to be copied: ibid., s. 191 (2). If inspection is refused or a copy is refused, the company and every officer of the company who is in default are liable on summary conviction to a fine not exceeding one-fifth of the statutory maximum, or, on conviction after continued contravention, to a daily default fine not exceeding one-fiftieth of the statutory maximum: ibid., ss. 191 (4), 730 and Sch. 24. Where a company is in default, the court may by order compel an immediate inspection of the register or direct that the copies required be sent to the person requiring them: ibid., s. 191 (5).

A register is deemed to be duly closed if closed in accordance with provisions contained in the articles or in the debentures during such period or periods, not exceeding in the whole 30 days in any year, as may be therein specified: ibid., s. 191 (6).

Remedies of debenture-holders

The remedies available to debenture-holders are: (a) sale; (b) appointment of a receiver; (c) foreclosure; (d) debenture-holders' action; (e) winding up petition; and (f) valuation of security.

(a) SALE: If the debenture-holder is the holder of a single debenture giving a charge over assets of the company, he will have an express power of sale or the implied power of sale given to a mortgagee by the Law of Property Act 1925, s. 103. If there is a debenture trust deed, the trustees will normally have an express or implied power of sale. (*See* DEBENTURE TRUST DEED). Sale may also be claimed in a debenture-holders' action. (*See* DEBENTURE HOLDERS' ACTION).

The holder of one of a series of debentures cannot sell the property unless the debentures contain an express power of sale: *Blaker v Herts and Essex Waterworks Co* (1889) 41 Ch D 399.

Any surplus of the proceeds of sale after payment of the principal, interest and costs due to the debenture-holders must be paid to the company: *Re Calgary and Medicine Hat Land Co Ltd, Pigeon v Calgary and Medicine Hat Land Co Ltd* [1908] 2 Ch 652, CA.

(b) APPOINTMENT OF RECEIVER: The debenture-holder may appoint a receiver if the 'conditions' of the debenture give him power to do so, or he may apply to the court in a debenture-holders' action to appoint one. (*See* DEBENTURE-HOLDERS' ACTION).

An appointment of a receiver by a debenture-holder takes effect when the document of appointment is handed to him by a person having the necessary authority in circumstances in which it may fairly be said that he was appointing a receiver, and the receiver accepts the proferred appointment, although the appointment may be tacit: *Cripps (Pharmaceuticals) Ltd v Wickenden* [1973] 2 All ER 606. The date of the instrument appointing the receiver is irrelevant except as a piece of evidence if the actual date of handing over is not known: ibid.

(c) FORECLOSURE: The debenture-holder may apply to the court for foreclosure, which may extend even to the uncalled capital of the company: *Sadler v Worley* [1894] 2 Ch 170. (*See* UNCALLED CAPITAL). But this remedy is not a usual one as it is necessary for all the debenture-holders of every class to be parties to the action: *Re Continental Oxygen Co, Elias v Continental Oxygen Co* [1897] 1 Ch 511.

(d) DEBENTURE-HOLDERS' ACTION: If his debenture is one of a series and legal proceedings are necessary, he will normally sue on behalf of himself and all other debenture-holders of the same class in a debenture-holders' action. (*See* DEBENTURE-HOLDERS' ACTION).

(e) WINDING UP PETITION: A debenture-holder may present a petition for winding up the company as he is a creditor for the amount of his principal and interest, but not for any premium payable on redemption unless the debenture expressly so provides: *Consolidated Goldfields of South Africa v Simmer and Jack East Ltd* (1913) 82 LJ Ch 214.

(f) VALUATION OF SECURITY: If the company is being wound up and his security is insufficient, the debenture-holder may value his security and prove for the balance of his debt or give up his security and prove for the whole debt.

The proceeds recovered by enforcing his security may be applied by the debenture-holder in payment of his costs, principal and interest up to the date of payment: *Wallace v Universal Automatic Machines Co* [1894] 2 Ch 547, CA. But if the security is insufficient and the company is insolvent, he cannot prove for interest which became due after winding up, nor can he get interest out of his security when arriving at a balance for which he can prove in the winding up: *Re London, Windsor and Greenwich Hotels Co, Quartermaine's Case* [1892] 1 Ch 639.

Debenture-holders' action. An action brought by a debenture-holder on behalf of himself and all other debenture-holders of the same class to enforce their rights under the debentures. The claim is usually for (i) a declaration that the debentures are a charge on the assets; (ii) accounts and inquiries to show what is due to the debenture-holders, what assets there are and what prior claims exist; (iii) the appointment of a receiver and manager; and (iv) enforcement of the debentures by sale or foreclosure. (*See* MANAGER: RECEIVER).

In case of a deficiency the assets realised by a debenture-holders' action are applied in the following order: (a) costs of realisation; (b) costs, including remuneration, of the receiver; (c) expenses of the debenture trust deed, including the trustee's remuneration; (d) the plaintiff's costs of the action; (e) preferential creditors, if the debentures are secured by a floating charge; and (f) the debenture-holders: *Re Glyncorrwg Colliery Co: Railway Debenture & General Trust Co v Glyncorrwg Colliery Co* [1926] Ch 951. (*See* DEBENTURE TRUST DEED).

Debenture trust deed. A deed charging specific property of the company by a legal mortgage or legal charge in favour of trustees for the debenture-holders and charging the rest of the assets of the company by a floating charge. (*See* DEBENTURE; FLOATING CHARGE).

Contents

The deed usually contains the following provisions:—(i) a legal charge on the freehold and leasehold property of the company; (ii) a floating charge over the rest of the company's assets; (iii) the company is to retain possession until it makes default in the payment of interest, etc., and then the trustees are to enter and sell; (iv) power to the trustees to sell or exchange any of the properties of the company at its request; (v) power to the trustees to convene meetings of debenture-holders; (vi) covenants by the company to insure, repair, etc.; (vii) provision for the remuneration of the trustees; and (viii) provisions for the exemption of the trustees from liability.

Debentures sometimes contain a clause that the rights of the debenture-holders may be modified with the consent of a majority of them, and that this consent shall bind all of them: *Sneath v Valley Gold Co Ltd* [1893] 1 Ch 477, CA. The modification may provide for postponement of payment of the principal or of interest (*Northern Assurance Co Ltd v Farnham United Breweries Ltd* [1912] 2 Ch 125) or for any other alteration of the rights of the debenture-holders, provided it is not unfair or oppressive (*Goodfellow v Nelson Line (Liverpool) Ltd* [1912] 2 Ch 324) or obtained by a bribe or special advantage given to some of the debenture-holders (*British America Nickel Corporation v O'Brien* [1927] AC 369, PC).

The remuneration of the trustees is usually a first charge on the assets: *Re Piccadilly Hotel Ltd, Paul v Piccadilly Hotel Ltd* [1911] 2 Ch 534. It usually is expressed to be payable 'during the continuance of the security' and 'notwithstanding the appointment of a receiver': *Re British Consolidated Oil Corporation Ltd, Howell v British Consolidated Oil Corporation Ltd* [1919] 2 Ch 81.

Any provision contained in a trust deed is void in so far as it would have the effect of exempting a trustee from or indemnifying him against liability for breach of trust where he fails to show the degree of care and diligence required of him as trustee, having regard to the provisions of the trust deed conferring on him any powers, authorities or discretions: Companies Act 1985, s. 192 (1). But this provision does not invalidate (a) any release otherwise validly given in respect of anything done or omitted to be done by a trustee before the giving of the release; or (b) any provision enabling such a release to be given (i) on the agreement of a majority of not less than three-fourths in value of the debenture-holders present and voting in person or, where proxies are permitted, by proxy at a meeting summoned for the purpose; and (ii) either with respect to specific acts or omissions or on the trustee dying or ceasing to act: ibid., s. 192 (2).

Copy of deed

A copy of any trust deed for securing an issue of debentures must be forwarded to every debenture-holder at his request on payment in the case of a printed trust deed of the sum of 20p (or such less sum as may be prescribed by the company), or, where the trust deed has not been printed, on payment of 10p (or such less sum as may be prescribed by the company) for every 100 words or fractional part of 100 words required to be copied: ibid., s. 191 (3). If a copy is refused or not forwarded, the company and every officer of the company who is in default is liable, on summary conviction, to a fine not exceeding one-fifth of the statutory maximum, or, on conviction after continued contravention, to a daily default fine not exceeding one-fiftieth of the statutory maximum: ibid., ss. 191 (4), 730 and Sch. 24. Where a company is in default, the court may by order direct that the copies required shall be sent to the person requiring them: ibid., s. 191 (5).

Advantages

The advantages of having a trust deed are that (i) if the company makes default, the trustees are there, ready to take the necessary steps instead of leaving it to the initiative of one of the debenture-holders to do so; (ii) the trustees may be given power to sell and thus to realise the security without the aid of the court; and (iii) a legal mortgage is vested in the trustees and where necessary the mortgage or charge is registered, thus preventing a subsequent legal mortgage from getting priority.

Declaration of solvency. A statutory declaration by the directors, where it is proposed to wind up a company voluntarily, to the effect that they have made a full inquiry into the affairs of the company, and that, having done so, they have formed the opinion that the company will be able to pay its debts in full within such period not exceeding 12 months from the commencement of the winding up as may be specified in the declaration: Companies Act 1985, s. 577 (1). Where there are more than 2 directors, the declaration must be made by the majority of them: ibid., s. 577 (1). (*See* COMMENCEMENT OF WINDING UP).

A declaration of solvency has no effect unless

(a) it is made within the 5 weeks immediately preceding the date of the passing of the resolution for winding up or on that date but before the passing of that resolution; and

(b) it embodies a statement of the company's assets and liabilities as at the latest practicable date before the making of the declaration: ibid., s. 577 (2).

The declaration by any directors must be delivered to the Registrar of Companies before the expiry of 15 days immediately following the date on which the resolution for winding up is passed: ibid., s. 577 (3).

If there is something which can be reasonably and fairly described as a 'statement of the company's assets and liabilities', and it subsequently appears that there are errors and omissions, this will not prevent the statement from being a valid one: *De Courcy v Clements* [1971] 1 All ER 681.

A director of a company making a declaration without having reasonable grounds for the opinion that the company will be able to pay its debts in full within the period specified is liable (i) on conviction on indictment to a term of imprisonment not exceeding 2 years or a fine or both; and (ii) on summary conviction to a term of imprisonment not exceeding 6 months or a fine not exceeding the statutory maximum or both: Companies Act 1985, ss. 577 (4), 730 and Sch. 24. If the company is wound up in pursuance of a resolution passed within 5 weeks after the making of the declaration, and its debts are not paid in full or provided for in full within the period specified, it is presumed (unless the contrary is shown) that the director did not have reasonable grounds for his opinion: ibid., s. 577 (5).

If a declaration required to be delivered to the Registrar of companies is not delivered within the time prescribed, the company and every officer in default is guilty of an offence and liable on summary conviction to a fine not exceeding one-fifth of the statutory maximum or, on conviction after continued contravention, to a daily default fine not exceeding one-fifth of the statutory maximum: ibid., ss. 577 (6), 730 and Sch. 24.

Deed of settlement. In the Companies Act 1985, s. 690 includes any contract of copartnery or other instrument constituting or regulating the company, not being an Act of Parliament, a royal charter, or letters patent: Companies Act 1985, s. 690 (4).

Default fine. A daily fine imposed where a person is convicted after continued contravention.

Where the Act imposes liability to a default fine on conviction after continued contravention, then, if, after a person has been summarily convicted of that offence, the original contravention is continued, he is liable on a second or subsequent summary conviction of that offence to the fine specified in the enactment for each day on which the contravention is continued instead of to the penalty which may be imposed on the first conviction of that offence: Companies Act 1985, s. 730 (4).

Deferred debt. A debt (e.g. one in respect of which a rate of interest varying with the profits of a business is payable) which has to be paid after the preferred debts and the ordinary debts have been paid in full. (*See* ORDINARY DEBT; PREFERENTIAL PAYMENTS).

Department of Trade and Industry. The Government department responsible for the supervision, operation and reform of Company and Partnership Law.

Department of Trade and Industry, powers of inspection and investigation of company. *See* INSPECTION AND INVESTIGATION OF COMPANY.

Director. A person in charge of the overall direction of the affairs of a company.

I. *Appointment, Removal, Resignation and Retirement*

APPOINTMENT (a) How appointed

(i) *Appointment of the first directors.* The first directors may be named in the articles of association. If they are not so named, the first directors are appointed by the subscribers to the memorandum of association. (*See* MEMORANDUM OF ASSOCIATION; SUBSCRIBER). This must be done by (i) the majority at a meeting of subscribers (*York Tramways Co v Willows* (1882) 8 QBD 685, CA; or (ii) a writing signed by all the subscribers unless the articles otherwise provide. (*John Morley Building Co v Barras* [1891] 2 Ch 386).

(ii) *Appointment of subsequent directors.* The way in which the appointments of subsequent directors are to be made is usually specified by the articles, e.g. by the company in general meeting or by the continuing directors from time to time.

Table A, art. 79 states: 'The directors may appoint a person who is willing to act to be a director, either to fill a vacancy or as an additional director, provided that the appointment does not cause the number of directors to exceed any number fixed by or in accordance with the articles as the maximum number of directors. A director so appointed shall hold office only until the next following annual general meeting and shall not be taken into account in determining the directors who are to retire by rotation at the meeting. If not reappointed at such annual general meeting, he shall vacate office at the conclusion thereof.' (*See* ANNUAL GENERAL MEETING; ROTATION OF DIRECTORS).

The power of the company in general meeting to appoint directors is not taken away by the usual provisions in the articles enabling the directors to fill vacancies or appoint additional directors: *Worcester Corsetry Ltd v Witting* [1936] Ch 640, CA.

If no provision is made, or if the directors fail to appoint anyone, the company in general meeting has power to appoint new directors: *Barron v Potter* [1914] 1 Ch 895.

Power may be given to an outsider to appoint directors: *British Murac Syndicate Ltd v Alperton Rubber Co Ltd* [1915] 2 Ch 186.

At a general meeting of a public company, a motion for the appointment of 2 or more persons as directors of the company by a single resolution must not be made, unless a resolution that it shall be so made has first been agreed to by the meeting without any vote being given against it: Companies Act 1985, s. 292 (1). (*See* ANNUAL GENERAL MEETING; EXTRAORDINARY GENERAL MEETING). A resolution moved in contravention of this provision is void, whether or not its being so moved was objected to at the time: Companies Act 1985, s. 292 (2). A motion for approving a person's appointment or for nominating a person for appointment is treated as a motion for his appointment: ibid., s. 292 (3).

(b) Age on appointment

In the case of a public company or a private company which is a subsidiary of a public company no person is capable of being appointed as a director if at the time of his appointment he has attained the age of 70: ibid., s. 293 (1). This rule, however, may be qualified by provisions in the company's articles: ibid., s. 293 (7).

But a person may be appointed at any age if his appointment is made or approved by the company in general meeting: ibid., s. 293 (5). But special notice is required of any resolution appointing or approving the appointment of a director for it to have effect: ibid., s. 293 (5). (*See* SPECIAL NOTICE). The notice given to the company and by the company to its members must state or have stated the age of the person to whom it relates: Companies Act 1985, s. 293 (5).

A person who is appointed or to his knowledge proposed to be appointed director of such a company at a time when he has attained any retiring age applicable to him as director either under s. 293 or under the company's articles must give notice of his age to the company: ibid., s. 294 (1). But this provision does not apply in relation to a person's reappointment on the termination of a previous appointment as director of the company: ibid., s. 294 (3). Any person who (a) fails to give notice of his age; or (b) acts as director under any appointment, is liable on summary conviction to a fine not exceeding one-fifth of the statutory maximum or, on conviction after continued contravention, to a daily default fine not exceeding one-fiftieth of the statutory maximum: ibid., ss. 294 (4), 730 and Sch. 24.

(c) Managing Director

The directors may appoint one of their number to be a managing director to deal with the day-to-day management of the company. (*See* MANAGING DIRECTOR).

(d) Service Contract

On his appointment the director and the company may enter into a service contract setting out the terms and conditions on which he is appointed and the duration of his employment (*See* DIRECTOR'S SERVICE CONTRACT).

REMOVAL: A company may by ordinary resolution remove a director before the expiration of his period of office, notwithstanding anything in its articles or in any agreement between it and him: Companies Act 1985, s. 303 (1). (*See* ORDINARY RESOLUTION). Special notice is required of any resolution to remove a director: Companies Act 1985, s. 303 (2).

(*See* SPECIAL NOTICE). On receipt of notice of an intended resolution to remove a director the company must forthwith send a copy of it to the director concerned, and he (whether or not he is a member of the company) is entitled to be heard on the resolution at the meeting: Companies Act 1985, s. 304 (1).

Nothing in the Act prevents the articles giving certain shares or classes of shares special voting rights e.g. special voting rights may be validly given to a director on a resolution to remove him from office: *Bushell v Faith* [1970] 1 All ER 53, HL.

Where notice is given of an intended resolution to remove a director, and the director concerned makes with respect to it representations in writing to the company (not exceeding a reasonable length), and requests their notification to members of the company, the company must, unless the representations are received by it too late for it to do so

(a) in any notice of the resolution given to members of the company state the fact of the representations having been made; and

(b) send a copy of the representations to every member of the company to whom notice of the meeting is sent (whether before or after receipt of the representations by the company): Companies Act 1985, s. 304 (2).

If a copy of the representations is not sent because received too late or because of the company's default, the director may (without prejudice to his right to be heard orally) require the representations to be read out at the meeting: ibid., s. 304 (3).

But copies of the representations need not be sent out and the representations need not be read out at the meeting if, on the application either of the company or of any other person who claims to be aggrieved, the court is satisfied that the rights conferred by the above provisions are being abused to secure needless publicity for defamatory matter: ibid., s. 304 (4). The court may order the company's costs on an application to be paid in whole or in part by the director even though he is not a party to the application: ibid., s. 304 (5).

Nothing in the above provisions is to be taken as depriving a person who has been removed of compensation or damages payable to him in respect of the termination of his appointment as director or of any appointment terminating with that as director: ibid., s. 303 (5).

A director who has been removed may be entitled to compensation if the articles or his service contract so provide: *Read v Astoria Garage (Streatham) Ltd* [1952] 2 All ER 292. (*See* DIRECTOR'S SERVICE CONTRACT). Where a director is removed and the company is liable to compensate him, he must mitigate the damages as far as possible: *Shindler v Northern Raincoat Co Ltd* [1960] 2 All ER 239; *Yetton v Eastwoods Froy Ltd* [1966] 3 All ER 353.

RESIGNATION: A director may resign his office in the manner provided by the articles. If the articles contain no provision, he can resign on reasonable notice.

A director, who has resigned, cannot withdraw his resignation: *Glossop v Glossop* [1927] 2 Ch 370.

Where the articles provide that a director may resign in writing, a verbal resignation accepted by the company in general meeting is effective and cannot be withdrawn: *Latchford Premier Cinema Ltd v Ennion* [1931] 2 Ch 409.

Where a director is appointed under a service agreement, he may resign in accordance with its provisions, if any: *Taupo Totara Timber Co Ltd v Rowe* [1977] 3 All ER 123, PC. (*See* DIRECTOR'S SERVICE CONTRACT).

RETIREMENT: The articles usually provide that a proportion of the directors shall retire by rotation year by year. (*See* ROTATION OF DIRECTORS).

In the case of a public company or a private company which is a subsidiary of a public company, a director must vacate his office at the conclusion of the annual general meeting next after he attains the age of 70: Companies Act 1985, s. 293 (3). This rule, however, may be qualified by provisions in the articles: ibid., s. 293 (7).

Where a person retires by virtue of this requirement, no provision for the automatic reappointment of retiring directors in default of another appointment applies: ibid., s. 293 (4). If at the meeting at which he retires the vacancy is not filled, it may be filled as a casual vacancy: ibid., s. 293 (4).

II. *Register of Directors*

Every company must keep at its registered office a register of its directors: Companies Act 1985, s. 288 (1). (*See* REGISTER OF DIRECTORS AND SECRETARIES).

III. *Director's particulars on letters etc.*

A company must not state, in any form, the name of any of its directors (otherwise than in the text or as a signatory) on any business letter on which the company's name appears unless it states on the letter in legible characters the Christian name or its initials and surname of every director of the company who is an individual and the corporate name of every director of the company who is an individual and the corporate name of every corporate director: Companies Act 1985, s. 305 (2) (a). This provision does not apply to a company which was registered before 23 November 1916: ibid., s. 305 (2) (a).

If a company makes default in complying with this requirement, the company and every officer of the company who is in default are liable on conviction on indictment to a fine and on summary conviction to a fine not exceeding the statutory maximum: ibid., ss. 305 (3), 730 and Sch. 24.

IV. *Remuneration*

Directors are not entitled to any remuneration apart from express agreement.

The articles may provide for their remuneration; if so, it cannot be changed or increased without a special resolution: *Boschoek Proprietary Co Ltd v Fuke* [1906] 1 Ch 148:; *Kerr v Marine Products Ltd* (1928) 44 TLR 292. (*See* SPECIAL RESOLUTION). Where the articles provide for remuneration, it becomes a debt due from the company to the directors, and may be sued for, and may be paid for out of capital if there are no profits: *Re Lundy Granite Co Ltd, Lewis's Case* (1872) 26 LT 673.

Where a director is to be paid such remuneration as the board of directors determines, and no resolution concerning the amount of his salary is passed by the board before the company goes into liquidation, he is entitled to nothing: *Re Richmond Gate Property Co Ltd* [1964] 3 All ER 936.

Table A, art. 82 states: 'The directors shall be entitled to such remuneration as the company may by ordinary resolution determine and, unless the resolution provides otherwise, the remuneration shall be deemed to accrue from day to day.'

Any provision in the articles as to the remuneration of the directors must be stated in the prospectus: Companies Act 1985, Sch. 3, Part 1, para. 1 (1) (b) (*See* PROSPECTUS).

In a note to the accounts of a company there must be shown, so far as the information contained in company's books and papers or the company has the right to obtain it from the persons concerned, the aggregate amount of the directors' emoluments: Companies Act 1985, s. 231, Sch. 5, Part V, para. 22 (1).

It is not lawful for a company to pay a director remuneration (whether as director or otherwise) free of income tax or otherwise calculated by reference to or varying with the amount of his income tax, or to or with any rate of income tax: Companies Act 1985, s. 311 (1). Any provision contained in a company's articles, or in any contract, or in any resolution of a company or a company's directors, for payment to a director of remuneration as above mentioned has effect as if it provided for payment, as a gross sum subject to income tax, of the net sum for which it actually provides: ibid., s. 311 (2).

When a company is making no profits, the directors may agree to waive their remuneration. There is sufficient consideration to support such an agreement if the several directors mutually agree to waive their claims: *West Yorkshire Darracq Agency Ltd v Coleridge* [1911] 2 KB 326.

Directors cannot get their travelling and other expenses unless this is expressly provided for: *Young v Naval, Military and Civil Service Co-operative Society of South Africa* [1905] 1 KB 687.

Table A, art. 83 states: 'The directors may be paid all travelling, hotel, and other expenses properly incurred by them in connection with their attendance at meetings of directors or committees of directors or general meetings or separate meetings of the holders of any class of shares or of debentures of the company or otherwise in connection with the discharge of their duties.'

V *Qualification shares*

The company's articles may require a director to have a specified number of qualification shares. (*See* QUALIFICATION SHARE). If he does not have them, he cannot be a director.

VI *Disqualification of director*

Where the court makes a disqualification order, the director ceases to hold office: Companies Act 1985, s. 295. (*See* DISQUALIFICATION ORDER).

If a director does not acquire or relinquishes his qualification shares, his office is vacated: Companies Act 1985, s. 291. (*See* QUALIFICATION SHARE).

In general, a director of a public company or a private company which is a subsidiary of a public company must vacate office on attaining the age of 70: Companies Act 1985, s. 293 (3).

A director becomes disqualified if he does anything which by the articles amounts to a disqualification.

Table A, art. 81 states: 'The office of a director shall be vacated if

(a) he ceases to be a director by virtue of any provision of the Act or he becomes prohibited by law from being a director; or

(b) he becomes bankrupt or makes any arrangement or composition with his creditors generally; or

(c) he is, or may be, suffering from mental disorder and either
   (i) he is admitted to hospital in pursuance of an application for admission for treatment under the Mental Health Act 1983; or
   (ii) an order is made by a court having jurisdiction (whether in the United Kingdom or elsewhere) in matters concerning mental disorder for his detention or for the appointment of a receiver or other person to exercise powers with respect to his property or affairs; or

(d) he resigns his office by notice to the company; or

(e) he shall for more than 6 consecutive months have been absent without permission of the directors from meetings of directors held during that period and the directors resolve that his office be vacated.'

If the articles state that a director is disqualified if he holds a place of profit under the company, and he is appointed as a paid trustee by the debenture holders, this constitutes disqualification: *Astley v New Tivoli Ltd* [1889] 1 Ch 151. Where a director 'absenting himself' is a disqualification, this refers only to voluntary absence: *Re London and Northern Bank, Mack's Claim* [1900] WN 114. Where the disqualification consists of 'making a secret profit', the disqualification does not prevent re-election after the transaction is complete: *Red Bodega Co Ltd* [1904] 1 Ch 276.

VII *Compensation for loss of office*
Where it is proposed that a director is to receive compensation for loss of office, the details of the proposed payment must be approved by the company: Companies Act 1985, ss. 312, 313. (*See* COMPENSATION FOR LOSS OF OFFICE).

VIII *Notification of director's shareholding*
A director of a company who is interested in the shares or debentures of the company must notify the company in writing of the number or amount and class of shares or debentures involved: Companies Act 1985, s. 324. (*See* DIRECTOR'S SHAREHOLDINGS).

IX *Powers of directors*
These are generally set out in the articles, and there is usually a clause giving them powers of management and all the powers of the company which are not required to be exercised by the company in general meeting. See e.g. *Re Pyle Works (No. 2)* [1981] 1 Ch 173.

Table A, art. 70 states: 'Subject to the provisions of the Act, the memorandum and articles and to any directions given by special resolution, the business of the company shall be managed by the directors who may exercise all the powers of the company. No alteration of the memorandum or articles and no such direction shall invalidate any prior act of the directors which would have been valid if that alteration had not been made or that direction had not been given. The powers given by this regulation shall not be limited by any special power given to the directors by the articles and a meeting of directors at which a quorum is present may exercise all powers exercisable by the directors.' (*See* QUORUM; SPECIAL RESOLUTION).

The directors may, by power of attorney or otherwise, appoint any person to be the agent of the company for such purposes and on such conditions as they determine, including authority to delegate all or any of his powers: Table A, art. 71.

The directors may delegate any of their powers to any committee consisting of one or more directors: ibid., art. 72. They may also delegate to any managing director (*see* MANAGING DIRECTOR) or any director holding any other executive office such of their powers as they consider desirable to be exercised by him: ibid., art. 72. Any such delegation may be made subject to any conditions the directors may impose, and either collaterally with or to the exclusion of their own powers and may be revoked or altered: ibid., art. 72. Subject to any such conditions, the proceedings of a committee with 2 or more members shall be governed by the articles regulating the proceedings of directors so far as they are capable of applying: ibid., art. 72.

The directors are the only persons who can deal with the matters thus assigned to them, and their decision cannot be overruled even by a general meeting of the company unless the articles are altered by a special resolution, or unless the directors are acting in their own interests against the interests of the company: *Automatic Self-Cleansing Filter Syndicate Ltd v Cuninghame* [1906] 2 Ch 34, CA; *Quin and Axtens Ltd v Salmon* [1909] AC 442, HL; *Scott v Scott* [1943] 1 All ER 582. They should, however, communicate their policy to the members and are bound to do so if their policy is attacked by any of them: *Marshall's Valve Gear Co v Manning, Wardle & Co Ltd* [1909] 1 Ch 267.

The members may enlarge the powers of the directors, and enable them to do anything which the company could do. Further, if the directors act beyond their powers, the members may ratify their act if it is within the powers of the company.

Directors may not delegate their powers unless the articles expressly give them power to do so: *Re Liverpool Household Stores Association Ltd* (1890) 59 LJ Ch 616.

The powers of the directors cease on the appointment of a liquidator in a volur.tary winding up unless they are expressly preserved: Companies Act 1985, s. 580 (2) (members' voluntary winding up), s. 591 (2) (creditors' voluntary winding up). (*See* LIQUIDATOR).

X *Duties of directors*

(i) DUTY TO HAVE REGARD TO INTERESTS OF EMPLOYEES: The matters to which the directors of a company are to have regard in the performance of their functions include the interests of the company's employees in general as well, as the interests of its members: Companies Act 1985, s. 309 (1).

This duty is owed by the directors to the company alone and is enforceable in the same way as any other fiduciary duty owed to a company by its directors: ibid., s. 309 (2).

(ii) DUTY OF CARE: A director is under a duty of care, the standard of which is that of an ordinary person in the conduct of his own affairs: *Re City Equitable Fire Insurance Co* [1925] Ch 407, CA. A director, who signs cheques, makes himself liable for negligence if the cheques ought not to have been paid, unless he takes reasonable care to satisfy himself of the purpose for which and the authority under which the cheques are to be signed: *Joint Stock Discount Co v Brown* (1869) LR 8 Eq 381. A director who habitually abstains from attending board meetings may become liable for the acts of his co-directors, but he is not bound to attend all board meetings: *Re Denham & Co* (1883) 25 Ch D 752. If the directors act within their powers in the *bona fide* exercise of their discretion, they are not liable for mere errors of judgment: *Re New Mashonaland Exploration Co* [1892] 3 Ch 577. A director is not liable if he can show that he acted without knowledge of the facts which made his act illegal, provided that he was not guilty of negligence: *Dovey v Cory* [1901] AC 477, HL.

A clause in the articles of association or in any contract with the company protecting directors from liability in case of negligence is void: Companies Act 1985, s. 310 (1), (2).

If, in any proceedings for negligence against a director, it appears to the court hearing the case that he is or may be liable in respect of the negligence but that he has acted honestly and reasonably and that, having regard to all the circumstances of the case, he ought fairly to be excused for the negligence, the court may relieve him, either wholly or partly, from his liability on such terms as it may think fit: ibid., s. 727 (1). *See Re Duomatic Ltd* [1969] 1 All ER 161.

If one of several directors has been made to pay damages for negligence, he is entitled to contribution from the others: *Ashurst v Mason* (1875) LR 20 Eq 225.

(iii) DUTY TO ACT HONESTLY: The directors must not make a profit from their position: *Regal (Hastings) Ltd v Gulliver* [1942] 1 All ER 378, HL; *Cook v Deeks* [1916] 1 AC 554, PC. Whether the company could have itself obtained a contract with a third party, which has been entered into by a director in breach of his duty to be honest, is irrelevant: *Industrial Development Consultants Ltd v Cooley* [1972] 2 All ER 162. If a director receives a secret profit from a third party without the consent of the company, the company is entitled to claim it from him: *Boston Deep Sea Fishing & Ice Co v Ansell* (1888) 39 Ch D 339, CA.

If he has acted honestly and reasonably and having regard to all the circumstances, he ought fairly to be excused, the court may relieve him from liability for breach of trust: Companies Act 1985, s. 727 (1).

(iv) DUTY TO DISCLOSE INTEREST IN CONTRACTS: It is the duty of a director of a company who is in any way, whether directly or indirectly, interested in a contract or proposed contract with the company to declare the nature of his interest at a meeting of the directors of the company: ibid., s. 317 (1).

In the case of a proposed contract, the declaration must be made at the meeting of the directors at which the question of entering into the contract is first taken into consideration, or if the director was not at the date of that meeting interested in the proposed contract, at the next meeting of the directors held after he became so interested: ibid., s. 317 (2). In a case where the director becomes interested in a contract after it is made, the declaration must be made at the first meeting of the directors held after the director becomes so interested: ibid., s. 317 (2).

Any director who fails to comply with the above provisions is liable on conviction on indictment to a fine, and on summary conviction to a fine not exceeding the statutory maximum: ibid., ss. 317 (7), 730 and Sch. 24.

Where a director fails to disclose his interest, the contract is voidable at the instance of the company: *Hely-Hutchinson v Brayhead Ltd* [1967] 3 All ER 98, CA.

The articles usually provide that a director must not vote at directors' meetings on contracts in which he is interested, but this does not necessarily prevent him from voting on the same question at a meeting of shareholders: *North-West Transportation Co v Beatty* (1887) 12 App Cas 589.

Table A, art. 85 states: 'Subject to the provisions of the Act and provided that he has disclosed to the directors the nature and extent of any material interest of his, a director notwithstanding his office

(a) may be a party to, or otherwise interested in, any transaction or arrangement with the company or in which the company is otherwise interested;

(b) may be a director or other officer of, or employed by, or a party to any transaction or arrangement with, or otherwise interested in any body corporate promoted by the company or in which the company is otherwise interested; and

(c) shall not, by reason of his office, be accountable to the company for any benefit which he derives from any such office or employment or from any such transaction or arrangement or from any interest in any such body corporate and no such transaction or arrangement shall be liable to be avoided on the ground of any such interest or benefit.'

A general notice given to the directors that a director is to be regarded as having an interest of the nature and extent specified in the notice in any transaction or arrangement in which a specified person or class of persons is interested is deemed to be a disclosure that the director has an interest in any such transaction of the nature and extent so specified: Table A, art. 86 (a).

An interest of which a director has no knowledge and of which it is unreasonable to expect him to have knowledge must not be treated as an interest of his: ibid., art. 86 (b).

Director, shadow. *See* SHADOW DIRECTOR.

Director's service contract. A contract entered into between a director and a company setting out his remuneration and the terms of service. Every company must keep at an appropriate place

(a) in the case of each director whose contract of service is in writing, a copy of that contract;

(b) in the case of each director whose contract of service with the company is not in writing, a written memorandum setting out its terms;

(c) in the case of each director who is employed under a contract of service with a subsidiary of the company, a copy of that contract or, if it is not in writing, a written memorandum setting out terms: Companies Act 1985, s. 318 (1).

All copies and memoranda kept by a company must be kept at the same place: ibid., s. 318 (2). (*See* SUBSIDIARY COMPANY). Appropriate places are (i) the company's registered office; (ii) the place where its register of members is kept (if other than its registered office); and (iii) its principal place of business provided that that is situated in England: ibid., s. 318 (3).

Every company must send notice in the prescribed form to the Registrar of Companies of the place where the copies and memoranda are kept, and of any change in that place except in a case where they have at all times been kept at its registered office: ibid., s. 318 (4). Every copy and memorandum must, during business hours (subject to such reasonable restrictions as the company may in general meeting impose, so that not less than 2 hours in each day are allowed for inspection) be open to the inspection of any member of the company without charge: ibid., s. 318 (7).

If the copies and memoranda are not kept as required by the above provisions, or if an inspection is refused, or if the company is in default for 14 days in complying with s. 318 (4) (supra), the company and every officer who is in default are liable on summary conviction to a fine not exceeding one-fifth of the statutory maximum, or, on conviction after continued contravention, to a default fine not exceeding one-fiftieth of the statutory maximum: ibid., ss. 318 (8), 730 and Sch. 24. Where an inspection is refused, the court may by order compel an immediate inspection: ibid., s. 318 (9).

A company must not incorporate in any agreement any term by which a director's employment cannot be terminated for a period of 5 years by the company by notice or can be so terminated only in specified circumstances, unless the term is first approved by the company in general meeting: ibid., s. 319 (1), (3).

A resolution of a company approving such a term must not be passed at a general meeting of the company unless a written memorandum setting out the proposed agreement incorporating the term is available for inspection by members of the company (a) at the company's registered office for not less than the period of 15 days ending with the date of the meeting; and (b) at the meeting itself: ibid., s. 319 (5). A term incorporated in an agreement in contravention of the above provision is void; and the agreement is deemed to contain a term entitling the company to terminate it at any time by the giving of reasonable notice: ibid., s. 319 (7).

Director's shareholdings. Shares in a company which are owned by a director of that company.

Duty to notify company

A director of a company who is interested in the shares or debentures of the company must notify the company in writing of the number or amount and class of shares or debentures involved: Companies Act 1985, s. 324. For the meaning of 'interested', see ibid., Sch. 13, Part I.

A similar notification must be given if he ceases to be interested: ibid., s. 324.

The provisions of s. 324 extend to the spouses and children of a director: ibid., s. 328.

A person who fails to discharge an obligation to notify the company, or who, in purported discharge of such an obligation, makes to a company a statement which he knows to be false, or recklessly makes to it a statement which is false, is liable on conviction on indictment to a term of imprisonment not exceeding 2 years or a fine or both, and on summary conviction to a term of imprisonment not exceeding 6 months or a fine not exceeding the statutory maximum or both: ibid., ss. 324 (7), 730 and Sch. 24.

If it appears to the Secretary of State that there are circumstances suggesting that contraventions may have occurred, in relation to shares in, or debentures of a company, of the above provisions, he may appoint one or more competent inspectors to carry out such investigations as are requisite to establish whether or not contraventions have occurred, and to report the result of their investigations to him: ibid., s. 446 (1). (*See* INSPECTION AND INVESTIGATION OF COMPANY).

Register of directors' interests

Every company must keep a register containing the above information when forwarded to the company by the director: Companies Act 1985, s. 325 (1), (2).

Further, whenever the company grants to a director a right to subscribe for shares in or debentures of the company, it must enter in the register against his name the date on which it is granted, the period during which it is exercisable, the consideration for the grant, and the description of shares or debentures involved, their number and the price to be paid for them: ibid., s. 325 (3).

Whenever such a right is exercised by a director, the company must enter in the register against his name that fact, the number of shares or debentures involved, and, if they were registered in his name, that fact, and, if not, the name of the person in whose name they were registered: ibid., s. 325 (4).

The company must send notice in the prescribed form to the Registrar of Companies of the place where the register is kept and of any change in that place except in a case in which it has at all times been kept at its registered office: ibid., Sch. 13, Part IV, para. 27.

The register must be open during business hours to the inspection of any member of the company without charge and of any other person on payment of 5p, or such less sum as the company may prescribe: ibid., Sch. 13, Part IV, para 25.

Any member of the company or other person may require a copy of the register or any part of it on payment of 10p, or such less sum as the company may prescribe, for every 100 words or fractional part of 100 words required to be copied: ibid., Sch. 13, Part IV, para. 26 (1).

The register must be produced at the commencement of the company's annual general meeting, and must remain open and accessible during the continuance of the meeting to any person attending it: ibid., Sch. 13, Part IV, para. 29.

Duty to notify Stock Exchange

Whenever a company in the case of which shares or debentures are listed on a recognised stock exchange is notified of the acquisition of its shares or debentures by a director, the company is under an obligation to notify that stock exchange of that matter: ibid., s. 329 (1). The stock exchange may publish, in such manner as it may determine, any such information received by it: ibid., s. 329 (1).

Directors, register of. *See* REGISTER OF DIRECTORS AND SECRETARIES.

Directors' report. A report by the directors concerning the finances and general activities of the company during the preceding financial year.

There must be attached to every balance sheet a report by the directors containing a fair review of the development of the business of the company and its subsidiaries during the financial year and of their position at the end of it and stating the amount, if any, which they recommend should be paid as dividend, and the amount (if any) which they propose to carry to reserves: Companies Act 1985, s. 235 (1). (*See* BALANCE SHEET; DIVIDEND; SUBSIDIARY COMPANY).

Additional matters to be stated

(a) MATTERS OF GENERAL NATURE: The directors' report must state the names of the persons who, at any time during the financial year, were directors of the company and the principal activities of the company and of its subsidiaries and any significant change in those activities in that year: Companies Act 1985, s. 235 (2).

It must also

(i) if significant changes in the fixed assets of the company or of any of its subsidiaries have occurred in the financial year, contain particulars of the changes, and, if, in the case of those assets as consist of interests in land, their market value differs substantially from the amount at which they are included in the balance sheet, and the difference is, in the directors' opinion, of such significance as to require that the attention of the members of the company or of holders of debentures should be drawn to it, indicate the difference with such degree of precision as is practicable;

(ii) state the extent, at the end of the financial year, according to the register of directors' shareholdings, of a director's holding of shares in, or debentures of, the company;

(iii) contain particulars of any important events affecting the company, an indication of likely future developments in the business of the company and of its subsidiaries in the field of research and development; and

(iv) in the case of companies of such classes as may be prescribed by regulations made by the Secretary of State contain such information as may be prescribed about the arrangements in force in that year for securing the health, safety and welfare at work of employees of the company and its subsidiaries and for protecting other persons against risk to health or safety arising out of or in connection with the activities at work of those employees: ibid., s. 261 (5), Sch. 7.

(ii) PARTICULARS OF ACQUISITION OF COMPANY'S OWN SHARES: The directors' report must give particulars of the acquisition of its own fully paid shares by a company or its nominee or by a person with financial assistance from the company: ibid., s. 261 (5), Sch. 7, Part II.

(c) TURNOVER AND PROFITABILITY OF EACH CLASS OF BUSINESS: Where the company has carried on business of two or more classes that in the opinion of the directors differ substantially from each other, there must be contained in the directors' report a statement of

(i) the proportions in which the turnover for that year is divided amongst those classes; and

(ii) as regards business of each class, the extent to which, in the opinion of the directors, the carrying on of business of that class contributed to, or restricted, the profit or loss of the company for that year: s. 261 (6), Sch. 10.

(d) AVERAGE NUMBER OF EMPLOYEES AND AMOUNT OF THEIR WAGES
The directors' report must contain a statement of

(i) the average number of persons employed by the company in each week in the year; and

(ii) the aggregate remuneration paid to them in the year: ibid., s. 18 (1).

(e) CONTRIBUTIONS FOR POLITICAL OR CHARITABLE PURPOSES: The directors' report must state the amount of money exceeding £200 given by way of contributions for political or charitable purposes: ibid., s. 261 (6), Sch. 7, Part I, paras. 3 to 5. (*See* MONEY GIVEN FOR POLITICAL PURPOSES).

(f) EMPLOYMENT OF DISABLED PERSONS: In every directors' report, there must be contained a statement describing such policy as the company has applied during the financial year

(i) for giving full and fair consideration to applications for employment by the company made by disabled persons having regard to their particular aptitude and abilities;

(ii) for continuing the employment of, and for arranging appropriate training for, employees of the company who have become disabled persons during the period when they were employed by the company; and

(iii) otherwise for the training, career development and promotion of disabled persons employed by the company: Companies Act 1985, s. 261 (5), Sch. 7, Part III.

Penalty for failure to state above matters

In respect of any failure in the case of a company to comply with the above requirements, every person who was a director immediately before the end of the financial year is guilty of an offence and liable on conviction on indictment to a fine, and, on summary conviction, to a fine not exceeding the statutory maximum: ibid., ss. 235 (7), 730 and Sch. 24.

Checking consistency of directors' report

It is the auditors' duty, in preparing their report, to consider whether the information given in the directors' report relating to the financial year in question is consistent with those accounts: ibid., s. 237 (6), (*See* AUDITOR; AUDITORS' REPORT). If the auditors are of the opinion that the information given in the directors' report is not consistent with the company's accounts for the financial year, they must state that fact in the auditors' report: Companies Act 1985, s. 237 (6).

Right to receive copy of the report

The members of a company, the holders of debentures of a company and persons who, though not members or holders of debentures, are entitled to receive notices of general meetings, must be sent copies of the directors' report: ibid., s. 246 (1).

Directors, rotation of. *See* ROTATION OF DIRECTORS.

Disclaimer of onerous property. A liquidator's right to renounce liability in respect of land burdened with onerous covenants, and of shares and of unprofitable contracts.

Where any part of the property of a company which is being wound up consists of land (of any tenure) burdened with onerous covenants, of shares or stock in companies, of unprofitable contracts, or of any other property that is unsaleable, or not readily saleable, by reason of its binding its possessor to the performance of any onerous act or to the payment of any sum of money, the liquidator may with the leave of the court by writing signed by him, at any time within 12 months after the commencement of the winding up or such extended period as may be allowed by the court, disclaim the property: Companies Act 1985, s. 618 (1), (2), (3). (*See* COMMENCEMENT OF WINDING UP).

The disclaimer operates to determine, as from the date of disclaimer, the rights, interests and liabilities of the company and the company's property, in or in respect of the property disclaimed; but it does not (except so far as is necessary for the purpose of releasing the company and its property) from liability affect the rights or liabilities of any other person: Companies Act 1985, s. 618 (4).

The court, before or on granting leave to disclaim, may require such notices to be given to persons interested, and impose such terms as a condition of granting leave, and make such other order in the matter, as it thinks just: ibid., s. 619 (1).

The liquidator is not entitled to disclaim property where an application in writing has been made to him by any persons interested in the property requiring him to decide whether he will or will not disclaim, and he has not, within 28 days after the receipt of the application (or such further period as may be allowed by the court) given notice to the applicant that he intends to apply to the court for leave to disclaim: ibid., s. 619 (2). In the case of a contract, if the liquidator after such an application does not within that period or further period concerned disclaim the contract, the company is deemed to have adopted it: ibid., s. 619 (3).

The court may, on the application of any person who is, as against the liquidator, entitled to the benefit or subject to the burden of a contract made with the company, make an order rescinding the contract on such terms as to payment by or to either party of damages for the non-performance of the contract or otherwise as the court thinks just: ibid., s. 619 (4). Any damages payable under the order to such a person may be proved by him as a debt in the winding up: ibid., s. 619 (4).

The court may, on an application by any person who claims any interest in any disclaimed property, and on hearing any such persons as it thinks fit, make an order for the vesting of the property in or its delivery to any persons entitled to it, and on such terms as the court thinks just: ibid., s. 619 (5).

A person injured by the operation of a disclaimer is deemed a creditor of the company to the amount of the injury, and may prove the debt in the winding up: ibid., s. 619 (8).

Discount, issue at a. *See* ISSUE AT A DISCOUNT.

Disqualification order. An order made by the court disqualifying a person from being e.g. a director.

In the circumstances mentioned in ss. 296 to 300 (infra) a court may make against a person a disqualification order to the effect that he must not, without the leave of the Court

(a) be a director of a company; or

(b) be a liquidator of a company; or

(c) be a receiver or manager of a company's property; or

(d) in any way, whether directly or indirectly, be concerned or take part in the promotion, formation or management of a company, for a specified period beginning with the date of the order: Companies Act 1985, s. 295 (1). (*See* DIRECTOR; LIQUIDATOR; RECEIVER).

The maximum period to be specified is (a) in the case of an order made under s. 297 or made by court of summary jurisdiction, 5 years, and (b) in any other case, 15 years: Companies Act 1985, s. 295 (2).

A disqualification order may be made on grounds which are or include matters other than criminal convictions, notwithstanding that the person in respect of whom it is to be made may be criminally liable in respect of those matters: ibid., s. 295 (4).

If a person acts in contravention of a disqualification order, he is in respect of each offence liable on conviction on indictment, to imprisonment for a term not exceeding 2 years or a fine or both, and on summary conviction to a term of imprisonment not exceeding 6 months or to a fine not exceeding the statutory maximum, or to both: ibid., ss. 295 (7), 730 and Sched 24.

Disqualification on conviction of indictable offence
The court may make a disqualification order against a person where he is convicted of an indictable offence (whether on indictment or summarily) in connection with the promotion, formation, management or liquidation of a company, or with the receivership or management of a company's property: ibid., s. 296 (1).

Disqualification for persistent default under Companies Acts
The court may make a disqualification order against a person where it appears to it that he has been persistently in default in relation to provisions of the Act requiring any return, account or other document to be filed with, delivered or sent, or notice of any matter to be given, to the Registrar of Companies: ibid., s. 297 (1).

Disqualification for fraud in winding up
The court may make a disqualification order against a person if, in the course of the winding up of a company, it appears that he (a) has been guilty of an offence of fraudulent trading (*see* FRAUDULENT TRADING) (whether he has been convicted or not); or (b) has otherwise been guilty, while an officer or liquidator of the company or receiver or manager of its property, of any fraud in relation to the company or of any breach of his duty as such officer, liquidator, receiver or manager: ibid., s. 298 (1).

Disqualification on summary conviction
Where a person is convicted of a summary offence in consequence of a contravention of or failure to comply with any provision of the Act requiring a return, account or other document to be filed with, delivered or sent, or notice of any matter to be given, to the Registrar of Companies, the court by which he is convicted may make a

disqualification order against him if during the 5 years ending with the date of the conviction, he has had made against him, or has been convicted of, in total not less than 3 default orders and offences counting for the purpose of s. 299: ibid., s. 299 (1), (3).

Disqualification by reference to association with insolvent companies

The court may make a disqualification order against a person where, on an application, it appears to it that he

(i) is or has been a director of a company which has at any time gone into liquidation (whether while he was a director or subsequently) and was insolvent at that time, and

(ii) is or has been a director of another such company which has gone into liquidation within 5 years of the date on which the first-mentioned company went into liquidation,

and that his conduct as a director of any of those companies makes him unfit to be concerned in the management of a company: ibid., s. 300 (1).

The Secretary of State may require the liquidator or former liquidator of a company

(a) to furnish him with such information with respect to the company's affairs, and

(b) to produce and permit inspection of such books or documents of or relevant to the company,

as the Secretary of State may reasonably require for the purpose of determining whether to make an application in respect of a person who is or has been a director of that company: ibid., s. 300 (3).

If a person makes default in complying with such a requirement, the court may, on the Secretary of State's application, make an order requiring that person to make good the default within such time as may be specified: ibid., s. 300 (3).

Register of disqualification orders

The Secretary of State may make regulations requiring officers of courts to furnish him with such particulars as the regulations may specify of cases in which

(a) a disqualification order is made under any of ss. 296 to 300 (ante), or

(b) any action is taken by a court in consequence of which such an order is varied or ceases to be in force, or

(c) leave is granted by a court for a person subject to such an order to do anything which otherwise the order prohibits him from doing: ibid., s. 301 (1).

The regulations may specify the time within which, and the form and manner in which, such particulars are to be furnished: ibid., s. 301 (1).

The Secretary of State must, from the particulars so furnished, continue to maintain the register of orders and of cases in which leave has been granted as mentioned above, which was set up by him under the Companies Act 1976, s. 29: ibid., s. 301 (2).

When an order of which entry is made in the register ceases to be in force, the Secretary of State must delete the entry from the register and all particulars relating to it which have been furnished to him under the above provisions: ibid., s. 301 (3).

The register must be open to inspection on payment of such fee as may be specified by the Secretary of State in regulations: ibid., s. 301 (4).

Regulations must be made by statutory instrument subject to annulment in pursuance of a resolution of either House of Parliament: ibid., s. 301 (5).

Dissolution of company. A termination of the company's existence.

In a winding up by the court, when the company's affairs have been completely wound up, the court (if the liquidator makes an application in that behalf) must make an order that the company be dissolved from the date of the order, and the company is then dissolved accordingly: Companies Act 1985, s. 568 (1). (*See* LIQUIDATOR). A copy of the order must within 14 days from its date be forwarded by the liquidator to the Registrar of Companies who must record the company's dissolution: Companies Act 1985, s. 568 (2). If the liquidator makes default in complying with this requirement, he is liable on summary conviction to a fine not exceeding one-fifth of the statutory maximum or, on conviction after continued contravention, to a daily default fine not exceeding one-fiftieth of the statutory maximum: ibid., ss. 568 (3), 730 and Sch. 24.

In a members' voluntary winding up the Registrar, on receiving from the liquidator the account of the winding up and a return of the holding of a general meeting of the company, must register them, and on the expiration of 3 months from the registration of the return the company is deemed to be dissolved: ibid., s. 585 (5). (*See* LIQUIDATOR). But the court may, on the application of the liquidator or of any other person who appears to the court to be interested, make an order deferring the date at which the dissolution of the company is to take effect for such time as the court thinks fit: Companies Act 1985, s. 585 (5).

In a creditors' voluntary winding up the Registrar, on receiving from the liquidator the account of the winding up and a return of a general meeting of the company and of a meeting of the creditors, must forthwith register them, and on the expiration of 3 months from their registration the company is deemed to be dissolved: ibid., s. 595 (6). But the court may, on the application of the liquidator or of any other person who appears to the court to be interested, make an order deferring the date at which the dissolution of the company is to take effect for such time as the court thinks fit: ibid., s. 595 (6). (*See* LIQUIDATOR).

A company which has been struck off the register by the Registrar of Companies is dissolved after a specified time. (*See* STRIKING OFF REGISTER).

Declaring dissolution void

Where a company has been dissolved, the court may at any time within 2 years of the date of dissolution, on an application made for the purpose by the liquidator or by any other person who appears to the court to be interested, make an order, on such terms as the court thinks fit, declaring the dissolution to have been void: Companies Act 1985, s. 651 (1). Thereupon such proceedings may be taken as might have been taken if the company had not been dissolved: ibid., s. 651 (2). It is the duty of the person on whose application the order was made, within 7 days after its making (or such further time as the court may allow) to deliver to the Registrar of Companies for registration an office copy of the order: ibid., s. 651 (3). If the person fails to do so, he is liable on summary conviction to a fine not exceeding one-fifth of the statutory maximum or, on conviction after continued contravention, to a daily default fine not exceeding one-fiftieth of the statutory maximum: ibid., ss. 651 (3), 730 and Sch. 24.

'Liquidator' means a liquidator validly appointed before the dissolution of the company: *Re Wood and Martin (Bricklaying Contractors) Ltd* [1971] 1 All ER 732. Accordingly, where a person was appointed liquidator on a resolution that it should be wound up voluntarily, and it was discovered that it had already been struck off the register, he was not entitled to apply for the dissolution to be declared void: ibid.

A solicitor acting on behalf of a client and having neither a financial nor a proprietary interest is not a 'person interested': *Re Roehampton Swimming Pool Ltd* [1968] 3 All ER 661 at 665 (per Megarry J). It is not necessary to show that the 'interest' of the person is one which is firmly established or one likely to succeed: *Re Wood and Martin (Bricklaying Contractors) Ltd* (supra). Hence, a person whose appointment as liquidator was invalid was a 'person interested', for he had more than a shadowy interest in the company since there was a possibility of a claim being made by him on a *quantum meruit* basis if a validly appointed liquidator made use of the work which he had done, and of a claim against him by the Crown for intermeddling with property which was *bona vacantia*: ibid.

Effect of dissolution

When a company is dissolved, all property and rights whatsoever vested in or held in trust for the company immediately before its dissolution (including leasehold property but not including property held by the company on trust for any other person) are deemed to be *bona vacantia*, and accordingly belong to the Crown, or to the Duchy of Lancaster or to the Duke of Cornwall for the time being, as the case may be, and vest and may be dealt with in the same manner as other *bona vacantia* accruing to the Crown, to the Duchy of Lancaster or to the Duke of Cornwall: ibid., s. 654 (1). (*See* BONA VACANTIA).

Dissolution of partnership. The bringing of a partnership to an end.

A partnership may be dissolved (i) by the expiration of the period for which it is to last or by notice of dissolution; (ii) by the death or bankruptcy of a partner or a charge on his share; (iii) under a clause in the partnership agreement giving a right to claim dissolution if a specified event occurs; (iv) by illegality; (v) by an order of the court; (vi) by an order by an arbitrator.

(i) *Dissolution by expiration or notice*

Subject to any agreement between the partners, a partnership is dissolved

(a) if entered into for a fixed term, by the expiration of that term;
(b) if entered into for a single adventure or undertaking, by the termination of that adventure or undertaking;
(c) if entered into for an undefined time, by any partner giving notice to the other or others of his intention to dissolve the partnership: Partnership Act 1890, s. 32.

In the last-mentioned case the partnership is dissolved as from the date mentioned in the notice as the date of dissolution, or, if no date is so mentioned, as from the date of the communication of the notice: ibid., s. 32.

(ii) *Dissolution by death, bankruptcy or charge*

Subject to any agreement between the partners, every partnership is dissolved as regards all the partners by the death or bankruptcy of any partner: ibid., s. 33 (1).

(iii) *Dissolution under express clause*

Any circumstance such as unsoundness of mind, physical incapacity, incompatibility of temperament, or dishonesty (even outside the business) may by an express clause in the partnership agreement be a ground for dissolution without the intervention of the court. See e.g. *Carmichael v Evans* [1904] 1 Ch 486 (conviction of offence of travelling on railway without a ticket); *Peyton v Mindham* [1971] 3 All ER 1215 (incapacity to perform fair share of work).

(iv) *Illegality*

A partnership is in every case dissolved by the happening of any event which makes it unlawful for the business of the firm to carry it on in partnership: Partnership Act 1890, s. 34. See e.g. *R v Kupfer* [1915] 2 KB 321 (trading with the enemy); *Hudgell, Yeats & Co v Watson* [1978] 2 All ER 363, CA (lapse of solicitor's practising certificate).

(v) *Dissolution by order of court*

On an application by a partner the court may decree a dissolution of the partnership

(a) when a partner, other than the partner suing, becomes, other than by reason of mental disorder, permanently incapable of performing his part of the partnership contract;

(b) when a partner, other than the partner suing, has been guilty of such conduct as, in the opinion of the court, regard being had to the nature of the business, is calculated to prejudicially affect the carrying on of the business;

(c) when a partner, other than the partner suing, wilfully or persistently commits a breach of the partnership agreement, or otherwise so conducts himself in matters relating to the partnership business that it is not reasonably practicable for the other partner or partners to carry on the business in partnership with him;

(d) when the business of the partnership can only be carried on at a loss;

(e) whenever in any case circumstances have arisen, which, in the opinion of the court, render it just and equitable that the partnership be dissolved: Partnership Act 1890, s. 35.

Where a judge, after considering medical evidence, is satisfied that a person is incapable by reason of mental disorder of managing his property and affairs, the judge may make an order for the dissolution of a partnership of which the person is a member: Mental Health Act 1983, s. 96 (1) (g). 'Mental disorder' means 'mental illness, arrested or incomplete development of mind, psychopathic disorder and any other disorder or disability of mind': ibid., s. 1 (2).

(vi) *Order of arbitrator*

If the partnership articles contain a clause referring all matters in dispute to arbitration, and the dispute involves a claim for dissolution, the arbitrator is empowered to dissolve the partnership just as the court might: *Vawdrey v Simpson* [1896] 1 Ch 166.

Distribution. In Part VIII of the Companies Act 1985 the means every description of distribution of a company's assets to its member, whether in cash or otherwise, except distribution made by way of

(a) an issue of shares as fully or partly paid bonus shares;

(b) the redemption or purchase of any of the company's own shares out of capital (including the proceeds of any fresh issue of shares) or out of unrealised profits in accordance with Chapter VII of Part V;

(c) the reduction of share capital by extinguishing or reducing the liability of any of the members on any of the company's shares in respect of share capital not paid up, or by paying off paid up share capital; and

(d) a distribution of assets to members of the company on its winding up: Companies Act 1980, s. 45 (2). (*See* BONUS SHARE).

Dividend. The profit of trading divided among the members in proportion to their shares and in accordance with their rights as shareholders.

Dividends may be payable in respect of preference shares and ordinary shares, the payment first being made in respect of the former. (*See* ORDINARY SHARE; PREFERENCE SHARE).

There may be both one or more interim dividends as well as a final dividend. (*See* INTERIM DIVIDEND; FINAL DIVIDEND).

Shareholders cannot insist on the payment of dividends, even where the profits are amply sufficient, if the directors decline to declare a dividend, except in case of fraud: *Bond v Barrow Haematite Steel Co* [1902] 1 Ch 353. Dividends must be paid in cash unless the articles state that payment may also be made in, e.g. paid up shares or debentures, etc.: *Hoole v Great Western Railway Co* (1867) 3 Ch App 262.

Provisions of Table A

The company may by ordinary resolution declare dividends in accordance with the respective rights of the members, but no dividend must exceed the amount recommended by the directors: Table A, art. 102.

The directors may pay interim dividends (*see* INTERIM DIVIDEND) if it appears to them that they are justified by the profits of the company available for distribution; Table A, art. 103. If the share capital is divided into different classes, the directors may pay interim dividends on shares which confer deferred or non-preferred rights with regard to dividend as well as on shares which confer preferential rights with regard to dividend, but no interim dividend must be paid on shares carrying deferred or non-preferred rights, if at the time of payment, any preferential dividend is in arrear: ibid., art. 103. The directors may also pay at intervals settled by them any dividend payable at a fixed rate if it appears to them that the profits available for distribution justify the payment: ibid., art. 103. Provided the directors act in good faith they do not incur any liability to the holders of shares conferring preferential rights for any loss they may suffer by the lawful payment of an interim dividend on any shares having deferred or non-preferred rights: ibid., art. 103.

Except as otherwise provided by the rights attached to shares, all dividends must be declared and paid according to the amounts paid up on the shares on which the dividend is paid: ibid., art. 104. All dividends must be apportioned and paid proportionately to the amounts paid up on the shares during any portion or portions of the period in respect of which the dividend is paid; but, if any share is issued on terms providing that it is to rank for dividend as from a particular date, that share ranks for dividend accordingly: ibid., art. 104.

A general meeting declaring a dividend may, upon the recommendation of the directors, direct that it is to be satisfied wholly or partly by the distribution of assets: ibid., art. 105. Where any difficulty arises in regard to the distribution, the directors may settle the same and in particular may issue fractional certificates and fix the value for distribution of any assets and may determine that cash shall be paid to any member upon the footing of the value so fixed in order to adjust the rights of members and may vest any assets in trustees: ibid., art. 105.

Any dividend or other moneys payable in respect of a share may be paid by cheque sent by post to the registered address of the person entitled or, if 2 or more persons are the holders of the share or are jointly entitled to it by reason of the death or bankruptcy of the holder, to the registered address of that one of those persons who is first named in the register of members or to such person as the person or persons entitled may in writing direct: ibid., art. 106. (*See* REGISTER OF MEMBERS).

No dividend or other moneys payable in respect of a share shall bear interest against the company unless otherwise provided by the rights attached to the share: Table A, art. 107.

Any dividend which has remained unclaimed for 12 years from the date when it became due for payment, shall, if the directors so resolve, be forfeited and cease to remain owing by the company: ibid., art. 108.

Restriction on distribution of profits and assets

A company must not make a distribution except out of profits available for the purpose: Companies Act 1985, s. 263 (1). (*See* DISTRIBUTION).

A company's profits available for distribution are its accumulated, realised profits, so far as not previously utilised by distribution or capitalisation, less its accumulated, realised losses, so far as not previously written off in a reduction or reorganisation of capital duly made: Companies Act 1985, s. 263 (3). (*See* REDUCTION OF CAPITAL).

A company must not apply an unrealised profit in paying up debentures or any amounts unpaid on its shares: Companies Act 1985, s. 263 (4).

A public company may only make a distribution at any time (a) if at that time the amount of its net assets is not less than the aggregate of the company's called-up share capital and its undistributable reserves; and (b) if, and to the extent that, the distribution does not reduce the amount of those assets to less than that aggregate: ibid., s. 264 (1). (*See* CALLED UP SHARE CAPITAL; PUBLIC COMPANY; UNDISTRIBUTABLE RESERVES)

An investment company may also make a distribution at any time out of its accumulated, realised revenue profits, so far as not previously utilised by distribution or capitalisation, less its accumulated revenue losses (whether realised or unrealised), so far as not previously written off in a reduction or reorganisation of capital duly made

(a) if at that time the amount of its assets is at least equal to one and a half times the aggregate of its liabilities; and

(b) if, and to the extent that, the distribution does not reduce that amount to less than one and a half times that aggregate: Companies Act 1985, s. 265 (1). (*See* INVESTMENT COMPANY; REDUCTION OF CAPITAL).

Where an insurance company carries on long term business, any amount properly transferred to the profit and loss account of the company from a surplus in the fund or funds maintained by it in respect of that business and any deficit in that fund or those funds are to be respectively treated as a realised profit and a realised loss: Companies Act 1980, s. 42 (1).

Where development costs are shown as an asset in the company's accounts, any amount shown in respect of those costs is to be treated (a) for the purposes of s. 263, as a realised loss; and (b) for the purposes of s. 265, as a realised revenue loss: ibid., s. 269 (1).

Where a distribution, or part of one, made by a company to one of its members is made in contravention of the above provisions and, at the time of the distribution, he knows or has reasonable grounds for believing that it is so made, he is liable to repay it or that part, as the case may be, to the company, or (in the case of a distribution made otherwise than in cash) to pay the company a sum equal to the value of the distribution or part at that time: ibid., s. 277 (1). The above provisions are without prejudice to any obligation imposed apart from this section on a member of a company to repay a distribution unlawfully made to him: ibid., s. 277 (2).

Document includes summons, notice, order and other legal process, and registers: Companies Act 1985, s. 744.

E

Employees' share scheme. A scheme for encouraging or facilitating the holding of shares or debentures in a company by or for the benefit of (a) the *bona fide* employees or former employees of the company, the company's subsidiary or holding company or a subsidiary of the company's holding company; or (b) the wives, husbands, widows, widowers or children or step-children under the age of 18 of such employees or former employees: Companies Act 1985, s. 743.

Ex dividend. Without the dividend. A term used in connection with the purchase of shares resulting in the buyer not having a right to the dividend in respect of them. (*See* DIVIDEND; SHARE).

Exemption from requirement to use word 'limited' in name. The removal of the requirement that a limited company must use the word 'limited' as part of its name.

A company limited by guarantee is exempt from the requirement of the Companies Act 1985 relating to the use of the word 'limited' as part of its name if

(i) the objects of the company are to be the promotion of commerce, art, science, education, religion, charity or any profession and anything incidental or conducive to any of these objects; and

(ii) the company's memorandum or articles

    (a) require its profits (if any) or other income to be applied in promoting its objects;

    (b) prohibit the payment of dividends to its members; and

    (c) require all the assets which would otherwise be available to its members generally to be transferred on its winding up either to another body with objects similar to its own or to another body the objects of which are the promotion of charity and anything incidental or conducive to it (whether or not the body is a member of the company): Companies Act 1985, s. 30 (1), (2), (3). (*See* COMPANY LIMITED BY GUARANTEE).

Any such company which does not include the word 'limited' as part of its name is also exempt from the requirements relating to the publication of its name and the sending of lists of members to the Registrar of Companies: ibid., s. 30 (7).

A statutory declaration in the prescribed form in the case of a company to be formed made by a solicitor engaged in the formation of the company or by a person named as a director or secretary of the company in the statement delivered under s. 10 (2), may be delivered to the Registrar of Companies: ibid., s. 30 (4), (5). The Registrar may accept such a declaration as sufficient evidence of the matters stated in it, and may refuse to register a company by a name which does not include the word 'limited' unless such a declaration has been delivered to him: ibid., s. 30 (4).

A company which is exempted from the requirement of including the word 'limited' in its name, must not alter the memorandum or articles of association so that it ceases to comply with the requirements of s. 30 (3): ibid., s. 31 (1). A company which contravenes this provision and any officer who is in default are liable on summary conviction to a fine not exceeding the statutory maximum, or, on conviction after continued contravention, to a daily default fine not exceeding one-tenth of the statutory maximum: ibid., ss. 31 (5), 730 and Sch. 24.

If it appears to the Secretary of State that the company has carried on any business other than the promotion of any of the objects mentioned above, or has applied any of its profits or income otherwise than in promoting such objects, or has paid a dividend to any of its members, he may, in writing, direct the company to change its name by resolution of the directors within such period as may be specified in the direction so that its name ends with 'limited': ibid., s. 31 (2). A company which fails to comply with such a direction and any officer who is in default are liable on summary conviction to a fine not exceeding one-fifth of the statutory maximum: ibid., ss. 31 (6), 730 and Sch. 24. A company which has received a direction must not thereafter be registered by a name which does not include the word 'limited' without the approval of the Secretary of State: ibid., s. 31 (3).

Expert includes engineer, valuer, accountant and any other person whose profession gives authority to a statement made by him: Companies Act 1985, s. 62.

Ex rights. Without the rights. A term used to denote the fact that a buyer of shares is not entitled to subscribe for further shares in proportion to the number bought. (*See* RIGHTS ISSUE; SHARE).

Extraordinary general meeting. A general meeting other than an annual general meeting: Table A, art. 36. (*See* ANNUAL GENERAL MEETING).

The directors of a company must on a members' requisition, forthwith proceed duly to convene an extraordinary general meeting: Companies Act 1985, s. 368 (1). This applies not withstanding anything in the company's articles: ibid., s. 368 (1).

A members' requisition is a requisition of
(a) members of the company holding at the date of the deposit of the requisition not less than one-tenth of such of the paid-up capital of

the company as at that date carries the right of voting at general meetings of the company; or

(b) in the case of a company not having a share capital, members of it representing not less than one-tenth of the total voting rights of all the members having at the date of the requisition a right to vote at general meetings: ibid., s. 368 (2).

The requisition must state the objects of the meeting, and must be signed by the requisitionists and deposited at the registered office of the company, and may consist of several documents in like form each signed by one or more requisitionists: ibid., s. 368 (3).

If the directors do not within 21 days from the date of the deposit of the requisition proceed duly to convene a meeting, the requisitionists, or any of them representing more than one half of the total voting rights of all of them, may themselves convene a meeting, but any meeting so convened must not be held after the expiration of 3 months from that date: ibid., s. 368 (4).

A meeting convened by requisitionists must be convened in the same manner, as nearly as possible, as that in which meetings are to be convened by directors: ibid., s. 368 (5).

Any reasonable expenses incurred by the requisitionists by reason of the failure of the directors duly to convene a meeting must be repaid to the requisitionists by the company: ibid., s. 368 (6). Any sum so repaid must be retained by the company out of any sums due or to become due from the company by way of fees or other remuneration in respect of their services to such of the directors as were in default: ibid., s. 368 (6).

On the requisition of members pursuant to the provisions of the Act the directors must proceed to convene an extraordinary general meeting for a date not later than 8 weeks after receipt of the requisition: Table A, art. 37.

Extraordinary resolution. A resolution passed by a majority of not less than three-fourths of such members as (being entitled to do so) vote in person, or where proxies are allowed, by proxy, at a general meeting of which notice specifying the intention to propose the resolution as an extraordinary resolution has been given: Companies Act 1985, s. 378 (1). (*See* GENERAL MEETING: PROXY).

At any meeting at which an extraordinary resolution is submitted to be passed, a declaration of the chairman that the resolution is carried, is, unless a poll is demanded, conclusive evidence of the fact without proof of the number or proportion of the votes recorded in favour of or against the resolution: Companies Act 1985, s. 378 (4). (*See* POLL).

In computing the majority on a poll demanded on the question that an extraordinary resolution be passed, reference must be had to the number of votes cast for and against the resolution: Companies Act 1985, s. 378 (5).

Notice of a meeting is deemed duly given and the meeting duly held when the notice is given and the meeting held in the manner provided by the Act or the company's articles: ibid., s. 378 (6).

Extraordinary resolutions are required (i) where it is desired to wind up a company voluntarily on the ground that it cannot by reason of its liabilities continue its business, and that it is advisable to wind up (ibid., s. 572 (1) (c)); (ii) where, in the case of a member's voluntary winding up, the books and papers of the company and of the liquidators are to be disposed of (ibid., s. 640 (1) (b)); and (iii) where in the case of a member's voluntary winding up, the liquidator wishes to exercise any of the powers given by s. 539 (1) (d), (e), (f) [i.e. the power to pay any classes of creditors in full and to enter into certain compromises] (ibid., s. 598 (1) (a)).

A copy of every extraordinary resolution must within 15 days after it has been passed be forwarded to the Registrar of Companies and recorded by him: ibid., s. 380 (1), (4) (b). The copy must be either a printed copy or else a copy in some other form approved by him: ibid., s. 380 (1). If a company fails to comply with this sub-section, the company and every officer of the company who is in default are liable on summary conviction to a fine not exceeding one-fifth of the statutory maximum, or on conviction after continued contravention, to a daily default fine not exceeding one-fiftieth of the statutory maximum: ibid., ss. 380 (5), 730 and Sch. 24.

Where articles have been registered, a copy of every extraordinary resolution must be embodied in or annexed to every copy of the articles issued after the passing of the resolution: ibid., s. 380 (2). Where articles have not been registered, a printed copy of every extraordinary resolution must be forward to any member at his request on payment of 5p or such less sum as the company may direct: ibid., s. 380 (3). If a company fails to comply with s. 380 (2) or s. 380 (3), the company and every officer of the company who is in default is liable on conviction to a fine not exceeding one-fifth of the statutory maximum for each occasion on which copies are issued or, as the case may be, requested: ibid., ss. 380 (6), 730 and Sch. 24.

F

Final dividend. A dividend recommended by the directors of a company and approved at the annual general meeting. It may be paid in addition to one or more interim dividends. (*See* INTERIM DIVIDEND).

Financial assistance. In ss. 151 to 158 means

(a) financial assistance by way of gift;

(b) financial assistance given by way of guarantee, security or indemnity, other than an indemnity in respect of the indemnifier's own neglect or default, or by way of release or waiver;

(c) financial assistance given by way of a loan or any other agreement under which any of the obligations of the person giving the assistance are to be fulfilled at a time when in accordance with the agreement any obligation of any other party to the agreement remains unfulfilled, or by way of the novation of, or the assignment of rights arising under any loan or such other agreement; or

(d) any other financial assistance given by a company the net assets of which are thereby reduced to a material extent or which has no net assets: Companies Act 1985, s. 152 (1) (a).

Financial year means

(a) in relation to any body corporate to which Part VII applies, a period in respect of which any profit and loss account prepared under s. 227 is made up; and

(b) in relation to any other body corporate, a period in respect of which any profit and loss account of the body laid before it in general meeting is made up;

whether, in either case, that period is a year or not: Companies Act 1985, s. 742 (1) (d).

Firm. Persons who have entered into partnership with one another: Partnership Act 1890, s. 4 (1).

Firm name. The name under which their business is carried on by persons who have entered into partnership with one another: Partnership Act 1890, s. 4 (1).

Floating charge. A charge where (i) it is on a class of assets, present and future; (ii) the class is one which, in the ordinary course of business, is changing from time to time; and (iii) it is contemplated that until some steps are taken to enforce the charge the company is free to carry on its business in the usual way: *Re Yorkshire Woolcombers' Association*

Ltd, Houldsworth v Yorkshire Woolcombers' Association Ltd [1903] 2 Ch 284 at 295 (per Romer LJ).

When money becomes payable under a 'condition' in a debenture which gives a floating charge over the assets of a company, and the debenture-holder takes steps to enforce his security, the charge is said to 'crystallise'.

A floating charge requires to be registered: Companies Act 1985, ss. 395 (1), 396 (1) (f). (*See* REGISTRATION OF CHARGES). A floating charge is liable to be postponed to the rights of other persons, and other charges may gain priority over it. (*See* DEBENTURES).

Where a company is being wound up, a floating charge on its undertaking or property created within 12 months of the commencement of the winding up is invalid (unless it is proved that the company immediately after the creation of the charge was solvent), except to the amount of any cash paid to the company at the time of or subsequently to the creation of, and in consideration for, the charge, together with interest on that amount at the rate of 5 per cent per annum or such other rate as may for the time being be prescribed by order of the Treasury in a statutory instrument: ibid., s. 617 (1), (2). The statutory instrument is subject to annulment in pursuance of a resolution of either House of Parliament: ibid., s. 617 (2). (*See* COMMENCEMENT OF THE WINDING UP). The payment must be one made to the company: *Re Orleans Motor Co Ltd* [1911] 2 Ch 41; *Re Matthew Ellis Ltd* [1933] Ch 48; *Re Destone Fabrics Ltd* [1941] Ch 319.

Forfeiture of share. An expropriation by a company of a member's share.

Shares can only be forfeited for non-payment of calls or for similar reasons. (*See* CALLS). An attempt to forfeit shares for other reasons is illegal: *Hopkinson v Mortimer, Harley & Co Ltd* [1917] 1 Ch 646. Any clause in the articles is void which provides that a member shall forfeit his shares if he takes any proceedings against the company or which in any way restricts his right to present a petition for the winding up of the company: *Re Peveril Gold Mines Ltd* [1898] 1 Ch 122. The power to declare shares forfeited is in the nature of a trust to be exercised for the benefit of the company: *Re Esparto Trading Co* (1879) 12 Ch D 191.

If a call (*see* CALL) remains unpaid after it has become due and payable the directors may give to the person from whom it is due not less than 14 clear days' notice requiring payment of the amount unpaid together with any interest which may have accrued. The notice must name the place where payment is to be made and must state that if the notice is not complied with, the shares in respect of which the call was made will be liable to be forfeited: Table A, art. 18.

If the notice is not complied with, any share in respect of which it was given, may, before the payment required by the notice has been made, be forfeited by a resolution of the directors, and the forfeiture must include all dividends or other moneys payable in respect of the forfeited shares and not paid before the forfeiture: ibid., art. 19.

A forfeited share may be sold re-allotted or otherwise disposed of on such terms and in such manner as the directors determine either to the person who was before the forfeiture the holder or to any other person: ibid., art. 20. At any time before sale, re-allotment or other disposition the forfeiture may be cancelled on such terms as the directors think fit: ibid., art. 20.

A person any of whose shares have been forfeited, ceases to be a member in respect of them: ibid., art. 21. He must surrender to the company the share certificate (*see* SHARE CERTIFICATE) for the shares forfeited but remains liable to the company for all moneys which at the date of forfeiture were presently payable by him to the company in respect of those shares together with interest until payment: ibid., art. 21. But the directors may waive payment or enforce payment without any allowance for the value of the shares at the time of forfeiture or for any consideration received on their disposal: ibid., art. 21.

A statutory declaration by a director or the secretary that a share has been forfeited on a specified date is conclusive evidence of the facts stated in it as against all persons claiming to be entitled to the share: ibid., art. 22.

Forged transfer. A transfer, which is not a genuine one, made with a view of inducing the company to register shares standing in the name of the supposed transferor into that of the transferee.

If a transfer is forged and the company registers the transfer and gives a share certificate to the transferee, the true owner remains entitled to be put back on the register. (*See* SHARE CERTIFICATE).

The company does not incur any liability in damages by putting the transferee's name in the register, but if it issues a certificate and any person acts on the faith of it and suffers damage, the company will be liable: *Re Bahia and San Francisco Railway Co Ltd* (1868) LR 3 QB 584; *Bloomenthal v Ford* [1897] AC 156, HL.

A company often insures against liability in respect of a forged transfer.

When a company receives a transfer for registration, it usually writes to the transferor telling him of the proposed transfer and saying that the transfer will be registered unless he objects. This gives him an opportunity of preventing a forged transfer from taking effect, but the transferor is not bound to reply to the letter, and, if he does not, he will not be estopped from denying the validity of the transfer: *Barton v London and North Western Railway Co* (1889) 24 QBD 77, CA.

Where a transfer is forged, the person sending the transfer form to the company for registration is under a liability to indemnify the company for any loss which is sustained: *Sheffield Corporation v Barclay* [1905] AC 392, HL.

Under the Forged Transfer Acts 1891 and 1892, a company has power to make a cash payment out of its funds for any loss arising from a forged transfer of its shares. (*See* FORGED TRANSFER ACTS 1891 AND 1892).

Forged Transfer Acts 1891 and 1892. Two Acts preserving purchasers of shares from losses by forged transfers.

Where a company issues or has issued shares, stock or securities transferable by an instrument in writing or by an entry in any books or register kept by or on behalf of a company, the company has power to make compensation by a cash payment out of its funds for any loss arising from a transfer of any such shares, stock or securities in pursuance of a forged transfer or of a transfer under a forged power of attorney, whether the person receiving such compensation or any person through whom he claims, has or has not paid any fee or otherwise contributed to any fund out of which the compensation is paid: Forged Transfers Act 1891, s. 1 (1).

Any company may, if it thinks fit, provide, by fees not exceeding the rate of 5p for every £100 transferred (with a minimum charge equal to that of £25) to be paid by the transferee on entry of the transfer in the books of the company, or by insurance, reservation of capital, accumulation of income, or in any other manner which it may resolve on, a fund to meet such claims for compensation: ibid., s. 1 (2).

For the purpose of providing such compensation, any company may borrow on the security of its property: ibid., s. 1 (3). Any company may impose such reasonable restrictions on the transfer of its shares, stock or securities or with respect to powers of attorney for their transfer as it considers requisite for guarding against losses arising from forgery: ibid., s. 1 (4). Where a company compensates a person for any loss arising from forgery, the company, without prejudice to any other rights or remedies, has the same rights and remedies against the person liable for the loss as the person compensated would have had: ibid., s. 1 (5).

Foss v Harbottle, Rule in. *See* RULE IN FOSS V HARBOTTLE.

Founder's share. A share allotted to a person who first founded the company. The issue of such shares is now rare. The holder of such a share is usually entitled to a proportion of the profits if the dividend on the ordinary shares has been paid up to a specified amount.

The number of founders' shares, if any, and the nature and extent of the interest of the holders in the property and profits of the company must be stated in the prospectus: Companies Act 1985, Sch. 3, Part I, para 1 (1) (a). (*See* PROSPECTUS).

Fraudulent trading. Trading by a company in defraud of creditors or for a fraudulent purpose.

If in the course of the winding up of a company it appears that any business of the company has carried on business with intent to defraud creditors or for any fraudulent purpose, the court, on the application of the Official Receiver, or the liquidator or any creditor or contributory of the company, may declare that any persons who were knowingly parties are to the carrying on of the business in this manner to be personally liable without any limitation of liability responsible for all or any debts or other obligations of the company as the court may direct: Companies Act 1985, s. 630 (1), (2).

The expression 'party to the carrying on of a business' indicates no more than 'participates in' or concurs in, and some positive steps are required. A person cannot be said to be a party to the carrying on of a business if he takes no positive steps at all: *Re Maidstone Buildings Provisions Ltd* [1971] 3 All ER 363, at 368–369 (per Pennycuick J).

It is immaterial that only one creditor has been defrauded, provided that the transaction can properly be described as a fraud on a creditor perpetrated in the course of carrying on a business: *Re Gerald Cooper Chemicals Ltd* [1978] 2 All ER 49.

A creditor is a party to the carrying on of a business with intent to defraud creditors if he accepts money which he knows full well has, in fact, been procured by carrying on the business with intent to defraud creditors for the very purpose of making the payment: ibid.

The court can order the sum to go in discharge of the debt of any particular creditor, or that it shall go to a particular class of creditors or to the liquidator so as to go into the general assets of the company: *Re Cyona Distributors Ltd* [1967] 1 All ER 281 at 284, CA (per Lord Denning MR). When an application is made by a liquidator, the court will usually order the sum to go into the general assets, but it is not bound to do so: ibid., at 284 (per Lord Denning MR). When an application is made by a creditor who has been defrauded, the court has power to order the sum to be paid to that creditor. The creditor applies on his own account. He does not apply as being a trustee for the other creditors or for anyone else: ibid.

If any business of a company is carried on with intent to defraud creditors of the company or creditors of any other person, or for any fraudulent purpose, every person who was knowingly a party to the carrying on of the business in that manner is liable on conviction on indictment to 7 years' imprisonment or a fine or both, and on summary conviction to 6 months' imprisonment or to a fine or both: Companies Act 1985, ss. 458, 730 and Sch. 24. This applies whether or not the company has been, or is in the course of being wound up: ibid., s. 458.

Fraudulent trading

Where a person has been found guilty of fraudulent trading, the court may make an order that he shall not, without the leave of the court, be a director or be concerned in the management of a company for any period up to 15 years: ibid., s. 295. (*See* DISQUALIFICATION ORDER).

G

Gazette, The means, as respects companies registered in England and Wales, the *London Gazette*: Companies Act 1985, s. 744.

General partner. A member of a limited partnership who is liable for all debts and obligations of the firm: Limited Partnerships Act 1907, s. 4 (2). (*See* LIMITED PARTNERSHIP).

Goodwill. An asset of a business defined as (i) 'nothing more than the probability of the old customers resorting to the old place': *Crutwell v Lye* (1810) 17 Ves 335 at 346 (per Lord Eldon); (ii) 'a connection formed by years of work': *Ginesi v Cooper & Co* (1880) 14 Ch D 596 at 599 (per Jessel MR); (iii) 'the whole advantage whatever it may be, of the reputation and connection of the firm, which may have been built up by years of honest work or gained by lavish expenditure of money': *Trego v Hunt* [1896] AC 7 at 24 (per Lord Macnaghten); (iv) 'the advantage, whatever it may be, which a person gets by continuing to carry on, and being entitled to represent to the outside world, that he is carrying on a business which has been carried on for some time previously': *Hill v Fearis* [1905] 1 Ch 466 at 471 (per Warrington J).

Generally, and in the absence of agreement, the goodwill of a partnership must be sold: *Pawsey v Armstrong* (1881) 18 Ch D 698. But a medical practitioner providing general medical services under the National Health Service cannot sell the goodwill or any part of the goodwill of his medical practice: National Health Service Act 1977, s. 54 (1). The sale of the goodwill does not prevent the seller from carrying on a business in competition with that of the purchaser, but the former may be restrained from soliciting any person who was a customer of the old firm: *Gillingham v Beddow* [1900] 2 Ch 242. Where goodwill forms part of the partnership property, and one of the partners dies, it should be valued on the basis that the surviving partners can carry on a rival business, but cannot use the firm name nor solicit its customers: *Re David and Matthews* [1899] 1 Ch 37. The partners may also be restrained from carrying on a similar business under the name of the old firm or from representing themselves as carrying on the old business: *Boorn v Wicker* [1927] 1 Ch 667. An executor, who is carrying out his testator's contract to sell the goodwill of a business, is under a duty to do nothing to destroy or depreciate the value of the goodwill which he has sold: ibid. The principle also applies to a case where a person has been taken into partnership on terms that, on the expiration of the partnership, the goodwill is to belong exclusively to the other partner: *Trego v Hunt* [1896] AC 7.

If the goodwill is not sold, each partner may not only canvass old customers, but, subject to any question as to endangering the other partner under the doctrine of 'holding out', may also use the firm name notwithstanding the obvious inconvenience of this course: *Burchell v Wilde* [1900] 1 Ch 551.

Group accounts. Accounts or statements dealing with the state of affairs and profit or loss of a company and its subsidiaries: Companies Act 1985, s. 229 (1).

Guarantee. In ss. 330 to 346 includes indemnity, and cognate expressions are to be construed accordingly: Companies Act 1985, s. 331 (2).

Guarantee, continuing. *See* CONTINUING GUARANTEE.

H

Harbour authority. For the purpose of the Forged Transfers Act 1891 'includes all persons, being proprietors of, or entrusted with the duty or invested with the power of constructing, improving, managing, regulating, maintaining, or lighting any harbour otherwise than for profit, and not being a joint stock company': Forged Transfers Act 1891, s. 4 (2).

Hire–purchase agreement. Has the same meaning as in the Consumer Credit Act 1974: Companies Act 1985, s. 744, i.e. 'an agreement, other than a conditional sale agreement, under which (a) goods are bailed in return for periodical payments by the person to whom they are bailed, and (b) the property in the goods will pass to that person if the terms of that agreement are complied with and one or more of the following occurs (i) the exercise of an option to purchase by that person, (ii) the doing of any other specified act by any party to the agreement, (iii) the happening of any other specified event' (Consumer Credit Act 1974, s. 189 (1)).

Holding company. A company controlling a subsidiary company.

A company is deemed to be another's holding company if, but only if, that other is its subsidiary: Companies Act 1985, s. 736 (5) (a). (*See* SUBSIDIARY COMPANY).

Holding out as a partner. A representation by a person that he is a partner.

Everyone who by words spoken or written or by conduct represents himself or knowingly suffers himself to be represented, as a partner in a particular firm, is liable as a partner to anyone who has on the faith of any such representation given credit to the firm, whether the representation has or has not been made or communicated to the person so giving credit by or with the knowledge of the apparent partner making the representation or suffering it to be made: Partnership Act 1890, s. 14 (1). But where after a partner's death the partnership is continued in the old firm–name, the continued use of that name, or of the deceased partner's name as part of it does not of itself make his executors or administrators, estate or effects liable for any partnership debts contracted after his death: ibid., s. 14 (2). (*See* FIRM NAME).

91

The word 'knowingly' does not mean mere carelessness in allowing himself to be represented as a partner: *Tower Cabinet Co Ltd v Ingram* [1949] 1 All ER 1033.

I

Inability to pay debts. A company is deemed unable to pay its debts
   (i) if a creditor (by assignment or otherwise) to whom the company
     is indebted in a sum exceeding £750 then due, has served on the
     company, by leaving it at the company's registered office, a
     written demand requiring the company to pay the sum so due and
     the company has for 3 weeks thereafter neglected to pay the sum
     due or to secure or compound for it to the reasonable satisfaction
     of the creditor; or
  (ii) if execution or other process issued on a judgment, decree or
     order of any court in favour of a creditor of the company is
     returned unsatisfied in whole or in part; or
 (iii) if it is proved to the satisfaction of the court that the company is
     unable to pay its debts and, in determining that question, the
     court must take into account the company's contingent and
     prospective liabilities: Companies Act 1985, s 518 (1).

The expression '3 weeks' means 3 clear weeks from the date of the
demand, i.e. the day on which the demand was made is excluded: *Re
Lympne Investments Ltd* [1972] 2 All ER 385. Section 223 is confined to a
debt which is payable. It does not apply where the debt is not yet due:
Re Bryant Investment Co Ltd [1974] 2 All ER 683. The existence of a
dispute on substantial grounds as to a debt defeats the contention that a
company has 'neglected' to pay the sum required by the statutory
notice: *Re London and Paris Banking Corporation* (1875) LR 19 Eq 444;
Re Lympne Investments Ltd (supra).

Incoming partner. A partner joining an existing partnership.

A person who is admitted as a partner into an existing firm does not
thereby become liable to the creditors of the firm for anything done
before he became a partner: Partnership Act 1890, s. 17 (1).

But by 'novation' he may take over the liabilities of the existing firm
and make himself liable to the creditors. Novation implies an
agreement with the creditors either expressed or inferred from
conduct: *British Homes Assurance Corporation Ltd v Paterson* [1902] 2 Ch
404 at 409 (per Farwell J).

Index of members. *See* REGISTER OF MEMBERS.

Index of names. A list of the names of a number of bodies kept by the
Registrar of Companies.

He must keep an index of (a) companies as defined by the Companies Act 1985; (b) oversea companies; (c) incorporated and unincorporated bodies to which any provision of the Companies Act 1985 applies; (d) limited partnerships registered under the Limited Partnerships Act 1907; and (e) societies registered under the Industrial and Provident Societies Act 1965: Companies Act 1985, s. 714 (1). 'Oversea companies' means companies which have complied with the Companies Act 1985, s. 691 and which do not appear to the Registrar not to have a place of business in Great Britain: ibid., s. 714 (1). The Secretary of State may by order in a statutory instrument vary sub-s. 1 by the addition or deletion of any class of body except any within sub-s. 1 (a) or (b): ibid., s. 714 (2).

Insider dealing. The taking advantage by a person of knowledge of the affairs of a company enabling him e.g. to buy or sell its shares at a profit.

(a) *Civil liability*

There is no civil liability in respect of insider dealing to the detriment of another person, e.g. where directors buy shares from a shareholder at a time when they are negotiating for the sale of the business to a third party at a high price and do not tell the shareholder of this fact, and they make a profit on the shares at his expense, they are under no civil liability to him: *Percival v Wright* [1902] 2 Ch 421.

(b) *Criminal liability*

In general, an individual who is, or at any time in the preceding 6 months has been, knowingly connected with a company must not deal on a recognised stock exchange in securities of that company if he has information which

(a) he holds by virtue of being connected with the company;

(b) it would be reasonable to expect a person so connected, and in the position by virtue of which he is so connected, not to disclose except for the proper performance of the functions attaching to that position; and

(c) he knows is unpublished price sensitive information in relation to those securities: Company Securities (Insider Dealing) Act 1985, s. 1(1). (*See* PRICE SENSITIVE INFORMATION; RECOGNISED STOCK EXCHANGE; SECURITIES).

Further, an individual who is, or at any time in the preceding 6 months has been, knowingly connected with a company must not deal on a recognised stock exchange in securities of any other company if he has information which

(a) he holds by virtue of being connected with the first company;

(b) it would be reasonable to expect a person so connected, and in the position by virtue of which he is so connected, not to disclose except for the proper performance of the functions attaching to that position;

(c) he knows is unpublished price sensitive information in relation to those securities of that other company; and

(d) relates to any transaction (actual or contemplated) involving both the first company and that other company, or involving one of them and securities of the other, or to the fact that any such transaction is no longer contemplated: Company Securities (Insider Dealing) Act 1985, s. 1 (2).

There is also a prohibition on the abuse of information obtained in an official capacity by a Crown servant or a former Crown servant: ibid., s. 2.

The above provisions apply to off-market deals: ibid., s. 4. There are also provisions relating to international bond issues: ibid., s. 6. (*See* INTERNATIONAL BOND ISSUE).

An individual who contravenes the provisions of ss. 1, 2, 4 or 5 is liable

(a) on conviction on indictment to imprisonment for a term not exceeding 2 years or a fine or both; and

(b) on summary conviction to imprisonment for a term not exceeding 6 months or a fine not exceeding the statutory maximum or both: Company Securities (Insider Dealing) Act 1985, s. 8 (1).

Proceedings for an offence under s. 8 must not be instituted except by the Secretary of State or by, or with the consent of, the Director of Public Prosecutions: ibid., s. 8 (2).

No transaction is void or voidable by reason only that it was entered into in contravention of ss. 1, 2, 4 or 5: ibid., s. 8 (3).

Insolvency Services Account. An account kept by the Secretary of State with the Bank of England into which must be paid all money received by him in respect of proceedings (a) under the Bankruptcy Act 1914; or (b) under the Companies Act 1985 in connection with the winding up of companies: Insolvency Act 1976, s. 3 (1), (3). All payments out of money standing to the credit of the Secretary of State in that account must be made by the Bank of England in such manner as he may direct: ibid., s. 3 (3).

Whenever the cash balance standing to the credit of the Insolvency Services Account is in excess of the amount which in the opinion of the Secretary of State is required for the time being to answer demands in respect of bankrupt's or companies' estates, he must notify the excess to the National Debt Commissioners, and must pay into the Insolvency Services Investment Account the whole or any part of that excess as the Commissioners may require for investment in accordance with the Insolvency Services (Accounting and Investment Act 1970): ibid., s. 3 (4).

Whenever any part of the money so invested is, in the opinion of the Secretary of State, required to answer any demand in respect of bankrupts' estates or companies' estates, he must notify to the National

Debt Commissioners the amount so required and the Commissioners must thereupon repay to him such sum as may be required to the credit of the Insolvency Services Account: ibid., s. 3 (5). For that purpose the Commissioners may direct the sale of such part of the securities in which the money has been invested as may be necessary: ibid., s. 3 (5).

Insolvency Services Investment Account. *See* INSOLVENCY SERVICES ACCOUNT.

Inspection and investigation of company. Powers given to the Secretary of State (1) to inspect a company's books and papers; (2) to investigate dealing by a director of a company in options to buy or sell its shares or debentures; (3) to investigate a director's interest in shares or debentures of the company; (4) to investigate the company's affairs; and (5) to investigate the membership of the company.

(1) Inspection of company's books and papers

(a) GENERAL POWERS: The Secretary of State may at any time, if he thinks there is good reason to do so, give directions to a company requiring it, at such time and place as may be specified in the directions, to produce such books or papers as may be so specified: Companies Act 1985, s. 447 (2). Further, he may at any time, if he thinks there is good reason to do so, authorise any officer of his, on producing (if required) evidence of his authority, to require the company to produce to the officer forthwith any books or papers which the officer may specify: ibid., s. 447 (3). Where the Secretary of State or an officer of his has power to require the production of any books or papers from any body, he or the officer has the like power to require production of those books or papers from any person who appears to him or the officer to be in possession of them: ibid., s. 447 (4). But where any such person claims a lien on books or papers produced by him, the production is without prejudice to the lien: ibid., s. 447 (4). Any power to require a body or other person to produce books or papers includes a power

(a) if the books or papers are produced,
    (i) to take copies of them or extracts from them; and
    (ii) to require that person, or any other person who is a present or past officer of, or is or was at any time employed by, the body in question, to provide an explanation of any of them;
(b) if the books or papers are not produced, to require the person who was required to produce them to state, to the best of his knowledge and belief, where they are: ibid., s. 447 (5).

If the requirement to produce books or papers or provide an explanation or make a statement is not complied with, the body or other person on whom the requirement was imposed is guilty of an offence and liable on conviction on indictment to a fine, and on summary conviction, to a fine not exceeding the statutory maximum:

ibid., ss. 447 (6), 730 and Sch. 24. But where a person is charged with an offence in respect of a requirement to produce any books or papers, it is a defence to prove that they were not in his possession or under his control and that it was not reasonably practicable for him to comply with the requirement: ibid., s. 447 (7).

A statement made by a person in compliance with such a requirement may be used in evidence against him: ibid., s. 447 (8).

(b) ENTRY AND SEARCH OF PREMISES: If a justice of the peace is satisfied on information on oath laid by an officer of the Secretary of State, or laid under the Secretary of State's authority, that there are reasonable grounds for suspecting that there are on any premises any books or papers of which production has been required, and which have not been produced in compliance with that requirement, the justice may issue a warrant authorising any constable, together with any other persons named in the warrant and any other constables, to enter the premises specified in the information (using such force as is reasonably necessary for the purpose) and to search the premises and take possession of any books or papers appearing to be such books or papers, or to take any other steps which may appear necessary for preserving them and preventing interference with them: ibid., s. 448 (1), (2).

A warrant so issued continues in force until the end of 1 month after the date on which it is issued: ibid., s. 448 (3). Any books or papers of which possession is taken may be retained for a period of 3 months, or, if within that period criminal proceedings are commenced under s. 449 (a) or (b) (being proceedings to which the books or papers are relevant), until the conclusion of those proceedings: ibid., s. 448 (4).

A person who obstructs the exercise of a right of entry or search conferred by a warrant, or who obstructs the exercise of a right so conferred to take possession of any books or papers, is guilty of an offence and liable on conviction on indictment to a fine, and on summary conviction to a fine not exceeding the statutory maximum: ibid., ss. 448 (5), 730 and Sch. 24.

(c) PROVISIONS FOR SECURITY OF INFORMATION: No information or document relating to a body which is obtained under the above provisions must, without the previous consent in writing of that body, be published or disclosed, except to a competent authority, unless the publication or disclosure is required for the purposes of certain specified criminal proceedings: ibid., s. 449 (1). For the meaning of 'competent authority', see ibid., s. 449 (3).

A person who publishes or discloses any information or document in contravention of the above provision is guilty of an offence, and is liable on conviction on indictment to a term of imprisonment not exceeding 2 years or a fine, or both, and on summary conviction to a term of imprisonment not exceeding 6 months or a fine not exceeding the statutory maximum, or both: ibid., ss. 449 (3), 730 and Sch. 24.

(2) Investigation of director's dealing in options

If it appears to the Secretary of State that there are circumstances suggesting that contraventions of s. 323 (which penalises the dealing by a director in options to buy or sell listed shares in, or listed debentures of, the company or associated companies) may have occurred, he may appoint one or more competent inspectors to carry out such investigations as are requisite to establish whether or not such contraventions have occurred, and to report the results of their investigations to him: ibid., s. 446 (1). The appointment of inspectors may limit the period to which his investigation is to extend or confine it to shares or debentures of a particular class or both: ibid., s. 446 (2). The inspectors may, and, if so directed by the Secretary of State, must make interim reports to him, and, on conclusion of the investigation must make to him a final report: ibid., s. 446 (5). Any such report must be written or printed, as the Secretary of State may direct, and he may cause it to be published: ibid., s. 446 (5). The expenses of an investigation are to be defrayed by the Secretary of State out of money provided by Parliament: ibid., s. 446 (7).

(3) Investigation of director's interest in shares

If it appears to the Secretary of State that there are circumstances suggesting that contraventions of s. 328 (which obliges a director of a company to notify it of his interest in shares in, or debentures of, the company or associated companies) may have occurred, he may appoint one or more competent inspectors to carry out such investigations as are requisite to establish whether or not such contraventions have occurred and to report the results of their investigations to him: ibid., s. 446 (1). The appointment of inspectors may limit the period to which their investigation is to extend or confine it to shares or debentures of a particular class or both: ibid., s. 446 (2). The inspectors may, and, if so directed by Secretary of State, must make interim reports to him, and, on the conclusion of the investigation, must make to him a final report: ibid., s. 446 (5). Any such report must be written or printed, as the Secretary of State may direct, and the Secretary of State may cause it to be published: ibid., s. 446 (5). The expenses of an investigation are to be defrayed by the Secretary of State out of money provided by Parliament: ibid., s. 446 (7). (*See* DIRECTOR'S SHAREHOLDINGS).

(4) Investigation of the company's affairs

INVESTIGATION ON APPLICATION OF COMPANY OR ITS MEMBERS: The Secretary of State may appoint one or more competent inspectors to investigate the affairs of a company and to report on them in such manner as he may direct: Companies Act 1985, s. 431 (1). The appointment may be made

(a) in the case of a company having a share capital, on the application either of not less than 200 members or of members holding not less than one-tenth of the shares issued;

(b) in the case of a company not having a share capital, on the application of not less than one-fifth in number of the persons on the company's register of members; and

(c) in any case, on the application of the company: ibid., s. 431 (2).

The application must be supported by such evidence as the Secretary of State may require for the purpose of showing that the applicant or applicants have good reason for requiring the investigation: ibid., s. 431 (3). The Secretary of State may, before appointing inspectors, require the applicant or applicants to give security, to an amount not exceeding £5,000, or such other sum as he may by order specify, for the payment of the costs of the investigation: ibid., s. 431 (4).

An order must be made by statutory instrument subject to annulment in pursuance of a resolution of either House of Parliament: ibid., s. 431 (4).

INVESTIGATION IN OTHER CASES: The Secretary of State must appoint one or more competent inspectors to investigate the affairs of a company and to report on them in such manner as he directs if the court by order declares that its affairs ought to be so investigated: ibid., s. 432 (1).

He may make such an appointment if it appears to him that there are circumstances suggesting

(i) that the company's affairs are being or have been conducted with intent to defraud its creditors or the creditors of any other person, or otherwise for a fraudulent or unlawful purpose, or in a manner which is unfairly prejudicial to some part of its members, or that any actual or proposed act or omission of the company (including an act or omission on its behalf) is or would be so prejudicial, or that it was formed for any fraudulent or unlawful purpose; or

(ii) that persons concerned with the company's formation or the management of its affairs have in connection with them been guilty of fraud, misfeasance or other misconduct towards it or towards its members; or

(iii) that the company's members have not been given all the information with respect to its affairs which they might reasonably expect; ibid., s. 432 (2).

INVESTIGATION INTO AFFAIRS OF RELATED COMPANIES: If inspectors think it necessary for the purposes of their investigation to investigate also the affairs of another body corporate which is or at any relevant time has been the company's subsidiary or holding company, or a subsidiary of its holding company or a holding company of its subsidiary, they have power to do so, and must report on the affairs of the other body corporate so far as they think the results of their investigation of its affairs are relevant to the investigation of the affairs of the first-mentioned company: ibid., s. 433 (1).

PRODUCTION OF DOCUMENTS, AND EVIDENCE ON INVESTIGATION: It is the duty of all officers and agents of the company and of all officers and agents of any other body corporate whose affairs are investigated to produce to the inspectors all books and documents of, or relating, to the company or the other body corporate which are in their custody or power, to attend before the inspectors when required to do so, and otherwise to give to the inspectors all assistance in connection with the investigation which they are reasonably able to give: ibid., s. 434 (1). The expression 'officers and agents' includes past as well as present officers or agents: ibid., s. 434 (4). The term 'agents' includes the bankers and solicitors of the company or other body corporate and persons employed by the company or other body corporate as auditors whether those persons are or are not officers of the company or other body corporate: ibid., s. 434 (4).

If the inspectors consider that a person other than an officer or agent of the company or other body corporate is or may be in possession of information concerning its affairs, they may require that person to produce to them any books or documents in his custody or power relating to the company or other body corporate, to attend before them and otherwise to give them all assistance in connection with the investigation which he is reasonably able to give: ibid., s. 434 (2). It is the duty of that person to comply with the requirement: ibid., s. 434 (2).

If an inspector has reasonable grounds for believing that a director, or past director, of the company or other body corporate whose affairs he is investigating maintains or has maintained a bank account of any description (whether alone or jointly with another person and whether in Great Britain or elsewhere) into or out of which there has been paid

(i) the emoluments or part of the emoluments of his office as such director, particulars of which have not been disclosed in the accounts; or

(ii) any money which has resulted from or been used in the financing of a transaction, arrangement or agreement

    (a) particulars of which have not been disclosed in a note to the accounts of any company; or

    (b) in respect of which any amount outstanding was not included in the aggregate amounts outstanding in respect of certain transactions, arrangements or agreements required to be disclosed in a note to the accounts of any company; or

    (c) particulars of which were not included in any register of certain transactions, arrangements and agreements required

to be maintained in respect of transactions between recognised banks and their directors (*see* RECOGNISED BANK); or
(iii) any money which has been in any way connected with an act or omission, which on the part of that director constituted misconduct (whether fraudulent or not) towards that company or body corporate or its members;

the inspector may require the director to produce to him all documents in the director's possession, or under his control, relating to that bank account: ibid., s. 435 (1), (2).

An inspector may examine on oath the officers and agents of the company or other body corporate, and any other person who the inspector considers is or may be in possession of any information concerning the affairs of the company or other body corporate, and may administer an oath accordingly: ibid., s. 434 (3).

If an officer or agent of the company or other body corporate or any other person who the inspector considers is or may be in possession of any information concerning the affairs of the company or other body corporate refuses to produce to the inspectors any book or document which it is his duty to produce, refuses to attend before the inspectors when required to do so, or refuses to answer any question which is put to him by the inspectors with respect to the affairs of the company or other body corporate, the inspectors may certify the refusal in writing to the court: ibid., s. 436 (2). The court may thereupon inquire into the case, and after hearing any witness who may be produced against or on behalf of the alleged offender and after hearing any statement which may be offered in defence, punish the offender in like manner as if he had been guilty of contempt of the court: ibid., s. 436 (3).

INSPECTORS' REPORT: The inspectors may, and, if so directed by the Secretary of State, must, make interim reports to the Secretary of State and on the conclusion of their investigation must make a final report to him: ibid., s. 437 (1). Any such report must be written or printed, as the Secretary of State directs: ibid., s. 437 (1).

Where the inspectors were appointed by an order of the court, the Secretary of State must furnish a copy of any report of theirs to the court, and, in any case, he may if he thinks fit
(a) forward a copy of any report made by the inspectors to the company's registered office;
(b) furnish a copy on request and on payment of the prescribed fee to
   (i) any member of the company or other body corporate which is the subject of the report;
  (ii) any person whose conduct is referred to in the report;
 (iii) the auditors of the company or body corporate;
 (iv) the applicants for the investigation;
  (v) any other person whose financial interests appear to the

101

Secretary of State to be affected by the matters dealt with in the report, whether as a creditor of the company or body corporate or otherwise; and

(c) cause any such report to be printed and published: ibid., s. 168 (2).

Although the proceedings before the inspectors are only administrative and not judicial or quasi-judicial, the characteristics of the proceedings require the inspectors to act fairly so that if they are disposed to condemn or criticise anyone in a report, they should first give him an opportunity to correct or contradict the allegation: *Re Pergamon Press Ltd* [1970] 3 All ER 535 at 439, CA (per Lord Denning MR); *Maxwell v Department of Trade and Industry* [1974] 2 All ER 122, CA.

EXPENSES OF INVESTIGATION OF COMPANY'S AFFAIRS: The expenses of and incidental to an investigation by inspectors appointed by the Secretary of State must be defrayed in the first instance by him: Companies Act 1985, s. 439 (1). But the following persons are liable to repay the Department

(a) a person who is convicted on a prosecution instituted as a result of the investigation;

(b) a body corporate dealt with by the inspectors' report where the inspectors were appointed otherwise than of the Secretary of State's own motion, except where it was the applicant for the investigation and except so far as the Secretary of State otherwise directs, and

(c) the applicant or applicants for the investigation where the inspectors were appointed under s. 431 (supra), to such extent (if any) as the Secretary of State may direct: ibid., s. 439 (1), (2), (4), (5).

The report of inspectors appointed otherwise than of the Secretary of State's own motion may, if they think fit, and must, if the Secretary of State so directs, include a recommendation as to the directions (if any) which they think appropriate, in the light of their investigation, to be given under the above provisions: ibid., s. 439 (6).

INSPECTORS' REPORT AS EVIDENCE: A copy of any report of inspectors, certified by the Secretary of State to be a true copy, is admissible in any legal proceeding as evidence of the opinion of the inspectors in relation to any matter contained in the report: ibid., s. 441 (1). A document purporting to be such a certificate must be received in evidence, and is deemed to be such a certificate, unless the contrary is proved: ibid., s. 441 (2).

WINDING UP PETITION: If it appears to the Secretary of State from a report made by inspectors under s. 437, or from information or documents obtained under s. 447 or s. 448, that it is expedient in the public interest that the company should be wound up, he may, unless the company is already being wound up by the court, present a petition for it to be so wound up if the court thinks it just and equitable: ibid., s. 440.

CIVIL PROCEEDINGS: If from any report made under s. 437 or from information or documents obtained under s. 447 or s. 448, it appears to the Secretary of State that any civil proceedings ought in the public interest to be brought by any company, the Secretary of State may bring proceedings in the name and on behalf of the company: ibid., s. 438 (1).

INFORMATION TENDING TO SHOW COMMISSION OF OFFENCE: Inspectors may at any time in the course of their investigation, without the necessity of making an interim report, inform the Secretary of State of matters coming to their knowledge as a result of the investigation tending to show that an offence has been committed: ibid., s. 433 (2).

(5) Investigation of membership of company

Where it appears to the Secretary of State that there is good reason to do so, he may appoint one or more competent inspectors to investigate and report on the membership of any company, and otherwise with respect to the company, for the purpose of determining the true persons who are or have been financially interested in the success or failure (real or apparent) of the company or able to control or materially to influence its policy: ibid., s. 442 (1).

The appointment of inspectors may define the scope of their investigations (whether as respects the matters or the period to which it is to extend or otherwise) and in particular may limit the investigation to matters connected with particular shares or debentures: ibid., s. 442 (2).

If application for an investigation with respect to particular shares or debentures of a company is made to the Secretary of State by members of the company, and the number of applicants or the amount of the shares held by them is not less than that required for an application for the appointment of an inspector under s. 431 (2) (a) and (b) (supra), he must appoint inspectors to conduct the investigation (unless he is satisfied that the application is vexatious): ibid., s. 442 (3) (a). The inspectors' appointment must not exclude from the scope of their investigation any matter which the application seeks to have included in it except in so far as the Secretary of State is satisfied that it is unreasonable for that matter to be investigated: ibid., s. 442 (3).

Subject to the terms of their appointment the inspectors' powers extend to the investigation of any circumstances suggesting the existence of an arrangement or understanding which, though not legally binding, is or was observed or likely to be observed in practice and which is relevant to the purposes of the investigation: ibid., s. 442 (4).

INFORMATION AS TO PERSONS INTERESTED IN SHARES OR DEBENTURES: If it appears to the Secretary of State that there is good reason to investigate the ownership of any shares in or debentures of a company, and that it is unnecessary to appoint inspectors for the purpose, he may require any person, whom he has reasonable cause to believe to have or to be able to obtain any information as to the present and past interests in those shares or debentures and the names and addresses of the persons interested and of any persons who act or have acted on their behalf in relation to the shares or debentures, to give any such information to the Secretary of State: ibid., s. 444 (1).

A person is deemed to have an interest in shares or debentures if he has any right to acquire or dispose of them or any interest in them or to vote in respect of them, or if his consent is necessary for the exercise of any of the rights of other persons interested in it, or if other persons interested in them can be required, or are accustomed, to exercise their rights in accordance with his instructions: ibid., s. 444 (2).

A person who fails to give any information required of him or who, in giving any such information, makes any statement which he knows to be false in a material particular, or recklessly makes any statement which is false in a material particular, is liable on conviction on indictment to a term of imprisonment not exceeding 2 years or a fine, or both, and on summary conviction to a term not exceeding 6 months or a fine not exceeding the statutory maximum or both: ibid., ss. 444 (3), 730 and Sch. 24.

POWER TO IMPOSE RESTRICTIONS ON SHARES OR DEBENTURES: If in connection with an investigation s. 442 or s. 444 it appears to the Secretary of State that there is difficulty in finding out the relevant facts about any shares (whether issued or to be issued) he may by order direct that the shares shall until further order be subject to restrictions: ibid., s. 445 (1).

These restrictions are that
(i) any transfer of the shares, or, in the case of unissued shares, any transfer of the right to be issued with them, and any issue of them, is void;
(ii) no voting rights are exercisable in respect of the shares;
(iii) no further shares are to be issued in right of them or in pursuance of any offer made to their holder;
(iv) except in a liquidation, no payment is to be made of any sums due from the company on the shares, whether in respect of capital or otherwise: ibid., s. 454 (1).

Where shares in a company are by order made subject to restrictions, application may be made to the court for an order directing that the shares be no longer so subject: ibid., s. 456 (1). If the order applying the restrictions was made by the Secretary of State, or he has refused to make an order diapplying them, the application may be made by any person aggrieved: ibid., s. 456 (2). If the order was made under s. 216 (non-disclosure of shareholding), it may be made by any such person or by the company: ibid., s. 456 (2).

A person who

(a) exercises or purports to exercise any right to dispose of any shares which, to his knowledge, are for the time being subject to the restrictions or of any right to be issued with any such shares; or

(b) votes in respect of any such shares (whether as holder or proxy), or appoints a proxy to vote in respect of them; or

(c) being the holder of any such shares, fails to notify of their being subject to the restrictions any person whom he does not know to be aware of that fact but does know to be entitled (apart from the restrictions) to vote in respect of those shares whether as holder or as proxy; or

(d) being the holder of any such shares enters into an agreement to transfer the shares;

is liable on conviction on indictment to a fine, and on summary conviction to a fine not exceeding the statutory maximum: ibid., s. 455 (1), 730 and Sch. 24.

If shares in any company are issued in contravention of the restrictions, the company and every officer of the company who is in default are liable on conviction on indictment to a fine, and on summary conviction to a fine not exceeding the statutory maximum: ibid., s. 455 (2), 730 and Sch. 24.

A prosecution must not be instituted except by or with the consent of the Secretary of State: ibid., ss. 455 (3), 732 (2).

All the above provisions apply in relation to debentures as they apply in relation to shares: ibid., s. 445 (2).

Instrument appointing a proxy. *See* PROXY.

Interest, appropriate rate of. *See* APPROPRIATE RATE.

Interim dividend. A dividend declared at any time between 2 annual general meetings: *Re Jowitt, Jowitt v Keeling* [1922] 2 Ch 442. (*See* DIVIDEND).

International bond issue. An issue of debentures of a company

(a) all of which are offered or to be offered by an off-market dealer to persons (whether principals or agents) whose ordinary business includes the buying or selling of debentures, and

(b) where debentures are denominated in sterling, not less than 50 per cent in nominal value of the debentures are or are to be so offered to persons who have not the requisite connection with the United Kingdom: Company Securities (Insider Dealing) Act 1985, s. 15 (1) (a).

(*See* OFF-MARKET DEALER).

Investment company. In s. 265 of the Act means a public company which has given notice in the prescribed form (which has not been revoked) to the Registrar of Companies of its intention to carry on business as an investment company and has since the date of that notice complied with the requirements

(a) that the business of the company consists of investing its funds mainly in securities, with the aim of spreading investment risk and giving members of the company the benefit of the results of the management of its funds;

(b) that none of the company's holdings in companies (other than companies which are for the time being investment companies) represents more than 15 per cent by value of the investing company's investment;

(c) that distribution of the company's capital profits is prohibited by its memorandum or articles of association;

(d) that the company has not retained, otherwise than in compliance With Part VIII of the Act, in respect of any accounting reference period, more than 15 per cent of the income it derives from securities: Companies Act 1985, s. 266 (1), (2).

Investment exchange. For the purposes of the Company Securities (Insider Dealing) Act 1985 means 'an organisation maintaining a system whereby an offer to deal in securities made by a subscriber to the organisation is communicated, without his identity being revealed, to other subscribers to the organisation, and whereby any acceptance of that offer by any of those other subscribers is recorded and confirmed': Company Securities (Insider Dealing) Act 1985, s. 13(2).

Issue at a discount. An issue of debentures or shares at less than their nominal value, e.g. an issue of shares with a nominal value of £1 at a price of 75p.

Shares must not be issued at a discount: Companies Act 1985, s. 100 (1). If shares are so issued, the allottee is liable to pay the company an amount equal to the amount of the discount, with interest at the appropriate rate: ibid., s. 100 (2). (*See* APPROPRIATE RATE). Shares must not be issued at a discount even by way of compromise (*Mother Lode Consolidated Gold Mines Ltd v Hill* (1903) 19 TLR 341), or in any other indirect way (*Mosely v Koffyfontein Mines Ltd* [1904] 2 Ch 108; *Mother Lode Consolidated Gold Mines Ltd v Hill* (supra)).

Because they do not form part of the capital of the company, debentures may be issued at a discount: *Re Regent's Canal Ironworks Co* (1876) 3 Ch D 43.

Issue at a premium. An issue of shares at more than their nominal value, e.g. an issue of shares with a nominal value of £1 at a price of £1.25. (*See* SHARE PREMIUM ACCOUNT).

Issue manager means
  (a) an off-market dealer acting as an agent of the issuing company for the purposes of an international bond issue; or
  (b) where the issuing company issues or proposes to issue the debentures to an off-market dealer under an arrangement in pursuance of which he is to sell them to other persons, that off-market dealer: Company Securities (Insider Dealing) Act 1985, s. 15 (1) (c). (*See* INTERNATIONAL BOND ISSUE PROSPECTUS).

Issued share capital. The nominal value of the shares actually issued.

J

Jobber means 'an individual, partnership or company dealing in securities on a recognised stock exchange and recognised by the Council of the Stock Exchange as carrying on the business of a jobber': Company Securities (Insider Dealing) Act 1985, s. 3 (1) (c).

L

Length of notice for calling meeting. A provision of a company's articles is void in so far as it provides for the calling of a meeting of the company (other than an adjourned meeting) by a shorter notice than

(a) in the case of the annual general meeting, 21 days' notice in writing; and

(b) in the case of a meeting other than an annual general meeting or a meeting for the passing of a special resolution, 7 days' notice in writing in the case of an unlimited company, and otherwise 14 days' notice in writing: Companies Act 1985, s. 369 (1). (*See* ANNUAL GENERAL MEETING; EXTRAORDINARY GENERAL MEETING; SPECIAL RESOLUTION; UNLIMITED COMPANY).

Except in so far as the articles of a company otherwise provide, a meeting of the company (otherwise than an adjourned meeting) may be called

(a) in the case of the annual general meeting by 21 days' notice in writing; and

(b) in the case of a meeting other than an annual general meeting or a meeting for the passing of a special resolution, by 7 days' notice in writing in the case of an unlimited company and otherwise, 14 days' notice in writing; Companies Act 1985, s. 369 (2).

A meeting of a company, notwithstanding that it is called by a shorter notice than that specified above or in the company's articles is deemed to have been duly called if it is so agreed

(a) in the case of a meeting called as the annual general meeting, by all the members entitled to attend and vote thereat; and

(b) in the case of any other meeting, by a majority in number of the members having a right to attend and vote at the meeting, being a majority together holding not less than 95 per cent in nominal value of the shares giving a right to attend and vote at the meeting or, in the case of a company not having a share capital, together representing not less than 95 per cent of the total voting rights at the meeting of all the members; ibid., s. 369 (3), (4).

But the persons who agree to a resolution being passed at short notice must have appreciated that the resolution was being passed on short notice, and have agreed to its being so passed with that consideration in their minds: *Re Pearce, Duff & Co Ltd* [1960] 3 All ER 222 at 224 (per Buckley J).

Where a shareholder discovers that a meeting was called without the length of notice required being given, and takes no effective steps to protest that it is void, a resolution passed at that meeting will be valid: *Re Bailey, Hay & Co Ltd* [1971] 3 All ER 693.

Table A, art. 38 states: 'An annual general meeting and an extraordinary general meeting called for the passing of a special resolution or a resolution appointing a person as a director shall be called by at least 21 clear days' notice. All other extraordinary general meetings shall be called by at least 14 clear days' notice but a general meeting may be called by shorter notice if it is so agreed
(a) in the case of an annual general meeting, by all the members entitled to attend and vote thereat; and
(b) in the case of any other meeting by a majority in number of the members having a right to attend and vote being a majority together holding not less than 95 per cent in nominal value of the shares giving that right. (*See* ANNUAL GENERAL MEETING; EXTRAORDINARY GENERAL MEETING; SPECIAL RESOLUTION).

Lien of partner. *See* PARTNER'S LIEN.

Lien on share. A right given to a company to retain the shares of a member until he has discharged his liabilities to the company. Such a lien is usually given by the articles.

Table A, art. 8 states: 'The company shall have a first and paramount lien on every share (not being a fully paid share) for all moneys (whether presently payable or not) payable at a fixed time or called in respect of that share. The directors may at any time declare any share to be wholly or in part exempt from the provisions of this regulation. The company's lien on a share shall extend to any amount payable in respect of it.' (*See* CALL).

Enforcement

The company is usually empowered to sell the shares if the member does not pay the amount due.

Table A, art. 9 states: 'The company may sell in such manner as the directors determine any shares on which the company has a lien if a sum in respect of which the lien exists is presently payable and is not paid within 14 clear days after notice has been given to the holder of the share or to the person entitled to it in consequence of the death or bankruptcy of the holder, demanding payment and stating that if the notice is not complied with the shares may be sold.'

To give effect to a sale the directors may authorise some person to execute an instrument of transfer of the shares sold to, or in accordance with the directions of, the purchaser: Table A, art. 10. The title of the transferee to the shares shall not be affected by any irregularity in or invalidity of the proceedings in reference to the sale: ibid., art. 10.

The net proceeds of the sale, after payment of the costs, shall be applied in payment of so much of the sum for which the lien exists as is presently payable: ibid., art. 11. Any residue shall (upon surrender to the company for cancellation of the certificate for the shares sold and subject to a like lien for any moneys not presently payable as existed upon the shares before the sale) be paid to the person entitled to the shares at the date of the sale: ibid., art. 11.

The company may enforce the lien against the registered shareholder even though he is only a trustee: *New London and Brazilian Bank v Brocklebank* (1882) 21 Ch D 302, CA. But the lien of the company will not prevail if the company had notice of the trust before the debt to the company was incurred: *Bradford Banking Co v Briggs & Co Ltd* (1886) 12 App Cas 29, HL.

The death of a member does not destroy the lien, and the lien is valid if it is first imposed after his death: *Allen v Gold Reefs of West Africa Ltd* [1900] 1 Ch 656, CA.

If the company has a lien on a member's shares, and he raises the money from another person to pay the debt, he may call on the company to assign the lien to that other person: *Everitt v Automatic Weighing Machine Co* [1892] 3 Ch 506.

If a member sells some of his shares only, the purchaser can insist on the company paying itself first out of the shares which are not sold: *Gray v Stone and Funnell* (1893) 69 LT 282.

Lifting the veil. *See* CORPORATE PERSONALITY, PRINCIPLE OF.

Limited partner. A member of a limited partnership who at the time of entering into it contributes to it a sum or sums as capital or property valued at a stated amount, and who is not liable for the debts or obligations of the firm beyond the amount so contributed: Limited Partnerships Act 1907, s. 4 (2). (*See* LIMITED PARTNERSHIP). A guarantee given by a person in respect of money advanced to the firm is not a contribution by him and does not make him a limited partner, and he will be liable as though he were a general partner: *Rayner & Co v Rhodes* (1926) 24 Ll L Rep 25. (*See* GENERAL PARTNER).

A limited partner must not during the continuance of the partnership, either directly or indirectly, draw out or receive back any part of his contribution, and if he does draw out or receive back any such part, he is liable for the debts and obligations of the firm up to the amount so drawn out or received back: Limited Partnerships Act 1907, s. 4 (3).

A body corporate may be a limited partner: ibid. s. 4 (4).

A statement showing the sum contributed by each limited partner, and whether paid in cash or how otherwise must be sent or delivered to the Registrar of Companies on the registration of the limited partnership: ibid. s. 8. If during the continuance of a limited partnership any change is made in or occurs in the sum contributed by

111

any limited partner, or in the liability of a limited partner becoming a general partner, a statement specifying the nature of the change must be delivered to the Registrar within 7 days: ibid., s. 9 (1). If default is made in compliance with this requirement, each of the general partners is liable on summary conviction to a fine not exceeding £1 for each day during which the default continues: ibid., s. 9 (2).

A limited partner must not take part in the management of the partnership business, and has no power to bind the firm, though he may by himself or his agent at any time inspect the books of the firm and examine into the state and prospects of the partnership business, and may advise with the partners on it: ibid., s. 6 (1). If a limited partner takes part in the management of the partnership business, he is liable for all debts and obligations of the firm incurred while he so takes part in the management as though he were a general partner: ibid., s. 6 (1).

Subject to any agreement express or implied between the partners,

  (i) a limited partner may, with the consent of the general partners, assign his share in the partnership, and upon such an assignment the assignee becomes a limited partner with all the rights of the assignor;

 (ii) the other partners are not entitled to dissolve the partnership by reason of any limited partner suffering his share to be charged for his separate debt;

(iii) a person may be introduced as a partner without the consent of the existing limited partners;

(iv) a limited partner is not entitled to dissolve the partnership by notice: ibid., s. 6 (5).

Notice of any arrangement or transaction under which the share of a limited partner will be assigned to any person must be forthwith advertised in the *London Gazette*: ibid., s. 10 (1). Until notice of the arrangement or transaction is so advertised, the arrangement is deemed, for the purposes of the Act, to be of no effect: ibid., s. 10 (1).

Limited partnership. A partnership consisting of one or more 'general partners' and one or more 'limited partners': Limited Partnerships Act 1907, s. 4 (2). (*See* GENERAL PARTNER; LIMITED PARTNER). The general rule is that a limited partnership must not consist of more than 20 persons: Limited Partnerships Act 1907, s. 4 (2). But the limit of 20 does not apply (i) to a partnership carrying on practice as solicitors and consisting of persons each of whom is a solicitor; (ii) to a partnership carrying on practice as accountants and consisting of persons each of whom falls within the Companies Act 1985, s. 389 (1) (a) or (b); (iii) to a partnership carrying on business as members of a recognised stock exchange and consisting of persons each of whom is a member of that exchange: Companies Act 1985, s. 717 (1). (*See* RECOGNISED STOCK EXCHANGE). Further, the Secretary of State may by regulations in a statutory instrument provide that the limit of 20 persons shall not apply to a partnership carrying on business of a description specified in the regulations: ibid., s. 717 (2). Thus, the limit of 20 persons does not apply to a limited partnership carrying on one or more of the following activities:— (i) surveying; (ii) auctioneering; (iii) valuing; (iv) estate agency; (v) land agency; and (vi) estate management: Limited Partnerships (Unrestricted Size) No. 1 Regulations 1971 (S.I. 1971 No. 782).

Every limited partnership must be registered as such in accordance with the provisions of the Limited Partnerships Act 1907, and in default thereof it is deemed to be a general partnership, and every limited partner is deemed to be a general partner: Limited Partnerships Act 1907, s. 5. The registration of a limited partnership is effected by sending by post or delivering to the Registrar of Companies a statement containing (i) the firm name; (ii) the general nature of the business; (iii) the principal place of business; (iv) the full name of each of the partners; (v) the term, if any, for which the partnership is entered into, and the date of its commencement; (vi) a statement that the partnership is limited, and the description of every limited partner as such; and (vii) the sum contributed by each limited partner, and whether paid in cash or how otherwise: Limited Partnerships Act 1907, s. 8. The form is set out in the Appendix to the Limited Partnership Rules 1907 (S.R. & O. 1907 No. 1020, as amended).

If during the continuance of a limited partnership any change is made or occurs in

  (i) the firm name;
  (ii) the general nature of the business;
 (iii) the principal place of business;
 (iv) the partners or the name of any partner;
  (v) the term or character of the partnership;
 (vi) the sum contributed by any limited partner;
(vii) the liability of any partner by reason of his becoming a limited instead of a general partner or a general instead of a limited partner,

a statement signed by the firm, specifying the nature of the change must within 7 days be sent by post or delivered to the Registrar of Companies: Limited Partnerships Act 1907, s. 9 (1). If default is made in compliance with these requirements, each of the general partners is liable on summary conviction to a fine not exceeding £1 for each day during which the default continues: ibid., s. 9 (2).

On receiving any statement made in pursuance of the Act the Registrar must cause it to be filed, and must send by post to the firm from which the statement has been received a certificate of the registration: ibid., s. 13. The Registrar must keep in proper books to be provided for the purpose a register and an index of all limited partnerships which have been registered and of all the statements registered in relation to them: ibid., s. 14. Any person may inspect the statements filed by the Registrar: ibid., s. 16 (1). There must be paid for each inspection such fees as may be appointed by the Department of Trade and Industry, not exceeding 5p for each inspection: ibid., s. 16 (1). Any person may require a certificate of the registration of any limited partnership, or a copy of or extract from any registered statement to be certified by the Registrar: ibid., s. 16 (1). There must be paid for such certificate of registration, certified copy or extract such fees as the Department of Trade and Industry may appoint, not exceeding 10p for the certificate of registration, and not exceeding $2\frac{1}{2}$p for each folio of 72 words: ibid., s. 16 (1). A certificate of registration or a copy of or extract from any statement registered under the Act, if duly certified to be a true copy under the hand of the Registrar or one of the assistant registrars, must be received in evidence in all legal proceedings, civil or criminal, and in all cases whatsoever: ibid., s. 16 (2).

A limited partnership is not dissolved by the death or bankruptcy of a limited partner, and the unsoundness of mind of a limited partner is not a ground for dissolution of the partnership unless his share cannot be otherwise ascertained and realised: ibid., s. 6 (2). In the event of the dissolution of a limited partnership its affairs must be wound up by the general partners unless the court otherwise orders: ibid., s. 6 (3).

Subject to any agreement express or implied between the partners,
(i) any difference arising as to ordinary matters connected with the partnership business may be decided by a majority of the general partners;
(ii) the other partners are not entitled to dissolve the partnership by reason of any limited partner suffering his share to be charged for his separate debt;
(iii) a person may be introduced as a partner without the consent of the existing limited partners: ibid., s. 6 (5).

Limited Partnerships Act 1907. An Act enabling persons to form a limited partnership. *See* LIMITED PARTNERSHIP.

Limited Partnership Rules 1907 (S.R. & O. 1907 No. 1020). The rules made by the Department of Trade and Industry under the Limited Partnerships Act 1907, s. 17. The rules concern (i) the fees to be paid to the Registrar of Companies; (ii) the duties to be performed by him; (iii) the performance by assistant registrars and other officers of acts required to be done by the Registrar of Companies; (iv) the

forms to be used; and (v) the conduct and regulation of registration.
Liquidator. A person appointed to conduct the winding up of a company.

(A) In a winding up by the court
(i) APPOINTMENT: (a) How made
The court may make any appointment and order required to give effect to any determination of the creditors and contributories as to the appointment of a liquidator: Companies Act 1985, s. 533 (4). If there is a difference between the determinations of the meetings of the creditors and contributories in respect of the appointment, the court must decide the difference and make such order as it may think fit: ibid., s. 533 (4).

A body corporate is not qualified for appointment as a liquidator of a company: ibid., s. 634 (1). Any appointment made in contravention of this provision is void: ibid., s. 634 (2). Any body corporate, which acts as liquidator of a company, is liable to conviction on indictment to a fine, and on summary conviction to a fine not exceeding the statutory maximum: ibid., ss. 634 (2), 730 and Sch. 24.

A person, who gives or agrees to offer to give to any member or creditor of a company any valuable consideration with a view to securing his own appointment, or to securing or preventing the appointment of some person other than himself, as the company's liquidator, is liable on conviction on indictment to a fine, and on summary conviction to a fine not exceeding the statutory maximum: ibid., ss. 635, 730 and Sch. 24.

As a general rule the court should not appoint a junior and inexperienced accountant as liquidator, and it is a rule of practice not to appoint an accountant of less than 5 years' standing, although the overall discretion of the court remains: *Re Icknield Development Ltd* [1973] 2 All ER 168.

If a liquidator is not appointed by the court, the Official Receiver is the liquidator of the company: Companies Act 1985, s. 533 (6).

A vacancy in the office of a liquidator appointed by the court must be filled by the court: ibid., s. 536 (3). The Official Receiver by virtue of his office is the liquidator during any vacancy: ibid., s. 533 (6).
(b) Style
A liquidator must be described, where a person other than the Official Receiver is liquidator, by the style of 'the liquidator', and where the Official Receiver is liquidator, by the style of 'the Official Receiver and liquidator' of the particular company in respect of which he is appointed (and not by his individual name) ibid., s. 533 (7).
(c) Notice of appointment and security
If a person other than the Official Receiver is appointed liquidator, he is incapable of acting as liquidator until he has notified his appointment to the Registrar of Companies and given security in the prescribed

manner to the satisfaction of the Secretary of State: ibid., s. 534 (a).

(d) Advertisement of appointment

Every appointment of a liquidator must be advertised by him in such manner as the court directs immediately after the appointment has been made, and he has given the required security: Companies (Winding-up) Rules 1949, (S.I. 1949 No. 330), r. 58 (6).

(e) Remuneration

Where a person other than the Official Receiver is appointed liquidator, he is to receive such salary or remuneration by way of percentage or otherwise as the court may direct, and if more such persons than one are appointed liquidators, their remuneration is to be distributed among them in such proportions as the court directs: Companies Act 1985, s. 536 (2). If the court gives no direction, the liquidator's remuneration is fixed by the committee of inspection: Companies (Winding-up) Rules 1949, r. 159 (1). (*See* COMMITTEE OF INSPECTION).

(ii) REGISTRATION, REMOVAL AND RELEASE: (a) Resignation

A liquidator appointed by the court may resign: Companies Act 1985, s. 536 (1).

A liquidator who desires to resign his office must summon separate meetings of the creditors and contributories: Companies (Winding-up) Rules 1949, r. 167. If the creditors and contributories by ordinary resolutions both agree to accept the resignation of the liquidator, he must file with the Registrar of Companies a memorandum of his resignation and must send a notice of it to the Official Receiver, and the resignation then takes effect: ibid., r. 167. In any other case the liquidator must report to the court the result of the meetings and must send a report to the Official Receiver: ibid., r. 167. Thereupon the court may, on the application of the liquidator or the Official Receiver, determine whether or not the resignation of the liquidator is to be accepted, and may give such directions and make such orders as in the court's opinion are necessary: ibid., r. 167.

On a liquidator resigning he must deliver to the Official Receiver, or the new liquidator, as the case may be, all books kept by him and all other books, documents, papers and accounts in his possession relating to the office of liquidator: ibid., r. 180 (1).

(b) Removal

A liquidator appointed by the court may be removed by the court on cause shown: Companies Act 1985, s. 536 (1). Thus he may be removed where he insists on acting in the interests of the shareholders alone, although the assets are insufficient to pay the creditors in full: *Re Rubber and Produce Investment Trust* [1915] 1 Ch 382. A contributory or a creditor, but not an outside person, can apply for the removal of the liquidator: *Re New De Koop Ltd* [1908] 1 Ch 589.

If a liquidator at any time retains for more than 10 days a sum not exceeding £100, or such other amount as the Secretary of State in any particular case authorises him to retain, then, unless he explains the retention to the Secretary of State's satisfaction, he is liable to be removed from his office by the Secretary of State: Companies Act 1985, s. 542 (4).

On a liquidator being removed from his office, he must hand over to the Official Receiver, or the new liquidator, as the case may be, all books kept by him and all other books, documents, papers and accounts in his possession relating to the office of liquidator: Companies (Winding-up) Rules 1949, r. 180 (1).

(c) Release

A liquidator in a winding up by the court, before making application to the Secretary of State for his release, must give notice of his intention to do so to all the creditors who have proved their debts, and to all the contributories, and must send with the notice a summary of all receipts and payments in the winding up: Companies (Winding-up) Rules 1949, r. 205 (1).

When the liquidator of a company which is being wound up by the court

(a) has realised all the company's property, or so much of it as can (in his opinion) be realised without needlessly protracting the liquidation, and has distributed a final dividend (if any) to the creditors and adjusted the rights of the contributories among themselves and made a final return to the contributories; or

(b) has resigned; or

(c) has been removed from his office,

the Secretary of State may, on the liquidator's application, cause a report on his accounts to be prepared: Companies Act 1985, s. 545 (2), (3).

On his complying with all the Secretary of State's requirements the Secretary of State must take into consideration the report and any objections which may be urged by any creditor or contributory or person interested against the release of the liquidator, and must grant or withhold the release, subject to an appeal to the High Court: ibid., s. 545 (3).

If the release of the liquidator is withheld, the court may, on the application of any creditor or contributory or person interested, make such order as it thinks just, charging the liquidator with the consequences of any act or default which he may have done or made contrary to his duty: ibid., s. 545 (4).

An order of the Secretary of State releasing the liquidator discharges him from all liability in respect of any act done or default made by him in the administration of the company's affairs or otherwise in relation to his conduct as liquidator: ibid., s. 545 (5). But any such order may be revoked on proof that it was obtained by fraud or by suppression or concealment of any material fact: ibid., s. 545 (5).

When the Department has granted a liquidator his release, a notice of the order granting the release must be gazetted: Companies (Winding-up) Rules 1949, r. 205 (2).

On a liquidator being released he must hand over to the Official Receiver or the new liquidator, as the case may be, all books kept by him, and all other books, documents, papers and accounts in his possession relating to the office of liquidator: ibid., r. 180 (1). His release does not take effect until he has done so: ibid., r. 180 (1).

(iii) POWERS:

(a) General Powers

With the sanction of the court or committee of inspection. The liquidator has power (a) to bring or defend any action or other legal proceeding in the name of and on behalf of the company; (b) to carry on the business of the company so far as may be necessary for its beneficial winding up; (c) to appoint a solicitor to assist him in the performance of his duties; (d) to pay any classes of creditors in full; (e) to make any compromise or arrangement with creditors or persons claiming to be creditors, or having or alleging themselves to have any claim (present or future, certain or contingent, ascertained or sounding only in damages) against the company, or whereby the company may be rendered liable; and (f) to compromise all calls and liabilities to calls, debts and liabilities capable of resulting in debts, and all claims (present or future, certain or contingent, ascertained or sounding only in damages) subsisting or supposed to subsist between the company and a contributory or alleged contributory or other debtor or person apprehending liability to the company, and all questions in any way relating to or affecting the assets or the winding up of the company, on such terms as may be agreed, and take any security for the discharge of any such call, debt, liability or claim and give a complete discharge in respect of it: Companies Act 1985, s. 539 (1). (*See* CALL).

Without such sanction. The liquidator in a winding up by the court has power, without such sanction (a) to sell any of the company's property by public auction or private contract, with power to transfer the whole of it to any person or to sell it in parcels; (b) to do all acts and to execute, in the name and on behalf of the company, all deeds, receipts and other documents, and for that purpose to use, when necessary, the company's seal; (c) to prove, rank and claim in the bankruptcy or insolvency of any contributory for any balance against his estate, and to receive dividends in the bankruptcy or insolvency in respect of that balance, as a separate debt due from the bankrupt or insolvent, and rateably with the other separate creditors; (d) to draw, accept, make and indorse any bill of exchange or promissory note in the name and on behalf of the company, with the same effect with respect to the company's liability as if the bill or note had been drawn, accepted, made or indorsed by or on behalf of the company in the course of its business; (e) to raise on the security of the assets of the company any money requisite; (f) to take out in his official name letters of administration to any deceased contributory, and to do in his official name any other act necessary for obtaining payment of any money due from a contributory or his estate which cannot conveniently be done in the name of the company (and in all such cases the money due, for the purpose of enabling the liquidator to take out the letters of administration or recover the money, is deemed to be due to the liquidator himself); (g) to appoint an agent to do any business which the liquidator is unable to do himself; and (h) to do all other things as may be necessary for winding up the company's affairs and distributing its assets: Companies Act 1985, s. 539 (2).

With the leave of the court in case of disclaimer. The liquidator may with the leave of the court, disclaim land subject to burdensome covenants, shares, unprofitable contracts, or any other property that is unsaleable: ibid., s. 618 (1). (*See* DISCLAIMER OF ONEROUS PROPERTY).

(b) Powers delegated by the court

Provision may be made by general rules for enabling or requiring all or any of the powers and duties conferred on the court in respect of the following matters:—

(a) the holding and conducting of meetings to ascertain the wishes of creditors and contributories;

(b) the settling of lists of contributories and the rectifying of the register of members where required, and the collection and application of the assets;

(c) the payment, delivery, conveyance, surrender or transfer of money, property, books or papers to the liquidator;

(d) the making of calls;

(e) the fixing of a time within which debts and claims must be proved; to be exercised or performed by the liquidator as an officer of the court, and subject to the court's control: Companies Act 1985, s. 567 (1).

But the liquidator must not, without the special leave of the court, rectify the register of members: ibid., s. 567 (2). Further, he must not make any call without either that special leave or the sanction of the committee of inspection: ibid., s. 567 (2). (*See* CALL; REGISTER OF MEMBERS).

Exercise and control of the liquidator's powers. The liquidator of a company which is being wound up by the court must, in the administration of the company's assets and in their distribution among its creditors, have regard to any directions that may be given by resolution of the creditors or contributories at any general meeting or by the committee of inspection: Companies Act 1985, s. 540 (1). (*See* COMMITTEE OF INSPECTION). Directions given by the creditors or contributories at any general meeting are deemed, in case of conflict, to override any directions given by the committee of inspection: Companies Act 1985, s. 540 (2).

The liquidator may summon general meetings of the creditors or contributories for the purpose of ascertaining their wishes: ibid., s. 540 (3). It is his duty to summon meetings at such times as the creditors or contributories by resolution (either at the meeting appointing the liquidator or otherwise) may direct, or whenever requested in writing to do so by one-tenth in value of the creditors or contributories, as the case may be: ibid., s. 540 (3).

He may apply to the court in the prescribed manner for directions in relation to any particular matter arising in the winding up: ibid., s. 540 (4). He must use his own discretion in the management of the estate and its distribution among the creditors: ibid., s. 540 (5). If any person is aggrieved by any act or decision of the liquidator, that person may apply to the court: ibid., s. 540 (6). The court may confirm, reverse or modify the act or decision complained of, and make such order as it thinks just: ibid., s. 540 (6).

The Secretary of State must take cognisance of the conduct of liquidators of companies which are being wound up by the court: ibid., s. 544 (1). If a liquidator does not faithfully perform his duties and duly observe all the requirements imposed on him by statute, rules or otherwise with respect to the performance of his duties, or if any complaint is made to the Secretary of State by any creditor or contributory, the Secretary of State must inquire into the matter, and take such action as he thinks expedient: ibid., s. 544 (1). The Secretary of State may at any time require the liquidator of a company which is being wound up by the court to answer any inquiry in relation to any winding up in which he is engaged, and may, if the Secretary of State thinks fit, apply to the court to examine him or any other person on oath concerning the winding up: ibid., s. 544 (2). The Secretary of State may also direct a local investigation to be made of the liquidator's books and vouchers: ibid., s. 544 (3).

(iv) DUTIES: The duties of the liquidator are (a) to take the property of the company into his custody; (b) to settle the list of contributories; (c) to admit or reject proofs of debts; (d) to make calls where necessary; (e) to pay the debts of the company;(f) to keep books and papers; (g) to report as to the state of the liquidation; (h) to insert advertisements; (i) to keep accounts; and (j) to distribute the balance of the assets (after all debts have been paid) among the members.

(a) Duty to take company's property into custody

When a winding-up order has been made, the liquidator must take into his custody or under his control all the property and things in action to which the company is or appears to be entitled: s. 537 (1).

When a company is being wound up by the court, the court may, on the application of the liquidator, by order direct that all or any part of the property of whatsoever description belonging to the company or held by trustees on its behalf is to vest in the liquidator by the official name: ibid., s. 538 (1). Thereupon, the property to which the order relates vests accordingly, and the liquidator may, after giving such indemnity (if any) as the court may direct, bring or defend in his official name any action or other legal proceeding which relates to that property or which it is necessary to bring or defend for the purpose of effectually winding up the company and recovering its property: ibid., s. 538 (1), (2).

(b) Duty to settle list of contributories

Unless the court dispenses with the settlement of a list of contributories, the liquidator must, with all convenient speed after his appointment, settle the list: Companies (Winding-up) Rules 1949, r. 80. He must appoint a time and place for that purpose: ibid., r. 80. The list must contain a statement of the address of and the number of shares or extent of interest to be attributed to each contributory, and the amount called up and the amount paid up in respect of such shares or interest: ibid., r. 80. It must also distinguish the several classes of contributories: ibid., r. 80. Thus, some are placed on the 'A' List and some on the 'B' List. (*See* CONTRIBUTORY).

The liquidator must give notice in writing of the time and place appointed for the settlement of the list to every person whom he proposes to enter in it: Companies (Winding-up) Rules 1949, r. 81. He must state in the notice to each person in what character and for what number of shares or interest he proposes to include that person in the list and what amount has been called up and what amount paid up in respect of such shares or interest: ibid., r. 81.

On the day appointed for settlement of the list, the liquidator must hear any person who objects to being settled as a contributory, and after such hearing must finally settle the list: ibid., r. 82. The liquidator must forthwith give notice to every person whom he has finally placed on the list of contributories stating in what character and for what number of shares or interest he has been placed on the list and what amount has been called up and what amount paid up in respect of such shares or interest: ibid., r. 83. The notice must inform such person that any application for the removal of his name from the list, or for a variation of the list, must be made to the court by summons within 21 days from the date of the service on the contributory or alleged contributory of notice of the fact that his name is settled on the list: ibid., r. 83.

Subject to the power of the court to extend the time or to allow an application to be made notwithstanding the expiration of the time limited for that purpose, no application to the court by any person who objects to the list as finally settled may be entertained after the expiration of 21 days from the date of service on such person of notice of the settlement of the list: ibid., r. 84 (1).

The liquidator may from time to time vary or add to the list of contributories: ibid., r. 85. Such variation or addition must be made in the same manner in all respects as the settlement of the original list: ibid., r. 85.

(c) Duty to admit or reject proofs of debts

It is the duty of the liquidator to admit or reject proofs of debts alleged to be owed by the company to the creditors.

In every winding up all debts payable on a contingency, and all claims against the company, present or future, certain or contingent, ascertained or sounding only in damages, are admissible to proof against the company: Companies Act 1985, s. 611 (1). A just estimate is to be made (so far as possible) of the value of such debts or claims as may be subject to any contingency or sound only in damages, or for some other reason do not bear a certain value: ibid., s. 611 (2).

In the winding up of an insolvent company, the same rules prevail and must be observed with regard to the respective rights of secured and unsecured creditors, and to debts provable and to the valuation of annuities and future and contingent liabilities, as are in force for the time being under the law of bankruptcy with respect to the estates of persons adjudged bankrupt: ibid., s. 612 (1). All those who in any such case would be entitled to prove for and receive dividends out of the company's assets may come in under the winding up and make such claims against the company as they respectively are entitled to: ibid., s. 612 (2).

Procedure. In a winding up by the court, every creditor must prove his debt unless the court in any particular winding up gives directions that any creditors or class of creditors are to be admitted without proof: Companies (Winding-up) Rules 1949, r. 91. A debt may be proved by delivering or sending through the post in a pre-paid letter to the Official Receiver or, if a liquidator has been appointed, to the liquidator (a) in any case in which the Official Receiver or liquidator so requires, an affidavit verifying the debt, and (b) in any other case, an unsworn claim to the debt: ibid., r. 92. A proof of a debt may be made by the creditor or by some person authorised by or on behalf of the creditor: ibid., r. 93. A proof must contain or refer to a statement of account showing the particulars of the debt and must specify the vouchers by which it can be substantiated: ibid., r. 94.

The liquidator must give the creditors notice of the time by which debts are to be proved: ibid., r. 106. He must examine every proof of debt lodged with him, and the grounds of the debt, and in writing admit or reject it, in whole or in part, or require further evidence in support of it: ibid., r. 107. If he rejects a proof, he must state in writing to the creditor the grounds of the rejection: ibid., r. 107.

(d) Duty to make calls

The liquidator may, with the special leave of the court or the sanction of the committee of inspection, make calls on all or any of the contributories for the time being settled on the list of contributories to the extent of their liability for payment of any money which he thinks necessary to satisfy the debts and liabilities of the company: Companies Act 1985, ss. 553 (1), 567. In making a call, he may take into consideration the probability that some of the contributories may partly or wholly fail to pay the call: ibid., s. 553 (2). (*See* COMMITTEE OF INSPECTION).

Procedure. When the liquidator is authorised by resolution or order to make a call on the contributories, he must file with the Registrar of Companies a document making the call in a form specified by the Rules: Companies (Winding-up) Rules 1949, r. 88. When a call has been made, a copy of the resolution of the committee of inspection or order of the court (if any), as the case may be, must forthwith be served on each of the contributories included in the call, together with a notice from the liquidator specifying the amount or balance due from him in respect of the call: ibid., r. 89. But such resolution or order need not be advertised unless for any special reason the court so directs: ibid., r. 89.

(e) Duty to pay the debts of the company

Whether the company's debts can be paid in full depends on whether the company is solvent or insolvent.

(i) *Where the company is solvent.* The liquidator is under a duty to pay the debts in full.

(ii) *Where the company is insolvent.* He must pay the secured creditors first and then those who are unsecured.

(1) Secured creditors: A secured creditor may

  (i) realise his security and prove for the balance (if any) of his debt; or

  (ii) give up his security and prove for the whole amount; or

  (iii) value his security and rank for dividend for the amount remaining after deducting the value: Bankruptcy Act 1914, Sch. 2, paras. 10–12.

(2) Unsecured creditors: After the costs of the liquidation have been paid, the liquidator must pay the debts due to unsecured creditors in the following order:—

  (i) the preferential debts. (*See* PREFERENTIAL PAYMENTS).

  (ii) the ordinary debts. (*See* ORDINARY DEBTS).

  (iii) deferred debts. (*See* DEFERRED DEBTS).

If any of these types of debt cannot be paid in full, they must be paid *pari passu*.

Procedure. Not more than 2 months before declaring a dividend, the liquidator must give notice of his intention to do so to the Department of Trade and Industry in order that the notice may be gazetted: Companies (Winding-up) Rules 1949, r. 119 (1). He must at the same time give notice to such of the creditors mentioned in the Statement of Affairs as have not proved their debts: ibid., r. 119 (1). The notice must specify the latest dates up to which proofs must be lodged: ibid., r. 119 (1). (*See* STATEMENT OF AFFAIRS).

Where any creditor, after the date mentioned in the notice of intention to declare a dividend as the latest date up to which proofs may be lodged, appeals against the decision of the liquidator rejecting a proof, the notice of appeal must, subject to the power of the court to extend the time in special cases, be given within 7 days from the date of the notice of the decision against which the appeal is made: ibid., r. 119 (2).

Immediately after the expiration of the time for appealing against the decision of the liquidator, he must proceed to declare a dividend: ibid., r. 119 (3). He must give notice to the Department of Trade and Industry (in order that it may be gazetted), and send a notice of dividend to each creditor whose proof has been admitted: ibid., r. 119 (3).

(f) Duty to keep books and papers

Every liquidator of a company which is being wound up by the court must keep, in the prescribed manner, proper books in which he must cause to be made entries or minutes of proceedings at meetings, and of such other matters as may be prescribed: Companies Act 1985, s. 541 (1). Any creditor or contributory may, subject to the control of the court, personally or by his agent inspect any such books: ibid., s. 541 (2).

The liquidator must keep a 'Record Book' in which he must record all minutes, all proceedings had and resolutions passed at any meeting of creditors or contributories, or of the committee of inspection, and all such matters as may be necessary to give a correct view of his administration of the company's affairs: Companies (Winding-up) Rules 1949, r. 171. (*See* COMMITTEE OF INSPECTION).

The Official Receiver, until a liquidator is appointed by the court, and thereafter the liquidator must keep a 'Cash Book' in which he must enter from day to day the receipts and payments made by him: ibid., r. 172 (1).

A liquidator other than the Official Receiver must submit the Record Book and the Cash Book, together with any other requisite books and vouchers, to the committee of inspection, if any, when required and not less than once every 3 months: ibid., r. 172 (2).

All books and papers of the company and of the liquidator, as between the contributories of the company, are *prima facie* evidence of the truth of all matters purporting to be recorded in them: Companies Act 1985, s. 639.

(g) Duty to Report as to State of Liquidation

If the winding up is not concluded within 1 year after its commencement, the liquidator must, at such intervals as may be prescribed, until the winding up is concluded, send to the Registrar of Companies a statement in the prescribed form and containing the prescribed particulars with respect to the proceedings in, and position of, the liquidation: ibid., s. 641 (1). If a liquidator fails to comply with this requirement, he is liable on summary conviction to a fine not exceeding one-fifth of the statutory maximum or, on conviction after continued contravention, to a default fine not exceeding one-fiftieth of the statutory maximum: ibid., ss. 641 (2), 730 and Sch. 24.

As to the procedure, see the Companies (Winding-up) Rules 1949, rr. 196–198.

(h) Duty to insert advertisements

Every appointment of a liquidator or committee of inspection must be advertised by the liquidator in such manner as the court directs: Companies (Winding-up) Rules 1949, r. 58 (6).

(i) Duty to keep accounts

Every liquidator of a company which is being wound up by the court must, at such times as may be prescribed but not less than twice in each year during his tenure of office, send to the Secretary of State (or as he directs) an account of his receipts and payments as liquidator: Companies Act 1985, s. 543 (1), (2). The account must be in the prescribed form, must be made in duplicate and must be verified by a statutory declaration in the prescribed form; and the Secretary of State may cause the accounts to be audited: ibid., s. 543 (3). The liquidator must furnish the Secretary of State with such vouchers and information as he requires, and the Secretary of State may at any time require the production of, and inspect, any books or accounts kept by the liquidator: ibid., s. 543 (4).

After the account has been audited, one copy of it must be filed by the Secretary of State, to be retained by him, and the other copy must be delivered to the court for filing: ibid., s. 543 (5). Each copy, when filed, must be open to the inspection of any person on payment of the prescribed fee: ibid., s. 543 (5). The liquidator must cause the account when audited or a summary of it to be printed, and must send a printed copy of the account or summary by post to every creditor and contributory: ibid., s. 543 (6). But the Secretary of State may in any case dispense with compliance with this requirement: ibid., s. 543 (6).

(j) Duty to distribute the balance

Where capital is to be returned to contributories, the liquidator must prepare a list of the persons to whom it must be paid, and the amounts payable to each, and this is appended as a schedule to the order made by the court authorising him to make the return to them: Companies (Winding-up) Rules 1949, r. 120. If too much is paid to the shareholders, they may be ordered to refund the amount: *Re Birkbeck Permanent Benefit Building Society* [1915] 1 Ch 91.

If the assets of the company are sufficient to pay the contributories in full, the surplus is divided according to the number of shares held and not according to the amounts paid on them: *Birch v Cropper, re Bridgewater Navigation Co Ltd* (1889) 14 App Cas 525, HL. If the assets are not sufficient, and the same amount has not been paid in respect of each share, an adjustment must be made by making a call on those shareholders whose shares are only partly paid: *Re Hodge's Distillery Co, ex parte Maude* (1870) 6 Ch App 51. (*See* CALL).

(B) *Voluntary Winding Up*

(i) APPOINTMENT: (a) How appointed

The method of appointment depends principally on whether the winding up is a members' voluntary winding up or a creditors' voluntary winding up. (*See* CREDITORS' VOLUNTARY WINDING UP; MEMBERS' VOLUNTARY WINDING UP).

(1) *Members' voluntary winding up*. The appointment is made by the company in general meeting: Companies Act 1985, s. 580 (1). A special resolution is not necessary nor need special notice be given of the intention to appoint a liquidator: *Re Trench Tubeless Tyre Co: Bethell v Trench Tubeless Tye Co* [1900] 1 Ch 408, CA. (*See* SPECIAL NOTICE; SPECIAL RESOLUTION). If a vacancy occurs by death, resignation or otherwise in the office of a liquidator appointed by the company, the company in general meeting may, subject to any arrangement with its creditors, fill the vacancy: Companies Act 1985, s 581 (1). For that purpose a general meeting may be convened by any contributory, or, if there is more than one liquidator, by the continuing liquidators: ibid., s. 581 (2). The meeting must be held in the manner provided by the Act or by the articles, or in such manner as may, on application by any contributory or by the continuing liquidators, be determined by the court: ibid., s. 581 (3). One member alone cannot validly constitute himself a general meeting for the purpose of appointing a liquidator: *Re London Flats Ltd* [1966] 3 All ER 889.

(2) *Creditors' voluntary winding up*. The creditors and the company at their respective meetings may nominate a person to be liquidator: Companies Act 1985, s. 589 (1). If the creditors and the company nominate different persons, the person nominated by the creditors is the liquidator, and if no person is nominated by the creditors, the person (if any) nominated by the company is liquidator: ibid., s. 589 (2). In the case of different persons being nominated, any

director, member or creditor of the company may, within 7 days after the date on which the nomination was made by the creditors, apply to the court for an order either directing that the person nominated as liquidator by the company is to be liquidator instead of or jointly with the person nominated by the creditors, or appointing some other person to be liquidator instead of the person appointed by the creditors: ibid., s. 589 (3).

If a vacancy occurs by death, resignation or otherwise in the office of a liquidator (other than a liquidator appointed by, or by the direction of the court) the creditors may fill the vacancy: ibid., s. 592.

(3) *Appointment by the court.* If from any cause whatever there is no liquidator acting, the court may appoint a liquidator: ibid., s. 599 (1). The court may, on cause shown, remove a liquidator and appoint another : ibid., s. 599 (2).

(b) Notice of Appointment

The liquidator must within 14 days after his appointment publish in the *Gazette* and deliver to the Registrar of Companies a notice of his appointment in the form prescribed by statutory instrument made by the Secretary of State: ibid., 600 (1). If the liquidator fails to comply with this requirement, he is liable on summary conviction to a fine not exceeding one-fifth of the statutory maximum or, on conviction after continued contravention, to a daily default fine not exceeding one-fiftieth of the statutory maximum: ibid., s. 600 (2).

A company is not entitled to rely against other persons on the appointment of a liquidator if (i) the appointment has not been officially notified at the material time and is not shown by the company to have been known at that time to the person concerned; or (ii) the material time fell on or before the 15th day after the date of official notification (or, where the 15th day was a non-business day, on or before the next day that was not) and it is shown that the person concerned was unavoidably prevented from knowing of the appointment at the time: Companies Act 1985, s. 42 (1). (*See* NON-BUSINESS DAY; OFFICIAL NOTIFICATION).

(c) Effect of Appointment

On the appointment of a liquidator in a members' voluntary winding up all the powers of the directors cease, except so far as the company in general meeting or the liquidator sanctions their continuance: Companies Act 1985, s. 580 (2). On the appointment of a liquidator in a creditors' voluntary winding up all the powers of the directors cease except so far as the committee of inspection (or, if there is no committee, the creditors) sanction their continuance: ibid., s. 591 (2).

(d) Remuneration

In a members' voluntary winding up the liquidator's remuneration may be fixed by the company in general meeting: ibid., s. 580 (1). In a creditors' voluntary winding up the committee of inspection or, if there is no committee, the creditors, may fix his remuneration: ibid., s. 591 (1). The remuneration of the liquidator is payable out of the assets of the company in priority to all other claims: ibid., s. 604.

If the appointment of the liquidator is defective, he cannot sue for his remuneration. But if the company or the new liquidator takes advantage of his services, he can claim a reasonable amount for his services: *Re Allison, Johnson and Foster Ltd, ex parte Birkenshaw* [1904] 2 KB 327.

(ii) REMOVAL: In either type of voluntary winding up the court may, on cause shown, remove a liquidator and appoint another: Companies Act 1985, s. 599 (2).

(iii) POWERS: *General extent.* When several liquidators are appointed, any power given by the Act may be exercised by such one or more of them as may be determined at the time of their appointment, or, in default of such determination, by any number not less than 2: ibid., s. 598 (5).

(a) Without sanction: A liquidator may without sanction:—(1) exercise all the powers given by the Act to a liquidator appointed by the court (except those mentioned below); (2) settle the list of contributories; (3) make calls; and (4) summon general meetings of the company for the purpose of obtaining the Court's sanction by special or extraordinary resolution or for any other purpose he may think fit: ibid., s. 598 (2), (3). (*See* EXTRAORDINARY RESOLUTION; SPECIAL RESOLUTION).

(b) With sanction: With the sanction (1) of an extraordinary resolution of the company in the case of a members' voluntary winding up or (2) of the court or the committee of inspection (or if there is no committee, a meeting of the creditors) in the case of a creditors' voluntary winding up, the liquidator may (a) pay any classes of creditors in full; (b) compromise with creditors; and (c) compromise calls, liabilities, debts and claims between the company and contributories and other debtors: ibid., ss. 598 (1), 539 (1) (d), (e) and (f).

With the sanction of a special resolution the liquidator may sell the assets of the company for shares on a reconstruction: ibid., s. 582. (*See* RECONSTRUCTION AND AMALGAMATION).

(c) With leave of the court: With leave of the court, the liquidator may disclaim onerous property: Companies Act 1985, s. 618. (*See* DISCLAIMER OF ONEROUS PROPERTY).

Application to have questions determined. The liquidator may apply to the court to determine any question arising in the winding up of a company, or to exercise, as respects the enforcing of calls or any other matter, all or any of the powers which the court might exercise if the company were being wound up by the court: Companies Act 1985, s. 602 (1). The court, if satisfied that the determination of the question or the required exercise of power will be just and beneficial, may accede wholly or partially to the application on such terms and conditions as it thinks fit or may make such other order on the application as it thinks just: ibid., s. 602 (2). A copy of an order made under the above provision staying the proceedings in the winding up must be forwarded forthwith by the company, or otherwise as may be prescribed, to the Registrar of Companies, who must enter it in his records relating to the company: ibid., s. 602 (3).

(iv) DUTIES: The principal duties of a liquidator in a voluntary winding up are: (i) to take the company's property into his custody; (ii) to settle the list of contributories; (iii) to admit or reject proofs of debts; (iv) to make calls where necessary; (v) to pay the company's debts; (vi) to distribute the balance; (vii) to keep books and papers; (viii) to report as to the state of the liquidation; (ix) to keep accounts; (x) to call a meeting at the end of each year; and (xi) to call a final meeting.

(i) *Taking company's property into custody.* The liquidator in a voluntary winding up is under the same duty to take the property of the company into his custody as if the company were being wound up by the court.

In a voluntary winding up all money (other than money representing unclaimed dividends) representing unclaimed or undistributed assets must be ascertained as at the date to which the statement of receipts and payments sent in to the Registrar of Companies is brought down, and the amount to be paid to the Insolvency Services Account is the minimum balance of such money which the liquidator has had in his hands or under his control during the 6 months immediately preceding the date to which the statement is brought down, less such part of it as the Secretary of State may authorise him to retain for the immediate purposes of the liquidation: Companies (Winding-up) Rules 1949, r. 199 (2). (*See* INSOLVENCY SERVICES ACCOUNT).

(ii) *Settling the list of contributories.* The liquidator's duties are the same as those in a winding up by the court.

The list of contributories settled by a liquidator in a voluntary winding up is *prima facie* evidence of the liability of the persons named in it to be contributories: ibid., Companies Act 1985, s. 598 (3) (a).

(iii) *Admission or rejection of proofs of debts.* The rules as to the admission or rejection of proofs of debts are the same as in the case of a winding up by the court except that (i) no notice of the date by which the creditors of the company are to prove their debts or claims need be given otherwise than by advertisement; and (ii) proofs need not be filed: Companies (Winding-up) Rules 1949, rr. 106–118.

(iv) *Making calls.* In a voluntary winding up the liquidator can make a call without the sanction of the court or of the committee of inspection: Companies Act 1985, s. 598 (3) (b).

(v) *Payment of debts.* All costs, charges and expenses properly incurred in the winding up, including the remuneration of the liquidator, are payable out of the assets of the company in priority to all other claims: ibid., s. 604. Subject to the provisions of the Act as to preferential payments, the property of a company must, on its winding up, be applied in satisfaction of its liabilities *pari passu*: ibid., s. 597. (*See* PREFERENTIAL PAYMENTS).

If the company is insolvent, interest on a debt ceases to run at the date of the commencement of the voluntary winding up: *Re Thomas Salt & Co Ltd* [1908] WN 63.

If the liquidator fails to pay a debt, the unpaid creditor may apply to the court: Companies Act 1985, s. 602 (1). He cannot claim payment from the liquidator personally under that section (*Re Hill's Waterfall Estate and Goldmining Co, ex parte Baylis* [1896] 1 Ch 947) or by an action commenced by writ (*Knowles v Scott* [1891] 1 Ch 717). But if the liquidator has destroyed the remedy of the creditor by allowing the company to be dissolved or by parting with all its assets, the liquidator becomes personally liable: *Pulsford v Devenish* [1903] 2 Ch 625.

(vi) *Distribution of balance.* After the debts of the company have been paid the property of the company must, unless the articles otherwise provide, be distributed among the members according to their rights and interests in the company: Companies Act 1985, s. 597.

(vii) *Keeping of books and papers.* The duty of the liquidator to keep books and papers is the same as in the case of a winding up by the court.

When a company has been wound up and is about to be dissolved, its books and papers and those of the liquidators may be disposed of (i) in the case of a members' voluntary winding up in such way as the company by extraordinary resolution directs; and (ii) in the case of a creditors' voluntary winding up in such way as the committee of inspection or, if there is no committee, as the creditors of the company, may direct: ibid., s. 640 (1). (*See* EXTRAORDINARY RESOLUTION). After 5 years from the company's dissolution no responsibility rests on the company, the liquidators or any person to whom the custody of the books and papers has been committed, by reason of any book or paper not being forthcoming to any person claiming to be interested in it: Companies Act 1985, s. 640 (2).

Provision may be made by general rules for enabling the Secretary of State to prevent, for such period (not exceeding 5 years from the dissolution of the company) as he thinks proper, the destruction of the books and papers of a company which has been wound up, and for enabling any creditor or contributory of the company to make representations to the Secretary of State and to appeal to the court from any direction which may be given by the Secretary of State in the matter: ibid., s. 640 (3). If any person acts in contravention of any general rules made for the purposes of the above provisions or of any direction of the Secretary of State under them, he is liable on summary conviction to a fine not exceeding one-fifth of the statutory maximum: ibid., ss. 640 (4), 730 and Sch. 24.

(viii) *Report on state of liquidation.* Where the liquidation continues for more than a year, the liquidator must make the same statements to the Registrar of Companies as in the case of a winding up by the court: ibid., s. 641 (1).

(ix) *Keeping of accounts.* In a voluntary winding up every person who has acted as liquidator of any company, whether the liquidation has been concluded or not, must furnish to the Secretary of State particulars of any money in his hands or under his control representing unclaimed or undistributed assets of the company and other particulars as the Secretary of State may require for the purpose of ascertaining or getting in any money payable into the Insolvency Services Account at the Bank of England: Companies (Winding-up) Rules 1949, r. 200. (*See* INSOLVENCY SERVICES ACCOUNT). The Department may require such particulars to be verified by affidavit: Companies (Winding-up) Rules 1949, r. 200.

The Secretary of State may at any time order the liquidator to submit an account verified by affidavit of the sums received and paid by him, and may direct and enforce an audit of the account: ibid., r. 201 (1).

(x) *Calling meeting at end of each year.* In a members' voluntary winding up, in the event of the winding up continuing for more than 1 year, the liquidator must summon a general meeting of the company at the end of the first year from the commencement of the winding up, and of each succeeding year, or at the first convenient date within 3 months from the end of the year or such longer period as the Secretary of State may allow: Companies Act 1985, s. 584 (1). (*See* COMMENCEMENT OF THE WINDING UP). He must lay before the meeting an account of his acts and dealings and of the conduct of the winding up during the preceding year: Companies Act 1985, s. 584 (1). If the liquidator fails to comply with the above provisions, he is liable on summary conviction to a fine not exceeding one-fifth of the statutory maximum: ibid., ss. 584 (2), 730 and Sch. 24.

In a creditors' voluntary winding up in the event of the winding up continuing for more than 1 year the liquidator must summon a general meeting of the company and a meetkng of the creditors at the end of the first year from the commencement of the winding up, and of each succeeding year, or at the first convenient date within 3 months from the end of the year or such longer period as the Secretary of State may allow: ibid., s. 594 (1). He must lay before the meetings an account of his acts and dealings and of the conduct of the winding up during the preceding year: ibid., s. 594 (1). If the liquidator fails to comply with the above provisions, he is liable on summary conviction to a fine not exceeding one-fifth of the statutory maximum: ibid., ss. 594 (2), 730 and Sch. 24.

(xi) *Calling final meeting.* (a) Members' voluntary winding up: As soon as the company's affairs are fully wound up, the liquidator must make up an account of the winding up, showing how it has been conducted and the company's property has been disposed of, and must call a general meeting of the company for the purpose of laying before it the account, and giving any explanation of it: ibid., s. 585 (1). The meeting must be called by advertisement in the *Gazette*, specifying the time, place and object of it, and published at least 1 month before the meeting: ibid., s. 585 (2). If the liquidator fails to call a general meeting of the company, he is liable on summary conviction to a fine not exceeding one-fifth of the statutory maximum: ibid., ss. 585 (7), 730 and Sch. 24.

Within 1 week after the meeting, the liquidator must send to the Registrar of Companies a copy of the account, and must make a return to him of the holding of the meeting and of its date: ibid., s. 585 (3). If the copy is not sent or the return is not made the liquidator is liable on summary conviction to a fine not exceeding one-fifth of the statutory maximum, or, on conviction after continued contravention, to a daily default fine not exceeding one-fiftieth of the statutory maximum: ibid., ss. 585 (3), 730 and Sch. 24.

(b) Creditors' voluntary winding up: As soon as the company's affairs are fully wound up, the liquidator must make up an account of the winding up, showing how it has been conducted, and the company's property has been disposed of: ibid., s. 595 (1). He must call a general meeting of the company and a meeting of the creditors for the purpose of laying the account before the meetings and giving any explanation of it: ibid., s. 595 (1). Each meeting must be called by advertisement in the *Gazette*, specifying the time, place and object of it, and published at least 1 month before it: ibid., s. 595 (2). If the liquidator fails to call a general meeting of the company or a meeting of the creditors, he is liable on summary conviction to a fine not exceeding one-fifth of the statutory maximum: ibid., ss. 595 (8), 730 and Sch. 24.

Within 1 week after the date of the meetings (or, if they are not held on the same date, after the date of the later one) the liquidator must send to the Registrar of Companies a copy of the account, and must make a return to him of the holding of the meetings and of their dates: ibid., s. 595 (3). If the copy is not sent or the return is not made, the liquidator is liable on summary conviction to a fine not exceeding one-fifth of the statutory maximum, or, on conviction after continued contravention, to a daily default fine not exceeding one-fiftieth of the statutory maximum: ibid., ss. 595 (4), 730 and Sch. 24.

Listed securities, in relation to a company, means any securities of the company listed on a recognised stock exchange: Company Securities (Insider Dealing) Act 1985, s. 12 (b). (*See* RECOGNISED STOCK EXCHANGE).

M

'Main objects' rule. A rule that where the 'objects' clause of a company's memorandum of association sets out the company's main object, and also lists other objects, those other objects are to be construed as being merely incidental to the main object: *Stephens v Mysore Reefs (Kangundy) Mining Co Ltd* [1902] 1 Ch 745. The 'main objects' rule can be excluded by making all the objects of the company independent main objects: *Cotman v Brougham* [1918] AC 514. Whether the 'main objects' rule has been so excluded is a matter of construction in each case: *Anglo–Overseas Agencies Ltd v Green* [1960] 3 All ER 244. If a company's 'main object' has gone, the company may be wound up: *Re Amalgamated Syndicate* [1897] 2 Ch 600. (*See* OBJECTS CLAUSE).

Maintenance of capital. The ensuring that at all times the capital of the company will constitute a fund available for the creditors of the company. The principle is illustrated by the following rules:

1. The capital may not be reduced except with the sanction of the court.
2. A company may not redeem its own shares.
3. A company may not, in general, purchase its own shares.
4. A company may not provide financial assistance for the purchase of its own shares.
5. Dividends may be paid out of the profits of the company.

(1) *Reduction of capital*

Subject to confirmation by the court, a company limited by shares or a company limited by guarantee and having a share capital may, if so authorised by its articles, by special resolution reduce its share capital in any way: Companies Act 1985, s. 135 (1). (*See* REDUCTION OF CAPITAL).

(2) *Redemption by company of its own shares*

In general, a company cannot redeem its own shares.

But a company limited by shares or limited by guarantee and having a share capital may, if authorised to do so by its articles, issue shares which are to be redeemed or are liable to be redeemed at the option of the company or of the shareholder: Companies Act 1985, s. 159 (1). A private company limited by shares or limited by guarantee and having a share capital may, if so authorised to do so by its articles, make a payment in respect of the redemption of its own shares otherwise than out of its distributable profits or the proceeds of a fresh issue of shares: ibid., s. 171 (1). (*See* REDEEMABLE SHARES).

(3) *Purchase by company of its own shares*

In general, a company limited by shares or limited by guarantee and having a share capital may not acquire its own shares (whether by purchase, subscription or otherwise): Companies Act 1985, s. 143 (1). But this provision does not apply to (a) the redemption or purchase of any shares in accordance with Part V, Chapter VII of the Act (*see* PURCHASE BY COMPANY OF ITS OWN SHARES); (b) the acquisition of any shares in a reduction of capital duly made (*see* REDUCTION OF CAPITAL); (c) the purchase of shares in pursuance of an order of the court (*see* OBJECTS CLAUSE; UNFAIR PREJUDICE TO MEMBERS); or (d) the forfeiture of shares, or the acceptance of shares surrendered in lieu, in pursuance of the articles, for failure to pay any sum payable in respect of the shares (*see* FORFEITURE OF SHARES; SURRENDER OF SHARE): ibid., s. 143 (3). If a company purports to act in contravention of s. 143, the company and every officer of the company who is in default are liable on conviction on indictment, in the case of a company to a fine, and in the case of an officer, to imprisonment for a term not exceeding 2 years or a fine, or both: ibid., ss. 143 (2), 730 and Sch. 24. On summary conviction, the company is liable to a fine not exceeding the statutory maximum, and an officer is liable to imprisonment for a term not exceeding 6 months or a fine not exceeding the statutory maximum or both: ibid., ss. 143 (2), 730 and Sch. 24. Further, where there is a contravention, the purported acquisition is void: ibid., s. 143 (2).

But under Part V, Chapter VII of the Act, a company may do so if certain requirements are fulfilled. (*See* PURCHASE BY COMPANY OF ITS OWN SHARES). A private company limited by shares or limited by guarantee and having a share capital may, if so authorised by its articles, make a payment in respect of the purchase of any of its own shares otherwise than out of the distributable profits of the company or the proceeds of a fresh issue of shares: Companies Act 1985, s. 171 (1). (*See* PURCHASE BY COMPANY OF ITS OWN SHARES).

(4) *Financial assistance for acquisition of its own shares*

In general, where a person is acquiring or is proposing to acquire shares in a company, it is not lawful for the company or any of its subsidiaries to give financial assistance directly or indirectly for the purpose of that acquisition before or at the same time as the acquisition takes place: Companies Act 1985, s. 151 (1). (*See* FINANCIAL ASSISTANCE). But s. 151 does not prohibit

(a) where the lending of money is part of the ordinary business of the company, the lending of money by the company in the ordinary course of its business;

(b) the provision by a company in accordance with an employees' share scheme of money for the acquisition of fully paid shares in the company or its holding company (*see* EMPLOYEES' SHARE SCHEME);

(c) the making by a company of loans to persons (other than directors) employed in good faith by the company with a view to enabling those persons to acquire fully paid shares in the company or its holding company to be held by themselves by way of beneficial ownership: Companies Act 1985, s. 153 (4).

There are certain relaxations of the provisions of s. 151 in relation to private companies: ibid., ss. 155 and 156.

(5) *Payment of dividends out of profits*

A company must not make a distribution except out of profits available for the purpose: ibid., s. 263 (1). (*See* DIVIDEND).

Manager. A person appointed to carry on the business of a company. On the appointment of a receiver the assets become specifically charged in favour of the debenture holders and the company's power to deal with them in the ordinary course of business ceases, although the company continues to exist until it is wound up: *Moss SS Co Ltd v Whinney* [1912] AC 254, HL.

If it is necessary to carry on the business, the court usually appoints the receiver to be manager and receiver. A manager is not usually appointed except to carry on the business for the purpose of selling it as a going concern: *Re Victoria Steamboats Ltd: Smith v Wilkinson* [1897] 1 Ch 158. If, however, there is no power to sell the business, a manager will not be appointed: *Marshall v South Staffordshire Tramways Co* [1895] 2 Ch 36, CA. A receiver and manager is not bound to adopt a contract which has been made between the company and a third party: *Airlines Airspares Ltd v Handley Page Ltd* [1970] 1 All ER 29.

A manager is appointed for a limited period, and if he acts after the expiration of this period, his expenses may be disallowed: *Re Wood Green and Hornsey Steam Laundry: Trenchard v Wood Green and Hornsey Steam Laundry* [1918] 1 Ch 423.

If a person obtains an order for the appointment of a manager of a company's property or appoints such a manager under powers contained in an instrument, he must, within 7 days of the order or of the appointment under those powers, give notice of the fact to the Registrar of Companies, and the Registrar must enter the fact in the register of charges: Companies Act 1985, s. 405 (1). (*See* REGISTER OF CHARGES). Where a person appointed manager of a company's property under the powers contained in an instrument ceases to act as such manager, he must, on so ceasing, give the Registrar of Companies notice to that effect, and the Registrar of Companies must enter the fact in the register of charges: Companies Act 1985, s. 405 (2). A notice must be in the prescribed form: ibid., s. 405 (3). If a person makes default in complying with the above provisions, he is liable on summary conviction to a fine not exceeding one-fifth of the statutory maximum, or on conviction after continued contravention, to a daily default fine not exceeding one-fiftieth of the statutory maximum; ibid., ss. 405 (4), 730 and Sch. 24.

Authority to borrow

The court may authorise the manager to borrow money which is to be a first charge on the property of the company in priority to all the debentures if it is required for the purpose of preserving the business: *Greenwood v Algeciras (Gibraltar) Railway Co* [1894] 2 Ch 205. The claims of the persons who lend the money will then have priority over the claims of the debenture holders (*Re Glasdir Copper Mines Ltd: English Electro-Metallurgical Co Ltd v Glasdir Copper Mines Ltd* [1906] 1 Ch 365), but will be postponed to the manager's right of indemnity (*Re A. Boynton Ltd: Hoffman v A Boynton Ltd* [1910] 1 Ch 519). Leave to borrow will be granted only where there is clear evidence of advantage: *Securities and Properties Corporation Ltd v Brighton Alhambra Ltd* (1893) 62 LJ Ch 566. If the manager exceeds the amount authorised, his right of indemnity does not extend to the excess even if he acted in good faith unless it was reasonably necessary for him to borrow without applying to the court: *Re British Power Traction & Lighting Co Ltd: Halifax Joint Stock Banking Co Ltd v British Power Traction & Lighting Co Ltd* [1907] 1 Ch 528.

Remuneration

The court may, on an application made by the liquidator of a company, by order fix the amount to be paid by way of remuneration to a person who, under the powers contained in an instrument, has been appointed as manager of the company's property: Companies Act 1985, s. 494 (1).

Managing director. One of the directors of the company appointed to deal with the day to day management.

The duration of his appointment, his remuneration and powers are defined by the directors. He is usually appointed under a service contract. (*See* DIRECTOR'S SERVICE CONTRACT). He can be removed under the Companies Act 1985, s. 303. He can claim damages for breach of his service contract: *Yetton v Eastwoods Froy Ltd.* [1966] 3 All ER 453.

Table A, art. 84 states: 'Subject to the provisions of the Act, the directors may appoint one or more of their number to the office of managing director . . . Any such appointment . . . may be made upon such terms as the directors determine and they may remunerate any such director for his services as they think fit . . . A managing director . . . shall not be subject to retirement by rotation.' (*See* ROTATION OF DIRECTORS).

Market purchase. A purchase by a company of any of its own shares which is made on a recognised stock exchange other than an off-market purchase: Companies Act 1985, s. 163 (3). (*See* OFF-MARKET PURCHASE).

Marketing arrangement, subject to a. *See* SUBJECT TO A MARKETING ARRANGEMENT.

Meeting, annual general. *See* ANNUAL GENERAL MEETING.

Meeting, extraordinary general. *See* EXTRAORDINARY GENERAL MEETING.

Members, overseas branch register of. *See* OVERSEAS BRANCH REGISTER.

Meeting, notice of. *See* LENGTH OF NOTICE FOR CALLING MEETING.

Meeting, notice of, length of. *See* LENGTH OF NOTICE FOR CALLING MEETING.

Member. A shareholder. The subscribers of a company's memorandum are deemed to have agreed to become members of the company and on its registration must be entered as members in its register of members: Companies Act 1985, s. 22 (1). Every other person who agrees to become a member of a company and whose name is entered in its register of members, is a member of the company: ibid., s. 22 (2). (*See* MEMORANDUM OF ASSOCIATION; REGISTER OF MEMBERS).

In general, a body corporate cannot be a member of a company which is its holding company; and any allotment or transfer of shares in a company to its subsidiary is void: Companies Act 1985, s. 23 (1). (*See* HOLDING COMPANY; SUBSIDIARY COMPANY).

Members, index of. *See* REGISTER OF MEMBERS.

Members, register of. *See* OVERSEAS BRANCH REGISTER; REGISTER OF MEMBERS.

Members, unfair prejudice to. *See* UNFAIR PREJUDICE TO MEMBERS.

Members' voluntary winding up. A winding up in the case of which a declaration of solvency has been made in accordance with the Companies Act 1985, s. 577: Companies Act 1985, s. 578. (*See* DECLARATION OF SOLVENCY).

Memorandum of association. A document registered with the Registrar of Companies on a company's formation and setting out essential details relating to it.

In general, the memorandum of every company must state

(a) the name of the company with 'limited' as the last word of the name in the case of a company limited by shares or by guarantee (*see* COMPANY LIMITED BY SHARES; COMPANY LIMITED BY GUARANTEE; NAME OF COMPANY);

(b) whether the registered office of the company is to be situate in England and Wales or in Scotland (*see* REGISTERED OFFICE);

(c) the objects of the company (*see* OBJECTS CLAUSE): Companies Act 1985, ss. 2 (1), 25.

But the name of a public company must end with the words 'public limited company': Companies Act 1985, s. 25 (1). (*See* PUBLIC COMPANY).

The memorandum of a company limited by shares or by guarantee must also state that the liability of its members is limited: Companies Act 1985, s. 2 (3).

The memorandum of a company limited by guarantee must also state that each member undertakes to contribute to the assets of the company if it should be wound up while he is a member, or within one year after he ceases to be a member, for payment of the debts and liabilities of the company contracted before he ceases to be a member, and of the costs, charges and expenses of winding up, and for adjustment of the rights of the contributories among themselves, such amount as may be required, not exceeding a specified amount: ibid., s. 2 (4). (*See* CONTRIBUTORY).

In the case of a company having a share capital

(a) the memorandum must also (unless it is an unlimited company) state the amount of share capital with which the company proposes to be registered and the division of the share capital into shares of a fixed amount;

(b) no subscriber of the memorandum may take less than one share; and

(c) there must be shown in the memorandum against the name of each subscriber the number of shares he takes: Companies Act 1985, s. 2 (5). (*See* UNLIMITED COMPANY).

Form of memorandum

The form of the memorandum of association of

(a) a public company, being a company limited by shares,

(b) a public company, being a company limited by guarantee and having a share capital,

(c) a private company limited by shares,

(d) a private company limited by guarantee and not having a share capital,

(e) a private company limited by guarantee and having a share capital, and

(f) an unlimited company having a share capital,

must be as specified respectively for such companies by regulations made by the Secretary of State, or as near to that form as circumstances admit: Companies Act 1985, s. 3 (1).

The regulations must be made by statutory instrument subject to annulment in pursuance of a resolution of either Houses of Parliament: ibid. s. 3 (2).

The regulations at present in force are the Companies (Tables A to F) Regulations 1985 (S.I. 1985, No. 805), as amended by the Companies (Tables A to F) (Amendment) Regulations 1985 (S.I. 1985, No. 1052).

Signature

The memorandum must be signed by each subscriber in the presence of at least one witness who must attest the signature; and that attestation is sufficient: ibid., s. 2 (6).

Restriction on alteration of memorandum

A company may not alter the conditions contained in its memorandum except in the cases, in the mode and to the extent for which express provision is made in the Act: ibid., s. 2 (7). Thus, alterations may be made in the company's name (*see* CHANGE OF NAME), objects (*see* OBJECTS CLAUSE), and capital (*see* REDUCTION OF CAPITAL).

But the statement in the memorandum as to whether the registered office of the company is situate in England or Scotland cannot be altered, for such an alteration would lead to a change of the company's nationality. If such a change is desired, re-registration of the company is required (*see* RE-REGISTRATION OF COMPANY).

Alteration of the memorandum by statute

Where an alteration is made in a company's memorandum by any statutory provision, whether contained in an Act of Parliament or in an instrument made under an Act, a printed copy of the Act or instrument must, not later than 15 days after that provision comes into force, be forwarded to the Registrar of Companies and recorded by him: Companies Act 1985, s. 18 (1).

Where a company is required by s. 18 or otherwise to send to the Registrar any document making or evidencing an alteration in the company's memorandum (other than a special resolution under s. 4, i.e. in the case of a change of the objects of the company), the company must send with it a printed copy of the memorandum as altered: ibid., s. 18 (2).

If a company fails to comply with s. 18, the company and any officer of the company who is in default is liable on summary conviction to a fine not exceeding one-fifth of the statutory maximum, or, on conviction after continued contravention, to a daily default fine not exceeding one-fiftieth of the statutory maximum: ibid., ss. 18 (3), 730 and Sch. 24.

Merger. *See* MERGER OF COMPANIES; NEWSPAPER MERGERS.

Merger of companies. A reference can be made to the Monopolies and Mergers Commission by the Secretary of State where it appears to him that it is or may be the fact that 2 or more enterprises, of which one at least was carried on in the United Kingdom or by or under the control of a body corporate in the United Kingdom, have ceased to be distinct enterprises, and the value of the assets taken over exceeds £15 million and at least a quarter of all the goods of any description which are supplied in the United Kingdom either

(a) are supplied by one and the same person or are supplied to one and the same person; or

(b) are supplied by the persons to whom the enterprises (so far as they continue to be carried on) are carried on, or are supplied to those persons: Fair Trading Act 1973, s. 64 (1).

Every reference must specify a period (not being longer than 6 months beginning with the date of the reference) within which a report on the reference is to be made: ibid., s. 70 (1). No action must be taken in relation to it unless the report is made before the end of that period or such further period as may be allowed by the Secretary of State: ibid., s. 70 (1).

In making their report on a reference the Commission must include in it definite conclusions on the questions comprised in it together with such an account of their reasons for those conclusions and such a survey of the general position with respect to the subject matter of the reference, and of the developments which have led to that position as in their opinion are expedient for facilitating a proper understanding of those questions and of their conclusions: ibid., s. 72 (1).

Where the Commission finds that a merger situation qualifying for investigation has been created, and that the creation of that situation operates or may be expected to operate against the public interest, they must specify in their report the particular effects, adverse to the public interest, which in their opinion the creation of that situation has or may be expected to have: ibid., s. 72 (2).

The Commission must consider what action, if any, should be taken for the purpose of modifying or preventing those adverse effects, and may, if they think fit, include in their report recommendations as to such action: ibid., s. 72 (2).

The Secretary of State may by order made by statutory instrument exercise his power for the purpose of remedying or preventing the adverse effects specified in the report: ibid., s. 73 (1).

A reference may be made to the Commission by the Secretary of State where it appears to him that it is or may be the fact that arrangements are in progress or in contemplation which, if carried into effect, will result in the creation of a merger situation qualifying for investigation: ibid., s. 75 (1).

Minimum number of members. At least 2 members are necessary to form a company: Companies Act 1985, s. 1 (1). If a company carries on business without having at least 2 members and does so for more than 6 months, a person who for the whole or any part of the period that it so carries on business after those 6 months

(a) is a member of the company, and

(b) knows that it is carrying on business with only 1 member,

is liable (jointly and severally with the company) for the payment of the company's debts contracted during the period or, as the case may be, that part of it: ibid., s. 24.

Minimum subscription. The minimum amount which in the opinion

of the directors must be raised by the issue of the shares in order to provide for
  (i) the purchase price of any property purchased or to be purchased which is to be defrayed in whole or in part out of the proceeds of the issue;
 (ii) any preliminary expenses payable by the company, and any commission so payable to any person in consideration of his agreeing to subscribe for, or of his procuring or agreeing to procure subscriptions for, any shares of the company;
(iii) the repayment of any moneys borrowed by the company in respect of any of the foregoing matters; and
(iv) working capital: Companies Act 1985, Sch. 3, Part I, para. 2 (a).

Minority shareholders. Shareholders who do not have voting control of a company, and must therefore comply with the wishes of the majority shareholders.

Minority shareholders are, however, protected (i) by the exceptions to the Rule in *Foss v Harbottle* (1843) 2 Hare 461 (*see* RULE IN FOSS V HARBOTTLE); (ii) by schemes of reconstruction and arrangement under the Companies Act 1985, Part XIII and s. 582 (*see* RECONSTRUCTION AND AMALGAMATION); (iii) by relief granted under the Companies Act 1985, s. 459 where they are unfairly prejudiced (*see* UNFAIR PREJUDICE OF MEMBERS); (iv) by the right to apply to have the affairs and membership of the company investigated (*see* INSPECTION AND INVESTIGATION OF COMPANY); and (v) by the right to apply for a resolution altering the objects of the company to be cancelled (*see* OBJECTS CLAUSE).

Minute books. *See* MINUTES.

Minute of reduction. A minute approved by the court, when the share capital of a company is reduced showing, with respect to the share capital as altered by the court's order (i) the amount of the share capital; (ii) the number of shares into which it is to be divided, and the amount of each share; and (iii) the amount, if any, at the date of the registration of the order and minute, deemed to be paid up on each share: Companies Act 1985, s. 138 (1). (*See* REDUCTION OF CAPITAL).

Minutes. The record of the proceedings of meetings.

Every company must cause minutes of all proceedings of general meetings, all proceedings at meetings of its directors and, where there are managers, all proceedings at meetings of its managers to be entered in books kept for that purpose: Companies Act 1985, s. 382 (1). Any such minute, if purporting to be signed by the chairman of the meeting at which the proceedings were had, or by the chairman of the next succeeding meeting, is evidence of the proceedings: ibid., s. 382 (2). Where minutes have been made of the proceedings of any general meeting of the company or meeting of directors or managers, then, until the contrary is proved, the meeting is deemed duly held and convened, and all proceedings had at the meeting to have been duly had; and all appointments of directors, managers or liquidators are deemed valid: ibid., s. 382 (4).

The books containing the minutes of proceedings of any general meeting must be kept at the company's registered office: ibid., s. 383 (1). During business hours (subject to such reasonable restrictions as the company may by its articles or in general meeting impose, so that not less than 2 hours in each day be allowed for inspection) the books containing the minutes are open to the inspection of any member without charge: ibid., s. 383 (1), (2). Any member is entitled to be furnished within 7 days after he has made a request to the company with a copy of the minutes at a charge of not more than $2\frac{1}{2}$p for every 100 words: ibid., s. 383 (3). If any inspection is refused or if a copy is not sent within the proper time, the company and every officer of the company who is in default are guilty of an offence: ibid., s. 382 (4). In the case of any such refusal or default, the court may by order compel an immediate inspection of all proceedings of general meetings or direct that the copies required be sent to the persons requiring them: ibid., s. 382 (5).

Misleading name, trading under. (*See* TRADING UNDER MISLEADING NAME.)

Money given for political purposes. A company is to be treated as giving money for political purposes if, directly or indirectly

(a) it gives a donation or subscription to a political party of the United Kingdom or of any part of it; or

(b) it gives a donation or subscription to a person who, to the company's knowledge, is carrying on, or proposing to carry on, any activities which can, at the time at which the donation or subscription was given, reasonably be regarded as likely to affect public support for such a political party.: Companies Act 1985, Sch. 7, Part I, para. 5 (2). (*See* DIRECTORS' REPORT).

Mortgage of share. The pledging of a share with another person as security for a debt.

This is usually accomplished by the owner of the share depositing with the mortgagee the share certificate together with a blank transfer i.e. a transfer with the name of the transferee left blank. (*See* SHARE; SHARE CERTIFICATE). If the money is not repaid, the mortgagee can put in his own name as transferee and get the transfer registered.

If by the articles of association a transfer of shares must be under seal, a blank transfer cannot be filled up without a power of attorney: *Powell v London and Provincial Bank* [1893] 2 Ch 555.

This form of mortgage is not a completely effective one for the transferor may obtain another share certificate from the company by

143

falsely pretending that he has lost the original one and then transfer the shares to a purchaser. To prevent this occurring, the mortgagee should serve a 'stop notice' on the company under R.S.C. Order 50. The effect is that if the mortgagor attempts to transfer the shares, the company must give the mortgagee notice that it will register the transfer to the purchaser unless the mortgagee takes proceedings within 8 days to prevent it.

N

Name, business. *See* BUSINESS NAME.

Name, change of. *See* CHANGE OF NAME.

Name clause. A clause in the memorandum of association stating the name of the company. (See MEMORANDUM OF ASSOCIATION; NAME OF COMPANY).

Name, company, of. *See* NAME OF COMPANY.

Name, exemption from requirement to use word 'limited' in. *See* EXEMPTION FROM REQUIREMENT TO USE WORD 'LIMITED' IN NAME.

Name, firm. *See* FIRM NAME.

Name, prohibition on registration of. *See* PROHIBITION ON REGISTRATION OF NAME.

Name of company. The appellation by which it is known.

(a) *Name likely to cause confusion*

In general, a company should not choose a name similar to that of an existing company, and may be restrained by injunction if the name chosen is likely to cause confusion between the two companies in the minds of the public: *Ewing v Buttercup Margarine Co Ltd* [1917] 2 Ch 1, CA. The court has jurisdiction to grant an injunction even though the name of the company is not actually registered e.g. where it is a foreign company: *Société Anonyme des Anciens Etablissements Panhard et Levassor v Panhard Levassor Motor Co Ltd* [1901] 2 Ch 513.

(b) *Prohibition of certain names*

A company is prevented from being registered with certain names: Companies Act 1985, s. 26 (1). (*See* PROHIBITION ON REGISTRATION OF NAME).

Further, without the authority of the Defence Council, the name of the company must not include the words 'Red Cross' or 'Geneva Cross': Geneva Conventions Act 1957, s. 6 (1). The name 'Anzac' must not be used without the authority of the Secretary of State for Foreign and Commonwealth Affairs: Anzac (Restriction on Trade Use of Word) Act 1916, s. 1. The names of certain organisations e.g. the Boy Scouts or Girl Guides must not be used or imitated in a company's name: Chartered Associations (Protection of Names and Uniforms) Act 1926, s. 1.

(c) *Name clause in memorandum of association*

The memorandum of association must state the name of the company: Companies Act 1985, s. 2 (1) (a). Further, the name of a public

145

company must end with the words 'public limited company': ibid., s. 25 (1). (*See* MEMORANDUM OF ASSOCIATION; NAME CLAUSE; PUBLIC COMPANY).

(d) *Exemption from requirement to use word 'limited'*

A private company limited by guarantee is exempt from the requirement to use the word 'limited' as part of its name if

(i) the objects of the company are the promotion of commerce, art, science, education, religion, charity or any profession and anything incidental or conducive to any of those objects; and

(ii) the company's memorandum or articles

(a) require its profits (if any) or other income to be applied in promoting its objects;

(b) prohibit the payment of dividends to its members; and

(c) require all the assets which would otherwise be available to its members generally to be transferred on its winding up either to another body with objects similar to its own or to another body the objects of which are the promotion of charity and anything incidental or conducive: Companies Act 1985, s. 30 (2), (3). (*See* DIVIDEND).

(e) *Publication of name*

Every company must paint or affix, and keep painted or affixed, its name on the outside of every office or place in which its business is carried on, in a conspicuous position in letters easily legible: Companies Act 1985, s. 348 (1). If a company does not paint or affix its name as required above, or does not keep its name painted or affixed in the manner directed, the company and every officer of the company who is in default are liable on summary conviction to a fine not exceeding one-fifth of the statutory maximum or, on conviction after continued contravention, to a daily default fine not exceeding one-fiftieth of the statutory maximum: ibid., ss. 348 (2), 730 and Sch. 24.

Further, the company must have

(i) its name engraved in legible characters on its seal;

(ii) its name mentioned in legible characters in all business letters of the company and in all its notices and other official publications, and in all bills of exchange, promissory notes, endorsements, cheques and orders for money or goods purporting to be signed by or on behalf of the company, and in all its bills of parcels, invoices, receipts and letters of credit: ibid., ss. 349 (1), 350 (1). (*See* SEAL).

If the company fails to comply with either of the two above requirements, the company is liable, on summary convictions, to a fine not exceeding one-fifth of the statutory maximum: Companies Act 1985, ss. 349 (2), 350 (1), 730 and Sch. 24.

In addition, if an officer of a company or a person on its behalf

(a) uses or authorises the use of any seal purporting to be a seal of the company on which its name is not engraved as required; or

(b) issues or authorises the issue of any business letter of the company, or any notice or other official publication of the company, or signs or authorises to be signed on behalf of the company any bill of exchange, promissory note, endorsement, cheque or order for money or goods on which its name is not mentioned in the required manner; or

(c) issues or authorises the issue of any bill of parcels, invoice, receipt or letter of credit of the company on which its name is not mentioned in the required manner;

he is liable on summary conviction to a fine not exceeding one-fifth of the statutory maximum: ibid., ss. 349 (3), 350 (2), 730 and Sch. 24.

But the court may hold that an officer of the company is not personally liable on a bill of exchange where an error with regard to the name of the company has been caused by the drawer of the bill: *Durham Fancy Goods Ltd v Michael Jackson (Fancy Goods) Ltd* [1968] 2 All ER 987.

(f) *Change of name*

A company may change its name by special resolution: Companies Act 1985, s. 28 (1). The Secretary of State has power to order a company to change its name: ibid., s. 28 (2), (3). (*See* CHANGE OF NAME).

(g) *Business name*

Where a company uses a name which is different from that under which it is incorporated, certain requirements must be fulfilled. (*See* BUSINESS NAME).

Names, index of. *See* INDEX OF NAMES.

Newspaper mergers. The merging of one newspaper with another. A transfer of a newspaper or of newspaper assets to a newspaper proprietor, whose newspapers have an average circulation per day of publication amounting together with that of the newspaper concerned in the transfer to 500,000 or more copies, is unlawful and void unless the transfer is made with written consent given by the Secretary of State: Fair Trading Act 1973, s. 58 (1).

In general, the Secretary of State's consent must not be given until he has received a report on the matter from the Monopolies and Mergers Commission: ibid., s. 58 (2).

Where an application is made to the Secretary of State for his consent to a transfer of a newspaper or of newspaper assets, he must, in general, within one month after receiving the application, refer the matter to the Commission for investigation and report: ibid., s. 59 (1).

A report of the Commission on a newspaper merger reference must be made within 3 months of the date of the reference or such further period as the Secretary of State allows: ibid., s. 60 (1). Only one such further period is allowed, and no such further period may be longer than 3 months: ibid., s. 60 (2).

In making their report on a newspaper merger reference the Commission must include in it definite conclusions on the questions comprised in the reference together with such an account of their reasons for the conclusions, and such a survey of the general position with respect to the transfer and of the developments which have led to that position as in their opinion are expedient for facilitating a proper understanding of those questions and of their conclusions: ibid., s. 61 (1).

Where the Commission finds that the transfer of a newspaper or of newspaper assets might operate against the public interest, the Commission must consider whether any (and, if so, what) conditions might be attached to the transfer in order to prevent the transfer from so operating, and may, if they think fit, include in their report recommendations as to such conditions: ibid., s. 61 (2).

Any person, who is knowingly concerned in, or privy to, a purported transfer of a newspaper or of newspaper assets which is unlawful, is guilty of an offence: ibid., s. 62 (1).

Nominal (or authorised) share capital. The nominal value of the shares which a company is authorised to issue by its memorandum of association.

Nominee shareholder. A person who is registered as the owner of shares in a company but who, in fact, holds them on behalf of and to the order of another person.

Non-cash asset means, any property or interest in property other than cash: Companies Act 1985, s. 739 (1). For this purpose 'cash' includes foreign currency: ibid., s. 739 (1).

Non-cumulative preference share. *See* PREFERENCE SHARE.

Non-trading partnership. A partnership not engaged in the buying and selling of goods: *Higgins v Beauchamp* [1914–15] All ER Rep 937. Such a partnership includes firms of (i) solicitors (*Hedley v Bainbridge* (1842) 3 QB 316); (ii) auctioneers (*Wheatley v Smithers* [1907] 2 KB 684, CA); and (iii) cinema proprietors (*Higgins v Beauchamp* (supra)). In the case of a non-trading partnership a partner cannot accept or issue negotiable instruments other than ordinary cheques nor borrow or pledge the partnership property: *Higgins v Beauchamp* (supra).

Notice, special. *See* SPECIAL NOTICE.

Novation. A tripartite agreement between a third party and the parties to a contract whereby they all agree that one of the parties shall be released from his obligations, and that these obligations shall be taken over by the third party. (*See* INCOMING PARTNER; RETIRING PARTNER).

O

Objects clause. A clause in the memorandum of association setting out the objects of the company.

The memorandum of every company must state the objects of the company: Companies Act 1985, s. 2 (1) (c). (*See* 'MAIN OBJECTS' RULE).

Alteration of objects

A company may, by special resolution, alter its memorandum with respect to the objects of the company, so far as may be required to enable it

(a) to carry on its business more economically or more efficiently; or

(b) to attain its main purpose by new or improved means; or

(c) to enlarge or change the local area of its operations; or

(d) to carry on some business which under existing circumstances may conveniently or advantageously be combined with the business of the company; or

(e) to restrict or abandon any of the objects specified in the memorandum; or

(f) to sell or dispose of the whole or any part of the undertaking of the company; or

(g) to amalgamate with any other company or body of persons: Companies Act 1985, s. 4. See *Re Hampstead Garden Suburb Trust Ltd* [1962] 2 All ER 879.

But if an application is made to the court in accordance with the provisions mentioned below for the alteration to be cancelled, the alteration has no effect except in so far as it is confirmed by the court: ibid., s. 4. An application may be made

(a) by the holders of not less in the aggregate than 15 per cent in nominal value of the company's issued share capital or any class of it, or, if the company is not limited by shares, not less than 15 per cent of the company's members; or

(b) by holders of not less than 15 per cent of the company's debentures, which are secured by a floating charge issued or first issued before 1 December 1947, or form part of the same series as any debentures so issued entitling the holders to object to an alteration of its objects: ibid., s. 5 (2), (8).

But an application cannot be made by any person who has consented to or voted in favour of the alteration: ibid., s. 5 (2). An application must be made within 21 days after the date on which the resolution altering the company's objects was passed, and may be made on behalf of the persons entitled to make the application by such one or more of their number as they may appoint in writing for the purpose: ibid., s. 5 (3).

On an application the court may make an order confirming the alteration either wholly or in part and on such terms and conditions as it thinks fit: ibid., s. 5 (4). It may, if it thinks fit, adjourn the proceedings in order that an arrangement may be made to its satisfaction for the purchase of the interests of dissentient members: ibid., s. 5 (4). An order may (if the court thinks fit) provide for the purchase by the company of the shares of any members of the company, and for the reduction accordingly of its capital and may make such alterations in the company's memorandum and articles as may be required in consequence of that provision: ibid., s. 5 (5).

Where a company passes a resolution altering its objects

(a) if no application is made for the alteration to be cancelled by the court, it must, within 15 days from the end of the period for making such an application, deliver to the Registrar of Companies a printed copy of its memorandum as altered; and

(b) if such an application is made, it must
   (i) forthwith give notice (in the prescribed form) of that fact to the Registrar; and
   (ii) within 15 days from the date of any order cancelling or confirming the alteration, deliver to the Registrar an office copy of the order and, in the case of an order confirming the alteration, a printed copy of the memorandum as altered: ibid., s. 6 (1).

The validity of an alteration of a company's memorandum with respect to the objects of the company cannot be questioned on the ground that it was not authorised by s. 4 except in proceedings taken for the purpose before the expiration of 21 days after the date of the resolution: ibid., s. 6 (4).

If a company makes default in giving notice or delivering any document to the Registrar of Companies as required above, the company and every officer of the company who is in default are liable on summary conviction to a fine not exceeding one-fifth of the statutory maximum, or on conviction after continued contravention, a default fine not exceeding one-fiftieth of the statutory maximum: ibid., ss. 6 (3), 730 and Sch. 24.

'Officer' includes a director, manager or secretary: Companies Act 1985, s. 744.

'Officer who is in default' means any officer of the company who knowingly and wilfully authorises or permits the default, refusal or contravention mentioned in the enactment: Companies Act 1985, s. 730 (5).

Official notification. In s. 42 means in relation to anything stated in a document of any of the descriptions contained in that section, the notification of that document in the *Gazette* and in relation to the appointment of a liquidator in a voluntary winding up the notification of it in the *Gazette* under s. 600, and 'officially notified' is to be construed accordingly: Companies Act 1985, s. 711 (2).

Official Receiver means the official receiver (if any) attached to the court for bankruptcy purposes, or, if there is more than one official receiver, then such one of them as the Secretary of State may appoint, or, if there is no such official receiver, then an officer appointed for the purpose by the Secretary of State: Companies Act 1985, s. 526 (1).

Official Receiver's report. A report sent to the court after he has received the statement of the company's affairs in a winding up by the court. (*See* STATEMENT OF AFFAIRS).

When a winding up order is made, the Official Receiver must, as soon as practicable after the receipt of the statement of affairs, (or, in a case where the court orders that no statement is to be submitted, as soon as practicable after the date of the order), submit a preliminary report to the court

(a) as to the amount of capital issued, subscribed and paid up, and the estimated amount of assets and liabilities; and

(b) if the company has failed, as to the causes of the failure; and

(c) whether in his opinion further inquiry is desirable as to any matter relating to the promotion, formation or failure of the company or the conduct of its business: Companies Act 1985, s. 530 (1).

The Official Receiver may also, if he thinks fit, make further reports (one or more) stating the manner in which the company was formed and whether in his opinion any fraud has been committed by any person in its promotion or formation, or by any officer of the company in relation to the company since its formation, and any other matters which in his opinion it is desirable to bring to the notice of the court: ibid., s. 530 (2).

If the Official Receiver states in any such further report that in his opinion a fraud has been committed, the court has power to order a public examination of the persons concerned: ibid., s. 530 (3). (*See* PUBLIC EXAMINATION).

Official seal. A seal kept by the company for the sealing of share certificates.

A company may have, for use for sealing securities issued by the company and for sealing documents creating or evidencing securities so issued, an official seal which is a facsimile of the common seal of the company with the addition on its face of the word 'Securities': Companies Act 1985, s. 40. (*See* SEAL).

Officially notified. *See* OFFICIAL NOTIFICATION.

Off-market dealer means a person who

(a) holds a licence under the Prevention of Fraud (Investments) Act 1958, s. 3; or

(b) is a member of a recognised stock exchange or recognised association of dealers in securities within the meaning of that Act; or

(c) is an exempted dealer within the meaning of that Act: Company Securities (Insider Dealing) Act 1985, s. 13 (3).

Off-market purchase. A purchase by a company of any of its own shares if (a) the shares are purchased otherwise than on a registered stock exchange; or (b) the shares are purchased on a recognised stock exchange but are not subject to a marketing arrangement on that stock exchange: Companies Act 1985, s. 163 (1). (*See* SUBJECT TO A MARKETING ARRANGEMENT).

Ordinary debt. A debt payable after the preferential debts have been paid in full. (*See* PREFERENTIAL PAYMENTS). If the ordinary debts cannot be paid in full, the liquidator must pay them *pari passu.*

Ordinary resolution. A resolution passed by a majority of persons present at a general meeting: *Bushell v Faith* [1970] 1 All ER 53 at 56, HL (per Lord Upjohn).

Ordinary share. A share entitling its holder to a dividend, if any, after the payment of the fixed dividend in respect of the preference shares. (*See* DIVIDEND: PREFERENCE SHARE).

Oversea company. A company incorporated outside Great Britain which establishes a place of business within Great Britain: Companies Act 1985, s. 744.

An oversea company within one month of the establishment of the place of business in Great Britain must deliver to the Registrar of Companies for registration (a) a certified copy of the charter, statutes or memorandum and articles of the company; and (b) a return in the prescribed form containing

(i) a list of the company's directors and secretary;

(ii) a list of the names and addresses of some one or more persons resident in Great Britain authorised to accept on the company's behalf service of process and any notices required to be served on it;

(iii) a list of the documents delivered in compliance with the above provisions;

(iv) a statutory declaration (made by a director or secretary of the company or by any person whose name and address are given in the list of persons authorised to accept service of process and any notices), stating the date on which the company's place of business in Great Britain was established: ibid., s. 691 (1).

If any alteration is made in

(a) the charter, statutes, or memorandum and articles of an oversea company; or

(b) the directors or secretary of an oversea company or the particulars contained the list of the directors and secretary; or

(c) the names and addresses of the person authorised to accept service on behalf of an oversea company,

the company must within the prescribed time deliver to the Registrar for registration a return containing the prescribed particulars of the alteration: ibid., s. 692 (1). If any change is made in the corporate name of an oversea company, the company must, within the prescribed time, deliver to the Registrar for registration a return containing the prescribed particulars of the change: ibid., s. 692 (2).

Every oversea company must

(a) in every prospectus inviting subscriptions for its shares or debentures in Great Britain state the country in which the company is incorporated. (*See* PROSPECTUS); and

(b) conspicuously exhibit on every place where it carries on business in Great Britain the company's name and the country in which it is incorporated; and

(c) cause the company's name and of the country in which it is incorporated to be stated in legible characters in all bill-heads and letter paper, and in all notices and other official publications of the company; and

(d) if the liability of the members of the company is limited, cause notice of that fact to be stated in legible characters in every such prospectus and in all bill-heads, letter paper, notices and other official publications of the company in Great Britain, and to be affixed on every place where it carries its business: ibid., s. 693.

Any process or notice required to be served on an oversea company is sufficiently served if addressed to any person whose name has been delivered to the Registrar and left at or sent by post to the address which has been so delivered: ibid., s. 695 (1).

A prospectus of an oversea company is subject to the same rules as to delivering the prospectus for registration and as to the contents of the prospectus as apply to companies registered in England, with some modifications: ibid., ss. 72 to 79.

An oversea company must register charges on property in England: ibid., s. 409.

Every oversea company must in respect of each accounting reference period of the company prepare such accounts made up by reference to such date or dates, and in such form containing such particulars and having annexed or attached to them such documents as would have been required if it had been a company formed and registered under the Act: ibid., s. 700 (1).

(*See* ACCOUNTING REFERENCE PERIOD: COMPANIES ACTS).

The Secretary of State may by order in a statutory instrument (a) modify the above requirements for the purpose of their application to oversea companies; and (b) exempt an oversea company from those requirements or from such of them as may be specified in the order: Companies Act 1985, s. 700 (4).

In respect of each accounting reference period of the company, an oversea company must deliver to the Registrar of Companies copies of the accounts and the other documents mentioned above: ibid., s. 700 (2). If such an account or other document is in a language other than English, there must be annexed to the copy so delivered a translation of it into English certified in the prescribed manner to be a correct translation: ibid., s. 700 (2).

Overseas branch register. A register of members resident in certain specified countries in which a company transacts business.

A company having a share capital whose objects comprise the transaction of business in any of the countries or territories specified in Part I of Sch. 14 to the Act may cause to be kept in such country or territory a branch register of members resident in that country or territory: Companies Act 1985, s. 362 (1). Such a branch register is to be known as an 'overseas branch register': ibid., s. 362 (2).

A company keeping an overseas branch register must give to the Registrar of Companies notice in the prescribed form of the situation of the office where any overseas branch register is kept and of any change in its situation, and, if it is discontinued, of its discontinuance: ibid., Sch. 14, Part II, para. 1 (1). Any such notice must be given within 14 days of the opening of the office or of the change or discontinuance, as the case may be: ibid., Sch. 14, Part II, para. 1 (2).

An overseas branch register is deemed to be part of the company's register of members ('the principal register'): ibid., Sch. 14, Part II, para. 2 (1). It must be kept in the same manner in which the principal register is required by the Act to be kept, except that the advertisement before closing the register must be inserted in a newspaper circulating in the district where the overseas branch register is kept: ibid., Sch. 14, Part II, para. 2 (2). (*See* REGISTER OF MEMBERS).

The company must (a) transmit to its registered office a copy of every entry in its overseas branch register as soon as may be after the entry is made, and (b) cause to be kept at the place where the company's principal register is kept a duplicate of its overseas branch register duly entered up from time to time: Companies Act 1985, Sch. 14, Part II, para. 4 (1). Every such duplicate is deemed for all purposes of the Act to be part of the principal register: ibid., Sch. 14, Part II, para. 4 (1).

The shares registered in an overseas branch register must be distinguished from those registered in the principal register; and no transaction with respect to any shares registered in an overseas branch register must, during the continuance of that registration, be registered in any other register: ibid., Sch. 14, Part II, para. 5.

A company may discontinue to keep an overseas branch register, and thereupon all entries in the register must be transferred to some other branch register kept by the company in the same country or territory, or to the principal register: ibid., Sch. 14, Part II, para. 6.

Subject to the provisions of the Act, any company may, by its articles, make such provisions as it thinks fit respecting the keeping of overseas branch registers: ibid., Sch. 14, Part II, para. 7.

P

Panel on Take-overs and Mergers. *See* CITY CODE ON TAKE-OVERS AND MERGERS.

Partner, general. *See* GENERAL PARTNER.

Partner, incoming. *See* INCOMING PARTNER.

Partner, limited. *See* LIMITED PARTNER.

Partner, outgoing. *See* RETIRING PARTNER.

Partner, retiring. *See* RETIRING PARTNER.

Partner, sleeping. *See* SLEEPING PARTNER.

Partner, usual authority of. *See* USUAL AUTHORITY OF PARTNER.

Partner's lien. A right vested in a partner to hold the whole or part of the partnership assets until certain payments are made to him.

Where a partnership contract is rescinded on the ground of the fraud or misrepresentation of one of the parties to it, the party entitled to rescind is, without prejudice to any other right, entitled to a lien on the surplus of the partnership assets after satisfying the partnership liabilities, for any sum of money paid by him for the purchase of a share in the partnership and for any capital contributed by him: Partnership Act 1890, s. 41 (a).

Partner's share in partnership, assignee of. *See* ASSIGNEE OF PARTNER'S SHARE IN PARTNERSHIP.

Partner's share in partnership, assignment of. *See* ASSIGNMENT OF PARTNER'S SHARE IN PARTNERSHIP.

Partners, continuing. *See* CONTINUING PARTNERS.

Partnership. The relation which subsists between persons carrying on a business in common with a view of profit: Partnership Act 1890, s. 1 (1). 'Business' includes every trade, occupation or profession: ibid., s. 45. But the relation between the members of any company or association which is

(i) registered under the Companies Act 1862 or any other Act for the time being in force and relating to the registration of joint stock companies; or

(ii) formed or incorporated by or in pursuance of any other Act of Parliament or letters patent or royal charter; or

(iii) a company engaged in working mines within and subject to the jurisdiction of the Stannaries,

is not a partnership within the meaning of the Partnership Act 1890: ibid., s. 1 (2).

Some partnerships are limited partnerships. (*See* LIMITED PARTNERSHIPS).

Existence of partnership

In determining whether a partnership does or does not exist, regard shall be had to the following rules:

(1) Joint tenancy, tenancy in common, joint property, common property or part ownership does not of itself create a partnership as to anything so held or owned, whether the tenants or owners do or do not share any profits by the use of it.

(2) The sharing of gross returns does not of itself create a partnership, whether the persons sharing such returns have or have not a joint or common right or interest in any property from which or from the use of which the returns are derived.

(3) The receipt by a person of a share of the profits of a business is *prima facie* evidence that he is a partner in the business, but the receipt of such a share, or of a payment contingent on or varying with the profits of a business, does not of itself make him a partner in the business: Partnership Act 1890, s. 2.

In particular

(a) the receipt by a person of a debt or other liquidated amount by instalments or otherwise out of the accruing business does not of itself make him a partner or liable as such;

(b) a contract for the remuneration of a servant or agent of a person engaged in the business does not of itself make the servant or agent a partner or liable as such;

(c) a person being the widow or child of a deceased partner, and receiving by way of annuity a portion of the profits made in the business in which the deceased person was a partner, is not by reason only of such receipt a partner in the business or liable as such;

(d) the advance of money by way of loan to a person engaged or about to engage in any business on a contract with that person that the lender shall receive a rate of interest varying with the profits, or shall receive a share of the profits arising from carrying on the business, does not of itself make the lender a partner with the person or persons carrying on the business or liable as such. Provided that the contract is in writing, and signed by or on behalf of all the parties to it;

(e) a person receiving by way of annuity or otherwise a portion of the profits of a business in consideration of the sale by him of the goodwill of the business is not by reason only of such receipt a partner in the business or liable as such: ibid., s. 2. (*See* GOODWILL).

Partnership Act 1890. An Act setting out the principles of the law of partnership. (*See* PARTNERSHIP).

It concerns (i) the nature of partnership (ss. 1–4); (ii) relations of partners to persons dealing with them (ss. 5–18); (iii) relations of partners to one another (ss. 19–31); (iv) dissolution of partnership and its consequences (ss. 32–44); and (v) supplemental (ss. 45–50).

Partnership articles. The contract between partners setting out the details of the relationship between them. The clauses in the contract will naturally vary with the type of profession or business concerned, but the following matters are dealt with in all types of partnership: (i) the nature and place of business; (ii) the firm name; (iii) the duration of the partnership; (iv) the provision of the capital; (v) the ascertainment and division of profits; (vi) the firm's bank account and the drawing of cheques; (vii) the management of the business; (viii) accounts; (ix) the death or retirement of a partner; (x) restriction on a partner carrying on a competing business; (xi) the reference of disputes to arbitration.

Rights and duties of partners

Subject to any agreement express of implied between the partners,

(1) all the partners are entitled to share equally in the capital and profits of the business, and must contribute equally towards the losses, whether of capital or otherwise, sustained by the firm;

(2) the firm must indemnify every partner in respect of payments made and personal liabilities incurred by him
 (a) in the ordinary and proper conduct of the business of the firm; or
 (b) in or about anything necessarily done for the preservation of the business or property of the firm;

(3) a partner making, for the purpose of the partnership, any actual payment or advance beyond the amount of capital which he has agreed to subscribe, is entitled to interest at the rate of 5 per cent per annum from the date of the payment or advance;

(4) a partner is not entitled, before the ascertainment of profits, to interest on the capital subscribed by him;

(5) every partner may take part in the management of the partnership business;

(6) no partner is entitled to remuneration for acting in the partnership business;

(7) no person may be introduced as a partner without the consent of all existing partners;

(8) any difference as to ordinary matters connected with the partnership business may be decided by a majority of the partners, but no change may be made in the nature of the partnership business without the consent of all existing partners;

(9) the partnership books are to be kept at the place of business of the partnership (or the principal place, if there is more than one), and every partner may, when he thinks fit, have access to and inspect and copy any of them: Partnership Act 1890, s. 24.

Some of the above rights do not apply in the case of limited partnerships. (*See* LIMITED PARTNER: LIMITED PARTNERSHIP).

Duty to render accounts

Partners are bound to render true accounts and full information of all things affecting the partnership to any partner or his legal representatives: Partnership Act 1890, s. 28. See e.g. *Law v Law* [1905] 1 Ch 140.

Accountability for private profit

Every partner must account to the firm for any benefit derived by him without the consent of the other partners from any transaction concerning the partnership, or from any use by him of the partnership property, name or business connection: Partnership Act 1890, s. 29. (*See* PARTNERSHIP PROPERTY). See e.g. *Pathirana v Pathirana* [1967] 1 AC 233.

Duty of partner not to compete with firm

If a partner, without the consent of the other partners, carries on any business of the same nature as and competing with that of the firm, he must account for and pay over to the firm all profits made by him in that business: Partnership Act 1890, s. 30. See e.g. *Aas v Benham* [1891] 2 Ch 244 and *Trimble v Goldberg* [1906] AC 494.

Partnership at will. A partnership containing no fixed term for its duration. Where no fixed term has been agreed on, any partner may determine the partnership on giving notice of his intention to do so to all the other partners: Partnership Act 1890, s. 26 (1). But a provision that the partnership is to be terminated 'by mutual agreement only' will prevent termination at the instance of a single partner: *Moss v Elphick* [1910] 1 KB 846. Whether a fixed term has been agreed on is a matter of construction in each case: *Abbott v Abbott* [1936] 3 All ER 823.

Partnership, dissolution of. *See* DISSOLUTION OF PARTNERSHIP.

Partnership, limited. *See* LIMITED PARTNERSHIP.

Partnership, non-trading. *See* NON-TRADING PARTNERSHIP.

Partnership property. All property and rights and interests in property originally brought into the partnership stock or acquired, whether by purchase or otherwise, on account of the firm, or for the purposes and in the course of the partnership business: Partnership Act 1890, s. 20 (1). See e.g. *Miles v Clarke* [1953] 1 All ER 779.

Partnership property must be held and applied by the partners exclusively for the purposes of the partnership and in accordance with the partnership agreement: Partnership Act 1890, s. 20 (1).

Where co-owners of an estate or interest in any land, not being itself partnership property, are partners as to profits made by the use of that land or estate, and purchase other land or estate out of the profits to be used in like manner, the land or estate so purchased belongs to them in the absence of an agreement to the contrary, not as partners, but as co-owners for the same respective estates and interests as are held by them in the land or estate first mentioned at the date of the purchase: ibid., s. 20 (3). See e.g. *Davis v Davis* [1894] 1 Ch 393.

Unless the contrary intention appears, property bought with money belonging to the firm is deemed to have been bought on account of the firm: Partnership Act 1890, s. 21. See e.g. *Wray v Wray* [1905] 2 Ch 349.

Where land has become partnership property, it must, unless the contrary intention appears, be treated as between the partners (including the representatives of a deceased partner) as personal and not real estate: Partnership Act 1890, s. 22.

A writ of execution cannot issue against any partnership property except on a judgment against the firm: s. 23 (1). See *Peake v Carter* (1916) 114 LT 273, CA.

Partnership property, application of. *See* APPLICATION OF PARTNERSHIP PROPERTY.

Payment in advance of calls. Payment by a member in advance of calls which may be made in respect of his shares. (*See* CALL).

Permissible capital payment. The payment out of its capital permissible in respect of the redemption of purchase by a company of any of its own shares: Companies Act 1985, s. 171 (3). (*See* PURCHASE BY COMPANY OF OWN SHARES; REDEEMABLE SHARES).

Petition for winding up. An application to the court by a petitioner for the making of an order for a company to be wound up by the court.

Persons who may petition

The persons who may present a petition are (a) a contributory; (b) a creditor; (c) the company; (d) the Secretary of State; (e) the Official Receiver; and (f) the Attorney-General where the company is a charity.

(a) CONTRIBUTORY: A contributory is not entitled to present a petition unless (i) the number of members is reduced below 2; or (ii) the shares in respect of which he is a contributory, or some of them, either were originally allotted to him or have been held by him, and registered in his name, for at least 6 months during the 18 months before the commencement of the winding up, or have devolved on him through the death of a former holder: Companies Act 1985, s. 519 (2). (*See* COMMENCEMENT OF WINDING UP).

The word 'contributory' includes a personal representative even though his membership is not registered in the register of members: *Re Bayswater Trading Co Ltd* [1970] 1 All ER 608. A petition can be presented by an allottee even though his membership is not registered: *Re J.N.Z. Ltd* [1977] 3 All ER 1104.

A petitioner has no *locus standi* to present a petition unless it can be shown that there will be surplus assets for distribution among the shareholders: *Re Expanded Plugs Ltd* [1966] 1 All ER 877. The smallness of a minority shareholder's holding is no bar to his presenting a petition if what he may hope to recover in a liquidation is likely to be appreciable in relation to the size of his holding: *Bryanston Finance Ltd v de Vries* (No. 2) [1976] 1 All ER 25 at 33, CA (per Buckley LJ).

When it is clear on the facts alleged in the petition that there will be nothing available for distribution among the shareholders, he cannot act as *amicus curiae* and present the petition merely with a view to bringing to the court's attention some state of affairs, which he considers is open to criticism, in the way in which the company's business is being conducted: *Re Othery Construction Ltd* [1966] 1 All ER 145. Further, he cannot act as the friend of creditors of the company in order to suggest that the company ought to be wound up to protect their interests: ibid.

(b) CREDITOR: A creditor whose claim is unliquidated cannot present a petition.

The court must not give a hearing to a petition presented by a contingent or prospective creditor until such security for costs has been given as the court thinks reasonable and until a *prima facie* case for winding up has been established to the satisfaction of the court: Companies Act 1985, s. 519 (5).

(c) COMPANY: The company itself may petition if it has passed a special resolution that it should be wound up by the court. (*See* SPECIAL RESOLUTION).

(d) SECRETARY OF STATE: If it appears to the Secretary of State from a report made by inspectors or from any information or documents obtained as a result of an inspection of the company's books that it is expedient in the public interest that the company should be wound up, he may, unless the company is already being wound up by the court, present a petition for it to be so wound up if the court thinks it just and equitable for it to be so: ibid., s. 440. (*See* INSPECTION AND INVESTIGATION OF COMPANY).

The decision to present a petition need not be made by the Secretary of State personally; it can properly be made by him acting through one of his officers: *Re Golden Chemical Products Ltd* [1976] 2 All ER 543.

Where the petition is based on the inspectors' report, the court is entitled to look at the report and act on it in the absence of any other evidence: *Re S.B.A. Properties Ltd* [1967] 2 All ER 615.

Where grave charges are levelled against individuals, the court will not, in the exercise of its jurisdiction under the Companies Act 1985 s. 440 be satisfied merely by *prima facie* evidence, but will require the petitioner to substantiate the case more fully: *Re A.B.C. Coupler and Engineering Co Ltd* (*No. 2*) [1962] 3 All ER 68, CA.

The court, without in the least abdicating any of its judicial and discretionary powers, ought to give special weight to the Secretary of State's view since he is acting not in his own interests but in those of the public: *Re Lubin, Rosen and Associates Ltd* [1975] 1 All ER 577 at 583 (per Megarry J).

Cross-examination of an officer of the Department of Trade and Industry which is directed to the question of what the Secretary of State considers 'the public interest' is not permissible: *Re Golden Chemical Products Ltd (No. 2)* (1976) *The Times*, 10 December.

The Secretary of State can petition for the winding up of an insurance company under the Insurance Companies Act 1982, s. 54.
(e) OFFICIAL RECEIVER: Where a company is being wound up voluntarily or subject to supervision, a petition may be presented by the Official Receiver. (*See* WINDING UP SUBJECT TO THE SUPERVISION OF THE COURT).

(f) ATTORNEY-GENERAL: The Attorney-General may present a petition for the winding up of a company which is a charity: Charities Act 1960, s. 30 (1).

Form and advertisement of petition
Every petition must be in the prescribed form: Companies (Winding-up) Rules 1949 (S.I. 1949 No. 330), r. 26. It must be presented at the office or chambers of the Registrar, who must appoint a time and place at which it is to be heard: ibid., r. 27. Unless the court otherwise directs, every petition must be advertised once in the *London Gazette* not less than 7 clear days after it has been served on the company and not less than 7 clear days before the day fixed for the hearing: ibid., r. 28 (1). Every petition must, unless presented by the company, be served on the company at its registered office, or if there is no registered office, at its principal or last known place of business, by leaving a copy with any member, officer or servant of the company: ibid., r. 29. Every petition must be verified by an affidavit: ibid., r. 30 (1). The affidavit must be made by the petitioner or by some person, such as a director, company secretary or similar officer, or a solicitor who has been concerned in the matter on behalf of the petitioner: ibid., r. 30 (2). The affidavit must be filed within 7 days after the petition is presented and is *prima facie* evidence of the statements in the petition: ibid., r. 30 (3). Every creditor of the company is entitled to be furnished by the solicitor of the petitioner with a copy of the petition within 24 hours after requiring, or paying the prescribed charge for, such a copy: ibid., r. 31.

After the presentation of a petition, on the application of a creditor, or of a contributory, or of the company, and on proof by affidavit of sufficient ground for the appointment of a provisional liquidator, the court, if it thinks fit and on such terms as in the opinion of the court are just and necessary, may make the appointment: ibid., r. 32 (1). (*See* PROVISIONAL LIQUIDATOR).

Restraining presentation of petition

The court will restrain the presentation of a proposed petition with the consequent necessity for advertisement, in a case where it might cause irreparable damage to innocent shareholders in the company (*Charles Forte Investments Ltd v Amanda* [1963] 2 All ER 940, CA), or would injure the goodwill of the company (*Mann v Goldstein* [1968] 2 All ER 769). It will also do so where the proceedings are vexatious and an abuse of the process of the court, e.g. where the petition is brought by an aggrieved member out of spite because he has had to resign his employment with a public company as a result of differences between him and the principal shareholder in a private company, who in effect controlled the public company, and it is shown that the petition is bound to fail or perhaps that there is a suitable alternative remedy to a petition: *Mann v Goldstein* (supra).

Action for maliciously presenting petition

An action will lie for maliciously presenting a petition, and no special damage need be proved for the presentation of the petition if it is from its very nature calculated to injure the credit of the company: *Quartz Hill Mining Co v Eyre* (1883) 11 QBD 674, CA.

Hearing of petition

After a petition has been presented, the petitioner or his solicitor must, on the day to be appointed by the Registrar, attend before him and satisfy him that the petition has been duly advertised, that the prescribed affidavit verifying the statements in it has been filed and the provisions of the Rules as to petitions have been duly complied with: Companies (Winding-up) Rules 1949, r. 33.

Every person who intends to appear on the hearing of the petition must give to the petitioner notice of his intention of doing so: ibid., r. 34 (1). The petitioner or his solicitor or London agent must prepare a list of the names and addresses of the persons who have given notice of their intention to appear on the hearing of the petition: ibid., r. 35. On the day appointed for the hearing, a fair copy of the list must be handed by the petitioner or his solicitor or London agent to the court prior to the hearing of the petition: ibid., r. 35.

Affidavits in opposition to a petition must be filed: ibid., r. 36 (1).

On hearing a petition, the court may dismiss it or adjourn the hearing conditionally or unconditionally or make an interim order or any other order that it thinks fit: Companies Act 1985, s. 520 (1).

Restraining proceedings against company

At any time after the presentation of a petition and before a winding up order has been made, the company, or any creditor or contributory, may apply to the court in which an action or proceeding against a company is pending for a stay of proceedings: ibid., s. 521 (1). The court may stay or restrain the proceedings on such terms as it thinks fit: ibid., s. 521 (1).

The court will usually do so when the petition stands over with a view to a scheme of arrangement being adopted: *Re Dynamics Corporation of America* [1972] 3 All ER 1046. (*See* SCHEME OF ARRANGEMENT).

Avoidance of dispositions

In a winding up by the court, any disposition of the company's property and any transfer of shares or alteration in the status of the company's members made after the commencement of the winding up is void unless the court otherwise orders: Companies Act 1985, s. 522. (*See* COMMENCEMENT OF THE WINDING UP).

Each case must be dealt with on its own facts and particular circumstances, and the court is free to act according to its opinion of what would be just and fair: *Re Steane's (Bournemouth) Ltd* [1950] 1 All ER 21 at 25 (per Vaisey J). It is for the applicant to make out a sufficient case for the court to make an order excluding the normal rule under s. 522; *Re Clifton Place Garage Ltd* [1969] 3 All ER 892 at 895 (per Megarry J).

Poll. A method of voting whereby each member can vote for or against a resolution according to the number of shares which he has.

Table A, art. 54 states: 'Subject to any rights or restrictions attached to any shares . . . on a poll every member shall have one vote for every share of which he is the holder.'

On a poll votes may be given either personally or by proxy: Table A, art. 59. (*See* PROXY). A member may appoint more than one proxy to attend on the same occasion: ibid.

A provision contained in a company's articles is void in so far as it would have the effect either

(a) of excluding the right to demand a poll at a general meeting on any question other than the election of the chairman of the meeting or the adjournment of the meeting; or

(b) of making ineffective a demand for a poll on any such question which is made either

   (i) by not less than 5 members having the right to vote at the meeting; or

   (ii) by a member or members representing not less than one-tenth of the total voting rights of all the members having the right to vote at the meeting; or

   (iii) by a member or members holding shares in the company conferring a right to vote at the meeting, being shares on which an aggregate sum has been paid up equal to not less than one-tenth of the total sum paid up on all the shares conferring that right: Companies Act 1985, s. 373 (1).

The instrument appointing a proxy to vote at a meeting of a company is deemed also to confer authority to demand or join in demanding a poll, and a demand by a person as proxy for a member is the same as a demand by the member: ibid., s. 373 (2).

On a poll taken at a meeting of a company or a meeting of any class of members of a company, a member entitled to more than one vote need not, if he votes, use all his votes or cast all the votes he uses in the same way: ibid., s. 374.

Preference share. A share giving its holder preferential rights in respect of dividends and sometimes in respect of the return of capital.

The holder is usually entitled to a fixed dividend, e.g. 8 per cent before any dividend is paid on the ordinary shares. But if so, he is (unless the articles expressly so provide) not entitled to more than 8 per cent, however prosperous the company may be: *Will v United Lankat Plantations Co Ltd* [1914] AC 11, HL.

Unless the preference shares are made 'preferential as to capital', they are paid off equally with the ordinary shares on the winding up of the company: *Welton v Saffery* [1897] AC 299, HL. But where the preference shares are made 'preferential as to capital', the assets of the company after payment of the company's debts will, apart from special provisions in the articles, be applied first in paying off the capital of the preference shares: *Re W. J. Hall & Co Ltd* [1909] Ch 211.

Whether the preference shareholders have any further rights in the capital if there is a surplus in a winding up after they and the ordinary shareholders have been paid off in full depends on the articles: *Re William Jones & Sons Ltd* [1969] 1 All ER 913. The onus is on the preference shareholders to show that, on the true construction of the articles, they are entitled to share in any surplus: *Scottish Insurance Corporation Ltd v Wilsons and Clyde Coal Co Ltd* [1949] 1 All ER 1068, HL. The principle is that where the articles set out the rights attached to a class of shares to participate in profits while the company is a going concern or to share in the assets of the company on a liquidation, *prima facie* the rights set out are exhaustive: *Re Isle of Thanet Electricity Supply Co Ltd* [1949] 2 All ER 1060, CA.

Arrears of dividend must not be paid by the liquidator up to the date of winding up unless such dividends have, in fact, been declared or unless the articles contain express provisions to this effect (*Re Crighton's Oil Co* [1902] 2 Ch 86, CA) or, on their true construction, give the preference shareholders a clear right to the dividend (*Re Catalinas Warehouses and Mole Co* [1947] 1 All ER 51).

Cumulative and non-cumulative preference shares

Where the preference shares are cumulative, then if the profits of the company in any year are insufficient to pay the fixed dividend on them, the deficiency must be made up out of the profits of subsequent years. But where the preference shares are 'non-cumulative', and the dividend has not been paid on them in a particular year, the deficiency is not made up out of the profits of subsequent years.

Preference shares are presumed to be cumulative, and ambiguous language in the articles will not be enough to make them non-cumulative: *Foster v Coles and M. B. Foster & Sons Ltd* (1906) 22 TLR 555. But they may be made non-cumulative by express provision in the articles or by any language which is sufficiently clear: *Staples v Eastman Photographic Materials Co* [1896] 2 Ch 303.

Guarantee of dividends by third party

Where a third party guarantees the dividends on preference shares, and is called on to pay under the guarantee, he cannot claim repayment from the company as a creditor, but he may stand in the place of the holders of preference shares to be recouped out of any dividends subsequently becoming payable to them for the period in respect of which he was called on to pay: *Re Walters' Deed of Guarantee: Walters' 'Palm' Toffee Ltd v Walters* [1933] Ch 321.

Preferential payments. Debts payable in priority to all other debts.

In a winding up the preferential debts listed in Sch. 19 must be paid in priority to all other debts, but with the exceptions and reservations specified in that Schedule: Companies Act 1985, s. 614 (1).

The debts mentioned in Sch. 19 are:—(i) debts to the Inland Revenue; (ii) debts due to Customs and Excise; (iii) local rates; (iv) social security debts; (v) debts due and in respect of a company's employees; and (vi) those due to a third party for advancing funds for wage-payments etc.

The debts to the Inland Revenue and to the Customs and Excise and in respect of local rates have priority only in respect of those due within the 12 months before

(a) in the case of a company ordered to be wound up compulsorily, the date of the appointment of a provisional liquidator, or if no such appointment has been made, the date of the winding-up order, unless in either case the company had commenced to be wound up voluntarily before that date; and

(b) otherwise, the date of the passing of the resolution for winding up the company: Companies Act 1985, Sch. 19, paras. 1, 4, 5, 7. (*See* PROVISIONAL LIQUIDATOR; WINDING UP).

As regards to and in respect of a company's employees priority is given in relation to all wages or salary of any clerk or servant in respect of services rendered to the company during four months next before the dates mentioned above: Companies Act 1985, Sch. 19, para. 9. The remuneration to which priority is to be given must not, in the case of each claimant, exceed £800: ibid., Sch. 19, para. 12 (1).

The preferential debts rank equally among themselves and must be paid in full, unless the assets are insufficient to meet them, in which case they abate in equal proportions: ibid., s. 614 (2) (a).

So far as the assets of the company available for payment of general creditors are insufficient to meet them, the preferential debts have priority over the claims of holders of debentures under any floating charge created by the company, and must be paid accordingly out of any property comprised in or subject to that charge: ibid., s. 614 (2) (a). (*See* DEBENTURE; FLATONG CHARGE).

Pre-incorporation contract. A contract purporting to be made by a company or by a person acting as its agent before the company has been incorporated.

Where a contract purports to be made by a company or by a person as agent for a company, at a time when the company has not yet been formed, then, subject to any agreement to the contrary, the contract has effect as one entered into by the person purporting to act for the company or as agent for it, and he is personally liable on the contract accordingly: Companies Act 1985, s. 36 (4).

Premium. (1) A sum paid to a company for the purchase of a share in excess of its nominal value. (*See* ISSUE AT A PREMIUM; NOMINAL VALUE); (2) a sum paid by a person to a partner or partners for the privilege of joining a partnership.

Where one partner has paid a premium to another on entering into a partnership for a fixed term, and the partnership is dissolved before the expiration of that term otherwise than by the death of a partner, the court may order the repayment of the premium, or such part of it as it thinks just, having regard to the terms of the partnership contract and to the length of time during which the partnership has continued unless

(a) the dissolution is, in the judgment of the court, wholly or chiefly due to the misconduct of the partner who paid the premium, or

(b) the partnership has been dissolved by an agreement containing no provision for a return of any part of the premium: Partnership Act 1890, s. 40. (*See* DISSOLUTION OF PARTNERSHIP).

Where a partnership contract is rescinded on the ground of fraud or misrepresentation, the party entitled to rescind has a lien on the partnership assets for any premium which he has paid: ibid., s. 41. (*See* PARTNER'S LIEN).

Private company, means a company that is not a public company: Companies Act 1985, s. 1 (3). (*See* PUBLIC COMPANY).

Profits available for distribution, for the purposes of Part VIII, are its accumulated, realised profits, so far as not previously utilised by distribution or capitalisation, less its accumulated, realised losses, so far as not previously written off in a reduction or reorganisation of capital duly made: Companies Act 1985, s. 263 (3).

Prohibition on registration of name. The prevention of a company from being registered with certain names.

A company must not be registered by a name (a) which includes otherwise than at the end of the name the words 'limited', 'unlimited' or 'public limited company'; (b) which includes, otherwise than at the end of the name, an abbreviation of any of those words; (c) which is the same as a name appearing in the index kept by the Registrar; (d) the use of which by the company would in the opinion of the Secretary of State constitute a criminal offence; or (e) which in the opinion of the Secretary of State is offensive: Companies Act 1985, s. 26 (1). (*See* INDEX OF NAMES).

In determining whether one name is the same as another, there must be disregarded

 (i) the definite article, where it is the first word in the name;

 (ii) the following words and expressions where they appear at the end of the name: 'company', 'and company', 'company limited', 'and company limited', 'limited', 'unlimited', and 'public limited company';

 (iii) abbreviations of any of those words where they appear at the end of the name; and

 (iv) type and case of letters, accents, spaces between letters, and punctuation marks: ibid., s. 26 (3).

'And' and '&' are to be taken to be as the same: ibid., s. 26 (3).

Further, except with the approval of the Secretary of State, a company must not be registered by a name which (a) in the opinion of the Secretary of State would be likely to give the impression that the company is connected in any way with Her Majesty's Government or with any local authority; or (b) includes any word or expression for the time being specified in regulations made under s. 29: ibid., s. 26 (2).

Promoter. A person who forms a company. 'The term "promoter" is a term not of law, but of business, usefully summing up in a single word a number of business operations familiar to the commercial world, by which a company is brought into existence.': *Whaley Bridge Calico Printing Co v Green* (1880) 5 QBD 109 at 111 (per Bowen J). 'One who undertakes to form a company with reference to a given project and to set it going, and who takes the necessary steps to accomplish that purpose.': *Twycross v Grant* (1877) 2 CPD 469 at 541 (per Cockburn CJ). Whether a person is or is not a promoter is a question of fact in each case: *Emma Silver Mining Co v Lewis & Son.* Where a person is acting not on his own account, e.g. as a solicitor engaged by the promoter, he will not be deemed a promoter: *Re Great Wheal Polgooth Ltd* (1883) 51 LJ Ch 42.

Fiduciary position

'[Promoters] stand, in my opinion, undoubtedly in a fiduciary position. They have in their hands the creation and moulding of the company; they have the power of defining how, and when, and in what shape, and under what supervision, it shall start into existence and begin to act as a trading corporation. If they are doing all this in order that the company may, as soon as it starts into life, become through its managing director, the purchaser of the property of themselves, the promoters, it is, in my opinion, incumbent upon the promoters to take care that in forming the company they provide it with an executive, that is to say with a board of directors, who shall be both aware that the property which they are asked to buy is the property of the promoters, and who shall be competent and impartial judges as to whether the purchase ought or ought not to be made.': *Erlanger v New Sombrero Phosphate Co* (1878) 3 App Cas 1218, HL.

If a promoter wishes to sell his own property to the company, he should either (i) see that there is a board of independent persons appointed as directors of the new company (*Erlanger v New Sombrero Phosphate Co* (supra)); or (ii) disclose all the facts to the intended members or to the public by means of a prospectus (*Re Leeds and Hanley Theatre of Varieties Ltd* [1909] 2 Ch 809, CA). (*See* PROSPECTUS).

Where proper disclosure is not made, the company is entitled to set aside any contract which has been made with the promoter: *Erlanger v New Sombrero Phosphate Co* (supra). The promoter can be compelled by the company to hand over any secret profit which he has made: *Gluckstein v Barnes* [1900] AC 240.

A promoter cannot relieve himself of his liability by provisions to that effect in the articles of the company: *Omnium Electric Palaces v Bains* [1914] 1 Ch 322. If he acquires property after he has taken up the position of a promoter of a company, the facts may show that he acquired it as a trustee for the company, but apart from such facts, he may sell the property to the company, provided he makes the proper disclosure: ibid.

Promoter's expenses and remuneration
A promoter cannot claim expenses incurred in forming a company unless there is a contract to that effect: *Re National Motor Coach Co Ltd, Clinton's Claim* [1908] 2 Ch 515.

Any amount or benefit paid or given within the 2 preceding years or intended to be paid or given to any promoter, and the consideration for the payment or the giving of the benefit must be stated in the prospectus: Companies Act 1985, Sch. 3, Part I, para. 10 (1) (c). *See* PROSPECTUS).

Liability for mis-statement in prospectus
Where a prospectus invites persons to subscribe for a company's shares or debentures, any promoter is liable to pay compensation to all persons who subscribe for any shares or debentures on the faith of the prospectus for the loss or damage they may have sustained by reason of any untrue statement included in it: ibid., s. 67 (1). For this purpose the expression 'promoter' means a promoter who was a party to the

preparation of the prospectus, or of the portion of it containing the untrue statement, but does not include any person by reason of his acting in a professional capacity for persons engaged in procuring the formation of the company: ibid., s. 67 (3). (*See* PROSPECTUS).

Prospectus. An invitation to the public to subscribe for shares or debentures of a company. '"Prospectus" means any prospectus, notice, circular, advertisement, or other invitation, offering to the public for subscription or purchase any shares in or debentures of a company.': Companies Act 1985, s. 744.

The expression 'offering shares or debentures to the public', must, subject to any provision to the contrary, be read as including a reference to offering them to any section of the public, whether selected as members or debenture holders of the company concerned, or as clients of the person issuing the prospectus, or in any other manner: ibid., s. 59 (1). An offer or invitation is not to be treated as made to the public if it can properly be regarded, in all the circumstances, as not being calculated to result, directly or indirectly, in the shares or debentures becoming available for subscription or purchase by persons other than those receiving the offer or invitation, or otherwise as being a domestic concern of the persons receiving and making it: ibid., s. 60 (1). An offer of shares in or debentures of a private company, or an invitation to subscribe for such shares or debentures is to be regarded (unless the contrary is proved) as being a domestic concern if it is

(a) an offer or invitation made to an existing member of the company or an existing employee or a member of the family of such a member or employee or an existing debenture holder;

(b) an offer or invitation to subscribe for shares or debentures to be held under an employees' share scheme;

(c) an offer or invitation made on terms which permit the person to whom the offer or invitation is made to renounce his right to the allotment of shares or issue of debentures but only in favour of an existing member or an existing employee or a member of the family of such a member or employee or an existing debenture holder: ibid., s. 60 (3), (4), (5), (6), (7). (*See* EMPLOYEES' SHARE SCHEME).

Dating of prospectus

A prospectus issued by or on behalf of a company, or in relation to an intended company, must be dated: ibid., s. 63. That date must, unless the contrary.is proved, be taken as its date of publication: ibid., s. 63.

Matters to be stated and reports to be set out

Every prospectus must state the matters specified in Part I of Sch. 3 and the reports set out in Part II of that Schedule: Companies Act 1985, s. 56 (1).

The matters specified in Part I of Sch. 3 include (i) the number of shares (if any) fixed by the articles as the qualification of a director (*see* QUALIFICATION SHARE); (ii) the names and addresses of directors or proposed directors; (iii) where shares are offered to the public, the 'minimum subscription' (*see* MINIMUM SUBSCRIPTION); (iv) the time of the opening of the subscription lists (*see* TIME OF OPENING OF THE SUBSCRIPTION LISTS); (v) the amount payable on application and allotment of each share; (vi) particulars of any options to subscribe for shares; (vii) the number of shares issued as fully or partly paid up otherwise than in cash; (viii) the names and addresses of the vendors of any property acquired or to be acquired by the company which is to be paid for wholly or partly out of the proceeds of the issue; (ix) the amount of the purchase money, specifying the amount paid for goodwill (*see* GOODWILL); (x) the amount or rate of the underwriting commission (*see* UNDERWRITING COMMISSION); (xi) an estimate of the preliminary expenses; (xii) any amount or benefit paid or given to any promoter (*see* PROMOTER); (xiii) the date of and parties to any material contract; (xiv) the names and addresses of the auditors (*see* AUDITORS); (xv) where the share are of more than one class, the rights of voting and the rights as to capital and dividend attached to the several classes of shares.

The reports set out in Part II of Sch. 3 which are required to be stated in the prospectus are (1) the report of the auditors as to the assets and liabilities of the company at the last date to which the accounts were made up, the profits of the company and the rates of the dividends in each of the 5 years preceding the issue of the prospectus, and the rates of the dividends paid on all classes of shares for the same period: and (2) a report by accountants named in the prospectus as to the profits or losses and assets and liabilities during the same period of any business intended to be acquired with the issue of the shares.

It is unlawful to issue any form of application for shares in or debentures of a company unless the form is issued which complies with the above provisions: Companies Act 1985, s. 56 (2). If any person acts in contravention of these provisions, he is liable on conviction on indictment to a fine, and on summary conviction to a fine not exceeding the statutory maximum: ibid., ss. 56 (4), 730 and Sch. 24.

Expert's consent to issue of prospectus

A prospectus including a statement purporting to be made by an expert must not be issued unless (i) he has given and has not, before delivery of a copy of the prospectus for registration, withdrawn his written consent to the issue with the statement included in the form and context in which it is, in fact, included; and (ii) a statement that he has given and has not withdrawn his consent appears in the prospectus: ibid., s. 61 (1). If a prospectus is issued in contravention of the above provisions, the company and every person who is knowingly a party to the issue are liable on conviction on indictment to a fine, and on summary conviction to a fine not exceeding the statutory maximum: ibid., ss. 61 (2), 730 and Sch. 24. (*See* EXPERT).

Registration of prospectus

No prospectus must be issued unless on or before the date of its publication there has been delivered to the Registrar of Companies for registration a copy of it signed by every person who is named in it as a director or proposed director, and having indorsed on it or attached to it

(i) any consent to the issue of the prospectus required from any person as an expert; and

(ii) in the case of a prospectus issued generally

    (a) a copy of or memorandum of all material contracts referred to in the prospectus,

    (b) a statement signed by a person who has made a report required by the Act setting out any adjustments which he has made to it: Companies Act 1985, ss. 64 (1), 65 (1), (2), (3).

The prospectus must state that it has been delivered for registration and must specify any documents required to be endorsed on or attached to the copy delivered: ibid., s. 64 (3).

The Registrar must not register a prospectus unless it is dated and the copy is signed in the required manner, and unless it has endorsed on it or attached to it the documents specified above: ibid., s. 64 (4).

If a prospectus is issued without a copy of it having been delivered or without the copy having the required documents endorsed on it or attached to it, the company and every person who is knowingly a party to the issue of the prospectus are liable on summary conviction to a fine not exceeding one-fifth of the statutory maximum, or, on conviction after continued contravention, to a daily default fine not exceeding one-fiftieth of the statutory maximum: ibid., ss. 64 (5), 730 and Sch. 24.

Civil liability for mis-statements in prospectus

Where a prospectus invites persons to subscribe for a company's shares or debentures, the following persons are liable to pay compensation to all those who subscribe for any shares or debentures on the faith of the prospectus for the loss or damage they may have sustained by reason of any untrue statement included in it:—

(i) every person who is a director at the time of the issue of the prospectus;

(ii) every person who authorised himself to be named, and is named, in the prospectus as a director;

(iii) every promoter; and

(iv) every person who has authorised the issue of the prospectus: ibid.,

s. 67 (1), (2).

In this connection 'promoter' means a promoter who was a party to the preparation of the prospectus, or of the portion of it containing the untrue statement, but does not include any person by reason of his acting in a professional capacity for persons engaged in procuring the formation of the company: ibid., s. 67 (3). (*See* PROMOTER).

A statement included in a prospectus is deemed to be untrue if it is misleading in the form and context in which it is included: ibid., s. 71.

No person is liable if he proves

(i) that having consented to become a director, he withdrew his consent before the issue of the prospectus, and that it was issued without his authority or consent; or

(ii) that the prospectus was issued without his knowledge or consent, and that on becoming aware of its issue he forthwith gave reasonable public notice that it was issued without his knowledge or consent; or

(iii) that after the issue of the prospectus and before allotment under it, he, on becoming aware of any untrue statement in it, withdrew his consent to it and gave reasonable public notice of the withdrawal and the reason for it; or

(iv) that

   (a) he had reasonable ground to believe that the statement was true;

   (b) he had reasonable ground to believe that an expert making the untrue statement was competent to make it; and

   (c) the untrue statement purported to be a statement made by an official person or contained in what purported to be a copy of or extract from a public official document, and was a correct and fair representation of the statement, copy or extract: ibid., s. 68 (2). (*See* ALLOTMENT).

Where the untrue statement is made by an expert, he is not liable if he proves

(i) that he withdrew his consent in writing before delivery of a copy of the prospectus for registration; or

(ii) that after delivery of the copy of the prospectus for registration and before allotment under it, he, on becoming aware of the untrue statement, withdrew his consent in writing and gave reasonable public notice of the withdrawal, and of the reasons for it; or

(iii) that he was competent to make the statement and that he had reasonable ground to believe and did up to the time of the allotment of the shares or debentures believe that the statement was true: ibid., s. 68 (5).

Provisional liquidator. A person appointed as liquidator pending the making of a final appointment of a liquidator. (*See* LIQUIDATOR).

The court may appoint a liquidator provisionally at any time after the presentation of a winding up petition: Companies Act 1985, s. 532 (1). The appointment of a provisional liquidator may be made at any time before the making of a winding up order and either the Official Receiver or any other fit person may be appointed: ibid., s. 532 (2). (*See* OFFICIAL RECEIVER). Where a liquidator is provisionally appointed by the court, his powers may be limited by the order appointing him: Companies Act 1985, s. 532 (4).

Proxy. A person appointed by a shareholder to vote for him at a meeting.

A proxy is appointed by a written authority called a 'proxy paper' authorising him to vote at a specified meeting.

Any member of a company entitled to attend and vote at a meeting of it is entitled to appoint another person (whether a member or not) as his proxy to attend and vote instead of him: Companies Act 1985, s. 372 (1). A proxy appointed to attend and vote instead of a member of a private company also has the same right as a member to speak at the meeting: ibid., s. 372 (1). (*See* PRIVATE COMPANY). But unless the articles otherwise provide, (i) a member of a private company is not entitled to appoint more than one proxy to attend on the same occasion; and (ii) a proxy is not entitled to vote except on a poll: Companies Act 1985, s. 372 (2). (*See* POLL).

In every notice calling a meeting of a company having a share capital, there must appear, with reasonable prominence, a statement that a member entitled to attend and vote is entitled to appoint or, where that is allowed, one or more proxies, to attend and vote instead of him, and that a proxy need not also be a member: Companies Act 1985, s. 372 (3). If default is made in complying with this requirement as respects any meeting, every officer of the company who is in default is liable on summary conviction to a fine not exceeding one-fifth of the statutory maximum: ibid., ss. 372 (4), 730 and Sch. 24.

A provision contained in a company's articles is void in so far as it would have the effect of requiring the instrument appointing a proxy, or any other document necessary to show the validity of, or otherwise relating to, the appointment of a proxy, to be received by the company or any other person more than 48 hours before a meeting or adjourned meeting in order that the appointment may be effective: ibid., s. 372 (5).

If, for the purpose of any meeting of a company, invitations to appoint as proxy a person or one of a number of persons specified in the invitations are issued at the company's expense to some only of the members entitled to be sent a notice of the meeting and to vote at it by proxy, every officer of the company who knowingly and wilfully authorises or permits their issue is liable on summary conviction to a fine not exceeding one-fifth of the statutory maximum: ibid., ss. 372 (6), 730 and Sch. 24.

The instrument appointing a proxy to vote at a meeting of a company is deemed also to confer authority to demand or join in demanding a poll: ibid., s. 373 (2).

A form of proxy is set out in Table A, art. 60.

The cost of obtaining the signature of proxy papers may be paid out of the funds of a company: *Peel v London and North Western Railway Co* [1907] 1 Ch 5, CA. If a proxy paper is signed for a particular meeting, the date of the meeting may be filled in afterwards: *Sadgrove v Bryden* [1907] 1 Ch 318. A misprint or other palpable mistake on the face of the proxy paper does not entitle a company to reject it: *Oliver v Dalgleish* [1963] 3 All ER 330.

The instrument appointing a proxy and any authority under which it is executed or a copy of such authority certified notarially or in some other way approved by the directors may

(a) be deposited at the office or at such other place within the United Kingdom as is specified in the notice convening the meeting or in any instrument of proxy sent out by the company in relation to the meeting not less than 48 hours before the time for holding the meeting or adjourned meeting at which the person named in the instrument proposes to vote; or

(b) in the case of a poll (*see* POLL) taken more than 48 hours after it is demanded, be deposited as aforesaid after the poll has been demanded and not less than 24 hours before the time appointed for the taking of the poll; or

(c) where the poll is not taken forthwith but is taken more than 48 hours after it was demanded, be delivered at the meeting at which the poll was demanded to the chairman or to the secretary or to any director;

and an instrument of proxy which is not deposited or delivered in a manner so permitted is invalid: Table A, art. 62.

A vote given or poll demanded by proxy is valid notwithstanding the previous determination of the authority of the person voting or demanding a poll unless notice of the determination was received by the company at the office or at such other place at which the instrument of proxy was duly deposited before the commencement of the meeting or adjourned meeting at which the vote is given or the poll demanded or (in the case of a poll taken otherwise than on the same day as the meeting or adjourned meeting) the time appointed for taking the poll: ibid., art. 63.

Proxy paper. *See* PROXY.

Public company means a company limited by shares or limited by guarantee and having a share capital, being a company—

(a) the memorandum of which states that the company is to be a public company; and

(b) in relation to which the provisions of the Act as to the registration or re-registration of a company as a public company have been complied with: Companies Act 1985, s. 1 (3). (*See* REGISTRATION OF COMPANY; RE-REGISTRATION OF COMPANY).

Public examination. An examination in public by the court of promoters, directors, etc.

Where an order has been made for winding up a company by the court, and the Official Receiver has reported in a 'further report' that fraud has been committed, the court may order that any person who has taken part in the promotion or formation of the company, or has been an officer of the company, shall attend and be publicly examined as to the formation and business of the company, or the conduct of its business and as to his conduct: Companies Act 1985, ss. 563, 564. The court can make an order under s. 564 in a voluntary as well as in a compulsory winding up: *Re Campbell Coverings Ltd* [1953] 2 All ER 47.

Where the court makes an order that a person shall attend for public examination (the order being based on a report of the Official Receiver that in his opinion a fraud has been committed), and an appeal is made against the order, the question is whether the report was so flimsy, so sketchy or so unfair that the court exceeded its jurisdiction in making the order: *Tejani v Official Receiver* [1963] 1 All ER 429, PC.

The Official Receiver's report need not attribute to each person ordered to attend the public examination some particular piece of alleged fraud: ibid. (*See* OFFICIAL RECEIVER).

Purchase by company of its own shares. A company limited by shares or limited by guarantee and having a share capital may, if authorised to do so by its articles, purchase its own shares (including any redeemable shares): Companies Act 1985, s. 162 (1). (*See* REDEEMABLE SHARES). A company may not purchase its shares if, as a result of the purchase of the shares in question, there would no longer be any member of the company holding shares other than redeemable shares: Companies Act 1985, s. 162 (3).

Off-market purchase

A company may only make an off-market purchase of its own shares in pursuance of a contract approved in advance or under a contingent purchase contract: ibid., s. 164 (1). (*See* CONTINGENT PURCHASE CONTRACT; OFF-MARKET PURCHASE).

The terms of the proposed contract of purchase must be authorised by a special resolution of the company before the company enters into the contract: Companies Act 1985, s. 164 (2). In general, the authority conferred by any such resolution may be varied, revoked or from time to time renewed by special resolution of the company: ibid., s. 164 (3). But in the case of a public company the authority for a proposed contract of purchase conferred by any such resolution must specify a date on which the authority is to expire: ibid., s. 164 (4). The date specified in any special resolution of a public company to confer or renew authority for a proposed contract of purchase must not be later than 18 months after that on which the resolution is passed: ibid., s. 164 (4).

A special resolution of a company to confer, vary, revoke or renew authority is not effective if any member of the company holding shares to which the resolution relates exercises the voting rights carried by any of those shares in voting on the resolution, and the resolution would not have been passed if he had not done so: ibid., s. 164 (5).

Such a resolution is not effective unless (if the proposed contract of purchase is in writing) a copy of the contract, or (if not) a written memorandum of its terms, is available for inspection by members of the company both (a) at the company's registered office for not less than 15 days ending with the date of the meeting at which the resolution is passed; and (b) at the meeting itself: ibid., s. 164 (6).

A memorandum of contract terms so made available must include the names of any members holding shares to which the contract relates: ibid., s. 164 (6). A copy of the contract must have annexed to it a written memorandum specifying any such names which do not appear in the contract itself: ibid., s. 164 (6).

Contingent purchase contracts

A company may only make a purchase of its own shares in pursuance of a contingent purchase contract if the contract is approved by a special resolution of the company before the contract is entered into: ibid., s. 165 (2). (*See* CONTINGENT PURCHASE CONTRACT).

Market purchase

A company must not make a market purchase of its own shares unless the purchase has first been authorised by the company in general meeting: Companies Act 1985, s. 166 (1). (*See* MARKET PURCHASE).

A resolution authorising market purchases of a company's own shares may confer general authority for that purchase or authority limited to the purchase of shares of any particular class or description: Companies Act 1985, s. 166 (2) (a). The authority may be unconditional or subject to conditions: ibid., s. 166 (2) (b).

Any such authority must (a) specify the maximum number of shares authorised to be acquired; (b) determine both the maximum and the minimum prices which may be paid for the shares; and (c) specify a date on which it is to expire: ibid., s. 166 (3). The authority may be varied, revoked or from time to time renewed by the company in general meeting: ibid., s. 166 (4). In any resolution to confer or renew authority the date on which the authority is to expire must not be later than 18 months after which the resolution is passed: ibid., s. 166 (4).

Assignment or release of company's right

The rights of a company under any contract approved under s. 164 or s. 165 or any contract for a purchase authorised under s. 166 are not capable of being assigned: ibid., s. 167 (1).

An agreement by a company to release its rights under any contract approved under s. 164 or s. 165 is void unless the terms of the release agreement are approved in advance by a special resolution of the company before the agreement is entered into: ibid., s. 167 (2).

Disclosure of particulars of purchases and contracts

Within the period of 28 days beginning with the date on which any shares purchased by the company are delivered to it, the company must deliver to the Registrar of Companies for registration a return in the prescribed form stating with respect to shares of each class purchased the number and nominal value of those shares, and the date on which they were delivered to the company: ibid., s. 169 (1). In the case of a public company the return must also state (a) the aggregate amount paid by the company for the shares; and (b) the maximum and minimum prices paid in respect of shares of each class purchased: ibid., s. 169 (2). If default is made in delivering a return to the Registrar of Companies, every officer who is in default is liable (a) on conviction on indictment to a fine; (b) on summary conviction to a fine not exceeding the statutory maximum or, on conviction after continued contravention, to a daily default fine not exceeding one-tenth of the statutory maximum: ibid., ss. 169 (6), 730 and Sch. 24.

Where a company enters into any contract approved under s. 164 or s. 165 or any contract for a purchase authorised under s. 166 it must keep at its registered office

(a) if the contract is in writing, a copy of it; or

(b) if it is not in writing, a memorandum of its terms,

from the conclusion of the contract until the end of the period of 10 years beginning with the date on which the purchase of all the shares in pursuance of the contract is completed or (as the case may be) the date on which the contract otherwise determines: ibid., s. 169 (4).

Every copy and memorandum which are required to be kept must, during business hours (subject to such reasonable restrictions as the company may in general meeting impose, provided that not less than 2 hours in each day are allowed for inspection) be open to inspection without charge (a) by any member of the company; and (b) if it is a public company, by any other person: ibid., s. 169 (5).

If default is made in complying with s. 169 (4), or if an inspection required under s. 169 (5) is refused, the company and every officer of the company who is in default are liable on summary conviction to a fine not exceeding one-fifth of the statutory maximum or, on conviction after continued contravention, to a daily default fine not exceeding one-fiftieth of the statutory maximum: ibid., ss. 169 (7), 730 and Sch. 24.

In the case of a refusal of an inspection of a copy or memorandum, the court may by order compel an immediate inspection of it: ibid., s. 169 (8).

Purchase out of capital

A private company limited by shares or limited by guarantee and having a share capital may, if authorised to do so by its articles, make a payment in respect of the purchase of its own shares otherwise than out of its distributable profits or the proceeds of a fresh issue of shares: ibid., s. 171 (1). The payment which may be made by a company out of capital in respect of the purchase is to be such an amount as, taken together with (a) any available profits of the company; and (b) the proceeds of any fresh issue of shares made for the purposes of the purchase, is equal to the price of purchase, and the payment is known as the 'permissible capital payment for the shares': ibid., s. 171 (3). If the permissible capital payment for shares purchased by a company is less than their nominal amount, the amount of the difference must be transferred to the capital redemption reserve: ibid., s. 171 (4). (*See* CAPITAL REDEMPTION RESERVE).

(a) REQUIREMENTS: A payment out of capital by a company is unlawful unless

(i) it is approved by a special resolution of the company;

(ii) the directors have made a statutory declaration specifying the amount of the permissible capital payment for the shares, and stating that, having made full inquiry into the affairs and prospects of the company, they have formed the opinion

   (a) as regards its initial situation immediately following the date on which the payment out of capital is proposed to be made, that there will be no ground on which the company could then be found to be unable to pay its debts; and

   (b) as regards its prospects for the year immediately following that date, that, having regard to their intentions with respect to the management of the company's business during that year and to the amount and character of the financial resources which will in their view be available to the company during that year, the company will be able to continue to carry on business as a going concern (and will, accordingly, be able to pay its debts as they fall due) throughout that year;

(iii) publicity has been given for the proposed payment out of capital: ibid., ss. 173 (1), (2), (3), 175.

179

(i) *Special resolution*

The resolution for payment out of capital must be passed on, or within the week immediately following, the date on which the directors make the statutory declaration, and the payment out of capital must be made not earlier than 5 or more than 7 weeks after the date of the resolution: ibid., s. 174 (1).

The resolution is ineffective if any member of the company holding shares to which the resolution relates exercises the voting rights carried by any of those shares in voting on the resolution, and the resolution would not have been passed if he had not done so: ibid., s. 174 (2).

A resolution is ineffective unless the statutory declaration and auditors' report are available for inspection by members of the company at the meeting at which the resolution is passed: ibid., s. 174 (4).

Where a private company passes a special resolution approving any payment out of capital for the purchase of any of its shares,

(a) any member of the company other than one who consented to or voted in favour of the resolution, and

(b) any creditor of the company,

may within 5 weeks of the date on which the resolution was passed apply to the court for the cancellation of the resolution: ibid., s. 176 (1).

If an application is made, the company must

(a) forthwith give notice in the prescribed from of that fact to the Registrar of Companies; and

(b) within 15 days from the making of any order of the court on the hearing of the application, or such longer period as the court may by order direct, deliver an office copy of the order to the Registrar: ibid., s. 176 (3).

A company which fails to comply with this provision and any officer of the company who is in default are liable on summary conviction to a fine not exceeding one-fifth of the statutory maximum or, on conviction after continued contravention, to a daily default fine not exceeding one-fiftieth of the statutory maximum: ibid., ss. 176 (4), 730 and Sch. 24.

On the hearing of an application the court may, if it thinks fit, adjourn the proceedings in order that an arrangement may be made to the court's satisfaction for the purchase of the interests of dissentient members or for the protection of dissentient creditors, as the case may be; and the court may give such directions and make such orders as it thinks expedient for facilitating or carrying into effect any such arrangement: ibid., s. 177 (1).

On the hearing of an application the court must make an order on such terms and conditions as it thinks fit either confirming or cancelling the resolution: ibid., s. 177 (2). If the court confirms the resolution, it may, in particular, by order alter or extend any date or period of time specified in the resolution or in Part V, Chapter VII of the Companies Act 1985 which applies to the purchase of shares to which the resolution refers: ibid., s. 177 (2).

(ii) *Statutory declaration*

The directors' statutory declaration must be in the prescribed form and contain such information with respect to the nature of the company's business as may be prescribed, and must, in addition, have annexed to it a report addressed to the directors by the company's auditors stating that

(a) they have inquired into the company's state of affairs; and

(b) the amount specified in the declaration as the permissible capital payment for the shares in question is in their view properly determined in accordance with ss. 171 and 172; and

(c) they are not aware of anything to indicate that the opinion expressed by the directors as to any of the matters mentioned in s. 173 (3) is unreasonable in all the circumstances: ibid., s. 173 (5).

A director of a company who makes a declaration without having reasonable grounds for the opinion expressed in it is liable.

(a) on conviction on indictment, to imprisonment for a term not exceeding 2 years or a fine or both; and

(b) on summary conviction, to imprisonment for a term not exceeding 6 months or to a fine not exceeding the statutory maximum: ibid., ss. 173 (6), 730 and Sch. 24.

(iii) *Publicity for proposed payment*

Within the week immediately following the date of the resolution for payment out of capital the company must cause to be published in the *Gazette* a notice

(a) stating that the company has approved a payment out of capital for the purpose of acquiring its own shares by purchase;

(b) specifying the amount of the permissible capital payment for the shares in question and the date of the resolution;

(c) stating that the directors' statutory declaration and the auditors' report are available for inspection at the company's registered office; and

(d) stating that any creditor of the company may at any time within the 5 weeks immediately following the date of the resolution apply to the court for an order prohibiting the payment: ibid., s. 175 (1).

Within the week immediately following the date of the resolution the company must cause a notice to the same effect as that required above to be published in a newspaper circulating throughout England and Wales or give notice in writing to that effect to each of its creditors: ibid., s. 175 (2), (3).

Not later than the first notice date (i.e. the day on which the company first publishes the notice required by s. 175 (1), or first publishes or gives the notice required by s. 175 (2), whichever is the earlier) the company must deliver a copy of the statutory declaration of the directors, and the auditors' report to the Registrar of Companies: ibid., s. 175 (4), (5).

The statutory declaration and the auditors' report must be kept at the company's registered office throughout the period beginning with the first notice date and ending 5 weeks after the date of the resolution for payment out of capital, and must during business hours on any day during that period be open to the inspection of any member or creditor of the company without charge: ibid., s. 175 (6). If an inspection is refused, the company and every officer of the company who is in default are liable to a fine not exceeding one-fifth of the statutory maximum or, on conviction after continued contravention, to a daily default fine not exceeding one-fiftieth of the statutory maximum: ibid., ss. 175 (7), 730 and Sch. 24. In the case of a refusal of an inspection of a declaration or report, the court may by order compel an immediate inspection of them: ibid., s. 175 (8).

(b) LIABILITY OF PAST SHAREHOLDERS AND DIRECTORS: Where a company has made a payment out of capital in respect of the purchase of any of its shares and the company is being wound up, and the aggregate of the amount of its assets and the amounts paid by way of contribution to its assets (*see* CONTRIBUTORY) is not sufficient for payment of its debts and liabilities and the costs, charges and expenses of the winding up, then, if the winding up commenced within 1 year of the date on which the payment was made

(a) the person from whom the shares were purchased; and
(b) the directors of the company who signed the statutory declaration for the purposes of the purchase (except a director who shows that he had reasonable grounds for forming the opinion set out in the declaration);

are, so as to enable that insufficiency to be met, liable to the extent specified below: ibid., s. 504 (1), (2).

A person from whom any of the shares were purchased is liable to contribute an amount not exceeding so much of the payment as was made by the company in respect of his shares: ibid., s. 504 (3). The directors of the company are jointly and severally liable with that person to contribute that amount: ibid., s. 504 (3). A person who has contributed any amount may apply to the court for an order directing any other person jointly and severally liable in respect of that amount to pay him such amount as the court thinks just and equitable: ibid., s. 504 (4). A person, who is liable to contribute to a company's assets in the event of its being wound up, may by petition apply to the court for the winding up of the company on either of the grounds set out in paragraphs (f) and (g) of s. 517 (1): ibid., s. 519 (3).

(c) COMPANY'S FAILURE TO PURCHASE: A company is not liable in damages in respect of any failure on its part to purchase any of the shares: ibid., s. 178 (2).

But this provision is without prejudice to any right of the holder of the shares other than his right to sue the company for damages in respect of its failure: ibid., s. 178 (3). But the court must not grant an order for specific performance of the terms of purchase if the company shows that it is unable to meet the cost of purchasing the shares in question out of distributable profits: ibid., s. 178 (3).

Q

Qualification share. A share which a director must hold in order to be appointed or to continue as such.

It is the duty of every director who is by the company's articles required to hold a specified share qualification, and who is not already qualified, to obtain his qualification within 2 months after his appointment, or such shorter time as may be fixed by the articles: Companies Act 1985, s. 291 (1). For the purpose of any provision of the articles requiring a director to hold a specified share qualification, the bearer of a share warrant is not deemed to be the holder of the shares specified in the warrant: ibid., s. 291 (2). (*See* SHARE WARRANT). The office of director is vacated if he does not within 2 months from the date of his appointment (or within such shorter time as may be fixed by the articles) obtain his qualification, or if, after the expiration of that period or shorter time, he ceases at any time to hold his qualification: Companies Act 1985, s. 291 (3). A person vacating office under the above provision is incapable of being reappointed a director until he has obtained his qualification: ibid., s. 291 (4). If, after the expiration of 2 months or shorter time, any unqualified person acts as a director, he is liable on summary conviction to a fine not exceeding one-fifth of the statutory maximum, or, on conviction after continued contravention, to a daily default fine not exceeding one-fiftieth of the statutory maximum: ibid., ss. 291 (5), 730 and Sch. 24.

If the articles state that the qualification of a director is the holding of
right', it is sufficient if he holds
Proprietary Co Ltd v Fuke [1906]
shares in such a way that the
owner of the shares: *Sutton v*
Ch 502. Shares which are held
r person may be a sufficient
Ch 444. If a director takes his
he promoters, he must account
Canadian Oil Works Corporation,
director holds his qualification
promoter, he is liable to the
lly be the nominal value of the
Canal Ltd [1911] 1 Ch 346. (*See*

Where a qualification is fixed, it must be disclosed in the prospectus: Companies Act 1985, Sch. 3, Part I, para. 1 (b). (*See* PROSPECTUS).

Quasi-loan for the purpose of ss. 330 to 346 is a transaction under which one party ('the creditor') agrees to pay, or pays otherwise than in pursuance of an agreement, a sum for another ('the borrower'), or agrees to reimburse, or reimburses otherwise than in pursuance of an agreement, expenditure incurred by another party for another ('the borrower') (i) on terms that the borrower (or a person on his behalf) will reimburse the creditor; or (ii) in circumstances giving rise to a liability on the borrower to reimburse the creditor: Companies Act 1985, s. 331 (3).

Quorum. The minimum number of persons necessary to constitute a valid meeting.

(a) *Quorum of shareholders*

Table A, art. 40 states: 'No business shall be transacted at any meeting unless a quorum is present. Two persons entitled to vote upon the business transacted, each being a member or a proxy for a member or a duly authorised representative of a corporation shall be a quorum.'

If such a quorum is not present within half an hour from the time appointed for the meeting, or if during a meeting such a quorum ceases to be present, the meeting shall stand adjourned to the same day in the next week at the same time and place or to such time and place as the directors may determine: Table A, art. 41.

If the articles so provide, one member may be a quorum: *Re Fireproof Doors Ltd* [1916] 2 Ch 142. If the articles do not make other provision 2 members personally present are a quorum: Companies Act 1985, s. 370 (4). Where the Secretary of State or the court convenes a meeting, they may direct that one member present in person or by proxy shall be deemed to consitute a meeting: ibid., ss. 367 (2), 371 (2).

If the articles provide that a quorum must be present 'when the meeting proceeds to business', a resolution is valid although members have left the meeting so that a quorum is no longer present when the resolution is passed: *Re Hartley Baird Ltd* [1954] 3 All ER 695.

(b) *Quorum of directors*

Table A, art. 89 states: 'The quorum for the transaction of the business of the directors may be fixed by the directors, and unless so fixed at any other number shall be two. A person who holds office only as an alternate director shall, if his appointor is not present, be counted in the quorum.'

R

Receiver. A person appointed to take over the property of a company.

Appointment

A receiver may be appointed by (a) the debenture holders; or (b) the court.

(a) BY THE DEBENTURE HOLDERS: A receiver appointed by the debenture holders under a power in the debentures is the agent of the debenture holders, and they are liable on his contracts unless the document conferring the power to appoint a receiver expressly states that he is to be the agent of the company: *Robinson Printing Co Ltd v Chic Ltd* [1905] 2 Ch 123; *Griffiths v Secretary of State for Social Services* [1973] 3 All ER 1184. (*See* DEBENTURE). A receiver appointed under powers contained in any instrument is personally liable on any contract entered into by him in the performance of his functions (except in so far as the contract otherwise provides) and entitled in respect of that liability to indemnity out of the assets: Companies Act 1985, s. 492 (3). But this provision does not limit his liability on contracts entered into without authority or confer any right to indemnity in respect of that liability: ibid., s. 492 (3).

On a winding up the receiver ceases to be the agent of the company, if he was so previously, but does not thereby become the agent of the debenture holders, and incurs personal liability if he continues to act: *Gosling v Gaskell* [1897] AC 575, HL. Although the winding up deprives the receiver of power to bind the company by acting as its agent, it does not affect his power to hold and dispose of the company's property comprised in the debenture including the power to use the company's name for that purpose: *Snowman v David Samuel Trust Ltd* [1978] 1 All ER 616.

A receiver appointed by the debenture holders may apply to the court for directions in relation to any particular matter arising in connection with the performance of his functions: Companies Act 1985, s. 492 (1). On any such an application, the court may give such directions or make such order declaring the rights of persons before the court or otherwise, as it thinks just: ibid., s. 492 (2).

(b) BY THE COURT: A receiver may be appointed by the court in a debenture holders' action (*see* DEBENTURE HOLDERS' ACTION) if

(i) the principal money has become payable (*Re Carshalton Park Estate Ltd: Graham v Carshalton Park Estate Ltd* [1908] 2 Ch 62); or

(ii) the company is wound up even though the money is not expressly made payable in that event (*Re Crompton & Co Ltd: Player v Crompton & Co Ltd* [1914] 1 Ch 954); or

(iii) if the security is in jeopardy even if there has been no default in the payment of interest, and no winding up.

Thus, the court has considered that the security was in jeopardy where e.g. (a) a judgment creditor had levied execution (*Edwards v Standard Rolling Stock Syndicate* [1893] 1 Ch 574); (b) a judgment remained unsatisfied (*Re London Pressed Hinge Co Ltd: Campbell v London Pressed Hinge Co Ltd* [1905] 1 Ch 576); (c) a company's works had been closed and the employees discharged (*McMahon v North Kent Iron Works* [1891] 2 Ch 148); (d) a company had closed down its business or even one of its chief branches (*Re Braunstein and Marjolaine Ltd* (1914) 112 LT 25); (e) a company proposed to distribute its reserve fund among its members by way of dividend leaving the debentures insufficiently secured (*Re Tilt Cove Copper Co Ltd* [1913] 2 Ch 588); and (f) disputes on the board of directors had led to a dereliction by them of their duties (*Trade Auxiliary Co v Vickers* (1873) LR 16 Eq 303). But mere insufficiency of the security does not amount to jeopardy: *Re New York Taxi-Cab Co Ltd: Sequin v New York Taxi-Cab Co Ltd* [1913] 1 Ch 1.

Where application is made to the court to appoint a receiver on behalf of the debenture holders or other creditors of a company which is being wound up by the court, the Official Receiver may be appointed: Companies Act 1985, s. 491. (*See* OFFICIAL RECEIVER).

Where the receiver is appointed by the court, any interference with him is a contempt of court, and no proceedings can be commenced against him or in respect of the property in his hands without the leave of the court: *Re Metropolitan Amalgamated Estates Ltd: Fairweather v Metropolitan Amalgamated Estates Ltd* [1912] 2 Ch 497. He is the agent of the court, and is personally liable on contracts which he makes and is entitled to be indemnified out of the assets of the company in priority to the rights of the debenture holders: *Burt, Boulton and Hayward v Bull* [1898] 1 QB 276, CA.

A receiver appointed by the court is considered to have been appointed for the benefit of all persons interested in the shares, and must not break contracts merely because he thinks that this will suit the debenture holders: *Re Newdigate Colliery Ltd: Newdigate v Newdigate Colliery Ltd* [1912] 1 Ch 468, CA. But he is not bound to borrow money to perform contracts which can only be completed at a loss: *Re Thames Ironworks, Shipbuilding & Engineering Co Ltd: Farrer v Thames Ironworks, Shipbuilding & Engineering Co Ltd* (1912) 106 LT 674.

If the court has ordered the receiver to take proceedings, the plaintiff debenture holder has no right to stop such proceedings, the question being in the discretion of the court: *Viola v Anglo-American Cold Storage Co* [1912] 2 Ch 305.

The receiver cannot create a lien in favour of certain creditors without the leave of the court: *Moss SS Co Ltd v Whinney* [1912] AC 254, HL.

Notice of appointment and of ceasing to act

If a person obtains an order for the appointment of a receiver or appoints a receiver under any powers contained in an instrument, he must within 7 days from the date of the order or of the appointment under those powers, give notice of the fact to the Registrar of Companies, and the Registrar must enter the fact in the register of charges: Companies Act 1985, s. 405 (1).

Where a person appointed receiver under the powers contained in an instrument ceases to act as such receiver, he must, on so ceasing, give the Registrar of Companies notice to that effect, and the Registrar must enter the notice in the register of charges: ibid., s. 405 (2).

A notice must be in the prescribed form: ibid., s. 405 (3). If a person makes default in complying with the above requirements, he is liable on summary conviction to a fine not exceeding one-fifth of the statutory maximum or, on conviction after continued contravention, to a daily default fine not exceeding one-fiftieth of the statutory maximum: ibid., ss. 405 (4), 730 and Sch. 24.

Disqualification from acting as receiver

A body corporate is not qualified for appointment as receiver: ibid., s. 489. Any body corporate which acts as a receiver is liable on conviction on indictment to a fine, and on summary conviction to a fine not exceeding the statutory maximum: ibid., ss. 489, 730 and Sch. 24. If a person, being an undischarged bankrupt, acts as receiver on behalf of debenture holders, he is liable on conviction on indictment to imprisonment for a term not exceeding 2 years, or on summary conviction to imprisonment for a term not exceeding 6 months or to a fine not exceeding the statutory maximum or to both: ibid., ss. 490, 730 and Sch. 24. But this provision does not apply to a receiver where he acts under an appointment made by the court: ibid., s. 490.

Appointment of another receiver

Where a receiver has been appointed by the court, the court may put the liquidator in his place to act as both receiver and liquidator: *Re Joshua Stubbs Ltd: Barney v Joshua Stubbs Ltd* [1891] 1 Ch 475, CA. (*See* LIQUIDATOR).

The court will sometimes replace a receiver appointed by one debenture holder by a receiver appointed by the court: *Re Slogger Automatic Feeder Co Ltd: Hoare v Slogger Automatic Feeder Co Ltd* [1915] 1 Ch 133. Thus, it may do so if the appointment of the original receiver was not for the benefit of all the debenture holders: *Re Maskelyne*

British Typewriter Ltd: Stuart v Maskelyne British Typewriter Ltd [1898] 1 Ch 133, CA.

Notice on invoices and business letters

When a receiver has been appointed, every invoice, order for goods or business letter issued by or on behalf of the company or the receiver or liquidator of the company, being a document on which the name of the company appears, must contain a statement that a receiver has been appointed: Companies Act 1985, s. 493 (1). If default is made in complying with the above requirements, the company and any of the following persons who knowingly and wilfully authorises or permits the default, i.e. any officer of the company, any liquidator and any receiver are liable on summary conviction to a fine not exceeding one-fifth of the statutory maximum: ibid., ss. 493 (2), 730 and Sch. 24.

Remuneration

The remuneration of a receiver may be fixed by the terms of the debenture or by the debenture holders in accordance with its terms.

The court may, on an application made to it by the liquidator, by order fix the amount to be paid by way of remuneration to a person who, under powers contained in an instrument, has been appointed as receiver: ibid., s. 494 (1). The power of the court extends to fixing the remuneration for any period before the making of the order or the application: ibid., s. 494 (2) (a). It is exercisable even though the receiver has died or ceased to act before the making of the order or application: ibid., s. 494 (2) (b). Where the receiver has been paid or has retained for his remuneration for any period before the making of the order any amount in excess of that so fixed for that period, the court's power extends to requiring him or his personal representatives to account for the excess or such part of it as may be specified in the order: ibid., s. 494 (2).

Duties

Where a receiver is appointed on behalf of the holders of any debenture or secured by a floating charge, he must forthwith send to the company notice of his appointment in the prescribed form: ibid., s. 495 (1), (2). The company must within 14 days (unless the time is extended) make out and submit to the receiver a statement as to its affairs: ibid., s. 495 (2).

The company's statement of affairs must show as at the date of the receiver's appointment the particulars of the company's assets, debts and liabilities, the names, residences and occupations of its creditors, the securities held by them, the dates when the securities were given, and such further or other information as may be prescribed: ibid., s. 496 (1). The statement must be submitted by and be verified by affidavit of a director and secretary, or past directors, employees and officers of the company and persons who have taken part in the formation of the company may be required by the receiver to submit and verify the statement: ibid., s. 496 (2), (3). If a person without reasonable excuse makes default in complying with the above requirements as to the statement of affairs, he is liable on summary conviction to a fine not exceeding one-fifth of the statutory maximum or, on conviction after continued contravention, to a default fine not exceeding one-fiftieth of the statutory maximum: ibid., ss. 496 (6), 730 and Sch. 24.

Within 2 months after receiving the statement the receiver must send to the Registrar of Companies and to the court a copy of the statement and any comments he sees fit to make on it and a summary of the statement and of his comments, and must send to the company a copy of his comments and to the trustees for the debenture holders on whose behalf he was appointed a copy of the summary: ibid., s. 495 (3).

The receiver must also within 2 months after the end of each year and within 2 months after he ceases to act as receiver send to the Registrar, the trustees, the company and the debenture holders an abstract of his receipts and payments during the relevant period: ibid., s. 497.

If the receiver makes default in complying with the above provisions, he is liable on summary conviction to a fine not exceeding one-fifth of the statutory maximum or, on conviction after continued contravention, to a daily default fine not exceeding one-fiftieth of the statutory maximum: ibid., ss. 497 (7), 730 and Sch. 24.

The receiver must make the preferential payments required to be made by the Companies Act 1985, s. 614 (1) and Sch. 19 out of any assets coming into his hands in priority to any claim for principal or interest in respect of debentures of the company secured by a floating charge: ibid., s. 196 (1), (2). (*See* DEBENTURE; FLOATING CHARGE; PREFERENTIAL PAYMENT). If he fails to do this, he may be liable in damages: *IRC v Goldblatt* [1972] 2 All ER 202.

Effect of sale on contracts of employees

Where a receiver appointed by the debenture holders sells the company's business, the employees' contracts of service are terminated: *Re Foster Clark Ltd's Indenture Trusts: Loveland v Horscroft* [1966] 1 All ER 43. An employee's contract of service is also terminated where simultaneously with, or very soon after, the appointment of a receiver, the receiver enters into a new agreement with him which is inconsistent with the previous contract of service, or where the continuation of the previous employment is inconsistent with the role and functions of the receiver: *Griffiths v Secretary of State for Social Services* [1973] 2 All ER 1184 at 1198 (per Lawson J).

Recognised bank, in ss. 330 to 346 of the Companies Act 1985, means a company which is recognised as a bank for the purposes of the Banking Act 1979: Companies Act 1985, s. 331 (5).

Recognised stock exchange means any body of persons which is for the time being a recognised stock exchange for the purposes of the Prevention of Fraud (Investments) Act 1958: Companies Act 1985, s. 744.

Reconstruction and amalgamation. Terms which do not have a precise legal meaning. 'Reconstruction' occurs when a company transfers the whole of its undertaking and property to a new company under an arrangement by which the shareholders of the old company are entitled to receive shares or other similar interests in the new company. 'Amalgamation' implies the combination of two or more companies or the business of two or more companies into one company or into the control of one company.

(a) *Methods of reconstruction or amalgamation*

Reconstruction or amalgamation, as the case may be, may be effected by (i) a sale under the memorandum of association; (ii) a sale under the Companies Act 1985, s. 582; (iii) a scheme of arrangement under the Companies Act 1985, ss. 425–427 (*see* SCHEME OF ARRANGEMENT); and (iv) a sale of shares under the Companies Act 1985, s. 428–430. (*See* TAKE OVER).

(i) SALE UNDER THE MEMORANDUM: This method may be used where a company does not require further capital from the members, and where it is not necessary to make the winding up of the old company an essential part of the arrangement. The old company sells its undertaking to the new company for shares in the new company, and, after the transaction is complete, the shares of the new company are distributed among its members according to their rights.

(ii) SALE UNDER THE COMPANIES ACT 1985, s. 582. This method may be used when a company needs more capital and cannot get it without putting pressure on the existing members. A new company is formed and the old company is put into liquidation, and the liquidator sells its undertaking to the new company in such a way that each shareholder in the old company is entitled to shares in the new company, but these shares are only partly paid so that each member incurs a liability to a call in respect of them. (*See* CALL).

Where a company is proposed to be, or is being, wound up altogether voluntarily, and the whole or part of its business or property is proposed to be transferred to another company ('the transferee company'), the liquidator of the transferor company may, with the sanction of a special resolution of that company, receive in compensation for the transfer or sale, shares, policies or other like interests in the transferee company for distribution among the members of the transferor company: Companies Act 1985, ss. 582 (1), (2). The

191

liquidator may enter into any other arrangement whereby the members of the transferor company may, in lieu of receiving cash, shares, policies or other like interests (or in addition thereto) participate in the profits of, or receive any other benefit from, the transferee company: ibid., s. 582 (3). (*See* LIQUIDATOR; SPECIAL RESOLUTION).

A sale or arrangement is binding on the members of the transferor company: ibid., s. 582 (4).

Effect of winding up order

If an order is made within 1 year for winding up the company by or subject to the supervision of the court, the special resolution is not valid unless sanctioned by the court: ibid., s. 582 (7).

Dissentient members

If a member of the transferor company, who did not vote in favour of the special resolution, expresses his dissent from it in writing addressed to the liquidator, and left at the company's registered office within 7 days after the passing of the resolution, he may require the liquidator

(i) to abstain from carrying the resolution into effect; or

(ii) to purchase his interest at a price to be determined by agreement or by arbitration: ibid., s. 582 (5).

If the liquidator elects to purchase the member's interest, the purchase money must be paid before the company is dissolved and be raised by the liquidator in such manner as may be determined by special resolution: ibid., s. 582 (6).

The notice of dissent must comply in all material respects with the provisions of the Act e.g. it must contain express notice to the liquidator to abstain from carrying the resolution into effect or to purchase the shares: *Re Union Bank of Kingston-upon-Hull* (1880) 13 Ch D 808. But an informality which is merely technical may be waived by the liquidator: *Brailey v Rhodesia Consolidated Ltd* [1910] 2 Ch 95.

The executors of a deceased member have a right to dissent: *Llewellyn v Kasintoe Rubber Estates Ltd* [1914] 2 Ch 670, CA.

Any provision in the articles depriving members of their rights under s. 582 is void: *Payne v Cork Co Ltd* [1900] 1 Ch 308.

(iii) SCHEME OF ARRANGEMENT UNDER THE COMPANIES ACT 1985, ss. 425–427. The company may adopt a scheme of arrangement in connection with a reconstruction or amalgamation under the Companies Act 1985, ss. 425–427. Such a scheme needs the court's sanction. (*See* SCHEME OF ARRANGEMENT).

(iv) SALE OF SHARES UNDER THE COMPANIES ACT 1985, ss. 428–430: An amalgamation of one company with another may take place as a result of a take-over bid under the Companies Act 1985, ss. 428–430. (*See* TAKE OVER).

(b) *Mergers*

Mergers of newspaper companies and mergers of other companies in which a monopoly situation is shown to exist are controlled under the Fair Trading Act 1973. (*See* MERGER OF COMPANIES; NEWSPAPER MERGERS).

Redeemable shares. Shares redeemable at the option of the company or the shareholder.

A company limited by shares or limited by guarantee and having a share capital may, if authorised to do so by its articles, issue shares which are to be redeemed or liable to be redeemed at the option of the company or the shareholder: Companies Act 1985, s. 159 (1). No redeemable shares may be issued at a time when there are no issued shares of the company which are not redeemable: ibid., s. 159 (2). Redeemable shares may not be redeemed unless they are fully paid: ibid., s. 159 (3). The terms of redemption must provide for payment on redemption: ibid., s. 159 (3).

In general, redeemable shares may only be redeemed out of distributable profits of the company or out of the proceeds of a fresh issue of shares made for the purpose of the redemption, and any premium payable on redemption must be paid out of distributable profits of the company: ibid., s. 160 (1). If the redeemable shares were issued at a premium, any premium payable on their redemption may be paid out of the proceeds of a fresh issue of shares made for the purposes of the redemption, up to an amount equal to (a) the aggregate of the premiums received by the company on the issue of the shares redeemed; or (b) the current amount of the company's share premium account (including any sum transferred to that account in respect of premiums on the new shares), whichever is the less: ibid., s. 160 (2). In that such case the amount of the company's share premium account must be reduced by a sum corresponding (or by sums in the aggregate corresponding) to the amount of any payment made out of the proceeds of the issue of the new shares: ibid., s. 160 (2). (*See* SHARE PREMIUM ACCOUNT).

Redemption of shares may be effected on such terms and in such manner as may be provided by the company's articles: Companies Act 1985, s. 160 (3). Shares which are redeemed are to be treated as cancelled on redemption, and the amount of the company's issued share capital must be diminished by the nominal value of those shares: ibid., s. 160 (4). But the redemption of the shares by a company is not to be taken as reducing the amount of the company's authorised share capital: ibid., s. 160 (4). (*See* REDUCTION OF CAPITAL). Where a company is about to redeem any shares, it has power to issue shares up to the nominal amount of the shares to be redeemed as if those shares had never been issued: Companies Act 1985, s. 160 (5).

Redemption out of capital

A private company limited by shares or limited by guarantee and having a share capital may, if authorised to do so by its articles, make a payment in respect of the redemption of the shares otherwise than out of the distributable profits of the company or the proceeds of a fresh issue of shares: ibid., s. 171 (1). The payment which may be made by a company out of capital in respect of the redemption is to be such an amount as, taken together with (a) any available profits of the company and (b) the proceeds of any fresh issue of shares made for the purposes of the redemption, is equal to the price of redemption, and is known as the 'permissible capital payment for the shares': ibid., s. 171 (3). If the permissible capital payment for shares redeemed by a company is less than their nominal amount, the amount of the difference must be transferred to the capital redemption reserve: ibid., s. 171 (4). (*See* CAPITAL REDEMPTION RESERVE).

(a) REQUIREMENTS: A payment out of capital by a company is unlawful unless

(i) it is approved by a special resolution of the company;

(ii) the directors have made a statutory declaration specifying the amount of the permissible capital payment for the shares and stating that, having made full inquiry into the affairs and prospects of the company, they have formed the opinion

  (a) as regards its initial situation immediately following the date on which the payment out of capital is proposed to be made, that there will be no grounds on which the company could then be found to be unable to pay its debts; and

  (b) as regards its prospects for the year immediately following that date, that, having regard to their intentions with respect to the management of the company's business during that year and to the amount and character of the financial resources which will in their view be available to the company during that year, the company will be able to continue to carry on business as a going concern (and will, accordingly, be able to pay its debts as they fall due) throughout that year;

(iii) publicity has been given for the proposed payment out of capital: ibid., ss. 173 (1), (2), (3).

(i) *Special resolution*

The resolution for payment out of capital must be passed on, or within 1 week immediately following, the date on which the directors make the statutory declaration, and the payment out of capital must be made not earlier than 5 or more than 7 weeks after the date of the resolution: ibid., s. 174 (1).

The resolution is ineffective if any member of the company holding shares to which the resolution relates exercises the voting rights carried by any of those shares in voting on the resolution, and the resolution would not have been passed if he had not done so: ibid., s. 174 (2).

The resolution is ineffective unless the statutory declaration and auditors' report are available for inspection by members of the company at the meeting which the resolution is passed: ibid., s. 174 (4).

Where a private company passes a special resolution approving any payment out of capital for the redemption of any of its shares
(a) any member of the company other than one who consented to or voted in favour of the resolution; and
(b) any creditor of the company;
may within 5 weeks of the date on which the resolution was passed apply to the court for the cancellation of the resolution: ibid., s. 176 (1).

If an application is made, the company must
(a) forthwith give notice in the prescribed form of that fact to the Registrar of Companies; and
(b) within 15 days from the making of any order of the court on the hearing of the application, or such longer period as the court may by order direct, deliver an office copy of the order to the Registrar: ibid., s. 176 (3).

A company which fails to comply with this provision and any officer of the company who is in default are liable on summary conviction to a fine not exceeding one-fifth of the statutory maximum or, on conviction after continued contravention, to a default fine not exceeding one-fiftieth of the statutory maximum: ibid., ss. 176 (4), 730 and Sch. 24.

On the hearing of an application, the court may, if it thinks fit, adjourn the proceedings in order that an arrangement may be made to the court's satisfaction for the purchase of the interests of dissentient members or for the protection of dissentient creditors, as the case may be; and the court may give such directions and make such orders as it thinks expedient for facilitating or carrying into effect any such arrangement: ibid., s. 177 (1).

The court must make an order on such terms and conditions as it thinks fit either confirming or cancelling the resolution: ibid., s. 177 (2). If the court confirms the resolution, it may, in particular, by order alter or extend any date or period of time specified in the resolution or any provision of Part V, Chapter VII which applies to the redemption of shares to which the resolution refers: ibid., s. 177 (2).

(ii) *Statutory declaration*
The directors' statutory declaration must be in the prescribed form and contains such information with respect to the nature of the company's business as may be prescribed, and must, in addition, have annexed to it a report addressed to the directors by the company's auditors stating that

(a) they have inquired into the company's state of affairs; and

(b) the amount specified in that declaration as the permissible capital payment for the shares in question is in their view properly determined in accordance with ss. 171 and 172; and

(c) they are not aware of anything to indicate that the opinion expressed by the directors as to any of the matters mentioned in s. 173 (3) is unreasonable in all the circumstances: ibid., s. 173 (5).

A director of a company, who makes a declaration without having reasonable grounds for the opinion expressed in it, is liable

(a) on conviction on indictment, to imprisonment for a term not exceeding 2 years or a fine or both; and

(b) on summary conviction, to imprisonment for a term not exceeding 6 months or to a fine not exceeding the statutory maximum: ibid., ss. 173 (6), 730 and Sch. 24.

(iii) *Publicity for proposed payment*

Within the week immediately following the date of the resolution for payment out of capital the company must cause to be published in the *Gazette* a notice

(a) stating that the company has approved a payment out of capital for the purpose of acquiring its own shares by redemption;

(b) specifying the amount of the permissible capital payment for the shares in question and the date of the resolution for payment out of capital;

(c) stating that the statutory declaration of the directors and the auditors' report are available for inspection at the company's registered office; and

(d) stating that any creditor of the company may at any time within the 5 weeks immediately following the date of the resolution for payment out of capital apply to the court for an order prohibiting payment: ibid., s. 175 (1).

Within the week immediately following the date of the resolution the company must also either cause a notice to the same effect as that required above to be published in a newspaper circulating throughout England and Wales or give notice in writing to that effect to each of its creditors: ibid., s. 175 (2), (3).

Not later than the first notice date (i.e. the day on which the company first publishes the notice required by s. 175 (1) or first publishes or gives the notice required by s. 175 (2), whichever is the earlier) the company must deliver a copy of the statutory declaration of the directors and the auditors' report to the Registrar of Companies: ibid., s. 175 (4), (5).

The statutory declaration and auditors' report must be kept at the company's registered office throughout the period beginning with the first notice date and ending 5 weeks after the date of the resolution for payment out of capital, and must during business hours on any day during that period be open to the inspection of any member or creditor of the company without charge: ibid., s. 175 (6). If an inspection is refused, the company and every officer of the company who is in default are liable on summary conviction to a fine not exceeding one-fifth of the statutory maximum or, on conviction after continued contravention, to a daily default fine not exceeding one-fiftieth of the statutory maximum: ibid., ss. 175 (6), 730 and Sch. 24. In the case of a refusal of an inspection of a declaration or report, the court may by order compel an immediate inspection of them: ibid., s. 175 (8).

(b) LIABILITY OF PAST SHAREHOLDERS AND DIRECTORS: Where a company has made a payment out of capital in respect of the redemption of any of its shares and the company is being wound up and the aggregate of the amount of the company's assets and the amount paid by way of contribution to its assets (*see* CONTRIBUTORY) is not sufficient for payment of its debts and liabilities and the costs, charges and expenses of the winding up, then, if the winding up commenced within 1 year of the date on which the payment was made,

(a) the person from whom the shares were redeemed; and
(b) the directors of the company who signed the statutory declaration for the purposes of the redemption (except a director who shows that he had reasonable grounds for forming the opinion set out in the declaration);

are, so as to enable that insufficiency to be met, liable to contribute to the extent specified below: Companies Act 1985, s. 504 (1), (2).

A person from whom any of the shares were redeemed is liable to contribute to the assets of the company an amount not exceeding so much of the payment as was made by the company in respect of his shares: ibid., s. 504 (3). The directors of the company are jointly and severally liable with that person to contribute that amount: ibid., s. 504 (3). A person who has contributed any amount to the assets of a company may apply to the court for an order directing any other person jointly and severally liable in respect of that amount to pay to him such amount as the court thinks just and equitable: ibid., s. 504 (4). A person who is liable to contribute to the assets of the company in the event of its being wound up may by petition apply the court for the winding up of the company on either of the grounds set out in paragraphs (e) and (f) of the Companies Act 1985 ibid., s. 518 (3).

(c) COMPANY'S FAILURE TO REDEEM: A company is not liable in respect of any failure on its part to redeem any of s. 178 (2).

But this provision is without prejudice to any

the shares other than his right to sue the company for damages in respect of its failure: ibid., s. 178 (3). But the court must not grant an order for specific performance of the terms of redemption if the company shows that it is unable to meet the costs of redeeming the shares in question out of distributable profits: ibid., s. 178 (3).

Reduction of capital. A diminution or extinguishment of the share capital of the company affecting (i) the fund available to creditors; or (ii) the rights of different classes of shareholders as between themselves and the interest of the members of the public who may be induced to take shares in the company: *Poole v National Bank of China Ltd* [1907] AC 229 at 239, HL (per Lord Macnaghten).

Reasons for reduction

A company may wish to reduce its capital because, e.g. (i) its capital may be more than enough for its needs, and it plans to return some of it to its members; (ii) its paid up capital may be sufficient for its needs, and it is desired to relieve members of their liability for uncalled capital (*see* PAID UP CAPITAL; UNCALLED CAPITAL); (iii) some of the capital may, in fact, have been lost, and it may be doubtful how far the company ought to pay dividends without first making good the loss (*see* DIVIDENDS).

How reduction is effected

Subject to confirmation by the court, a company limited by shares or a company limited by guarantee and having a share capital may, if so authorised by its articles, by special resolution reduce its share capital in any way: Companies Act 1985, s. 135 (1). In particular the company may

(a) extinguish or reduce the liability on any of its shares in respect of share capital not paid up; or

(b) either with or without extinguishing or reducing liability on any of its shares, cancel any paid-up share capital which is lost or ... ; or

... ing or reducing liability on any ... hare capital which is in excess of

... ary, alter its memorandum by ... tal and of its shares accordingly:

... ndum contains power to reduce, ... : *Re Dexine Patent Packing and* ... o not do so, they must be altered ... t be effected before the special ... e passed: *Re Patent Invert Sugar*

Where creditors are not affected

Where creditors are not affected, the question whether each member shall have his shares proportionately reduced or whether some members shall retain their shares unreduced, the shares of others being extinguished on their receiving a just equivalent, is a purely domestic matter: *British and American Trustee and Finance Corporation Ltd v Couper* [1894] AC 399 at 408, HL (per Lord Watson). The only questions to be considered by the court in exercising its discretion are:— (i) ought the court to refuse its sanction to the reduction out of regard to the interests of those members of the public who may be induced to take shares in the company? and (ii) is the reduction fair and equitable as between different classes of shareholders?: *Poole v National Bank of China Ltd* [1907] AC 229 at 239, HL (per Lord Macnaghten).

One form of reduction is an 'all round reduction', i.e. the lost capital is written off all the shares in proportion to the nominal value. An 'all round reduction' might be considered fair and equitable where preference shares are preferential as to dividend only, but not where the preference extends to capital: *Re Barrow Haematite Steel Co* [1902] 2 Ch 846. (*See* PREFERENCE SHARE). But it may be written off one class of shares and not off others.

If capital which is surplus to the company's requirements is to be paid off, the normal practice is that the reduction is to be effected in the first place by paying off the class of shares which is entitled to priority in a winding up; and if capital is to be written off in consequence of a loss, the loss is to be borne in the first place by the class which would be paid off last in a winding up: *Prudential Assurance Co Ltd v Chatterley-Whitfield Collieries Ltd* [1949] 1 All ER 1094, HL.

A reduction of capital which is not in accordance with class rights is regular if it is effectually sanctioned in accordance with the articles: *Re Holders Investment Trust Ltd* [1971] 2 All ER 289 at 291 (per Megarry J). There is an effectual sanction to the modification of class rights if those holding a sufficient majority of that class vote in favour of the modification in the *bona fide* belief that they are acting in the interests of the general body of members of that class: ibid. The burden of proof depends on whether there is or is not any such sanction: ibid. If there is, the court will confirm the reduction unless the opposition proves that it is unfair: ibid. If there is not, the court will confirm the reduction only if it is proved to be fair: ibid.

Where creditors are affected

Where the proposed reduction of share capital involves either diminution of liability in respect of unpaid share capital or the payment to any shareholder of any paid-up share capital, and in any other case if the court so directs, every creditor of the company who at the date fixed by the court is entitled to any debt or claim which, if that date were the commencement of the winding up of the company, would be admissible in proof against the company, is entitled to object to the reduction: Companies Act 1985, s. 136 (2), (3). (*See* COMMENCEMENT OF THE WINDING UP).

The court must settle a list of creditors entitled to object, and for that purpose must ascertain, as far as possible without requiring an application from any creditor, the names of those creditors and the nature and amount of their debts or claims, and may publish notices fixing a day or days within which creditors not entered on the list are to claim to be entered or are to be excluded from the right of objecting to the reduction of capital: Companies Act 1985, s. 136 (4).

If a creditor entered on the list, whose debt or claim is not discharged or has not determined, does not consent to the reduction, the court, may, if it thinks fit, dispense with his consent on the company securing payment of his debt or claim by appropriating (as the court may direct)

(i) if the company admits the full amount of the debt or claim or, though not admitting it is willing to provide for it, then the full amount of the debt or claim;

(ii) if the company does not admit, and is not willing to provide for, the full amount of the debt or claim, or if the amount is contingent or not ascertained, then an amount fixed by the court after the like enquiry and adjudication as if the company were being wound up by the court: ibid., s. 136 (5).

If a proposed reduction of share capital involves either the diminution of any liability in respect of unpaid share capital or the payment to any shareholder of any paid-up share capital, the court may, if, having regard to any special circumstances of the case, it thinks proper to do so, direct that the above provisions are not to apply as regards any class or any classes of creditors: ibid., s. 136 (6).

The special circumstances to justify such a direction dispensing with settling the list of creditors must be such that the court is satisfied that, as far as can be reasonably foreseen, the relevant creditors will not be adversely affected by the reduction of capital: *Re Lucania Temperance Billiard Halls (London) Ltd* [1965] 3 All ER 879 at 882 (per Buckley J). The circumstances must be such that broadly speaking the creditors affected will at least be no worse off than if they were permitted to attend on the application for confirmation of the reduction of capital and to object: ibid. In that case the court could only override a creditor's objection if the company secured payment of his debt or claim by appropriating a sufficient fund to satisfy the requirements of s. 136 (5): ibid.

Powers of the court

The court, if satisfied, with respect to every creditor of the company who is entitled under the above provisions to object to the reduction of capital that either his consent to the reduction has been obtained or his debt or claim has been discharged or has determined, or has been secured, may make an order confirming the reduction on such terms and conditions as it thinks fit: ibid., s. 137 (1).

Where the court so orders, it may, if for any special reason it thinks proper to do so, make an order directing that the company must during such period (commencing on or at any time after the date of the order) as is specified in the order, add to its name as the last words 'as reduced': ibid., s. 137 (2) (a). The court may also make an order requiring the company to publish (as the court directs) the reasons for reduction of capital or such other information in regard to it as the court thinks expedient with a view to giving proper information to the public, and (if the court thinks fit) the causes which led to the reduction: ibid., s. 68 (2).

Where a company is ordered to add to its name the words 'and reduced', those words are deemed to be part of the company's name until the expiration of the period specified in the order: ibid., s. 137 (3).

Registration of the order and minute of reduction

The Registrar of Companies, on production to him of an order of the court confirming the reduction of a company's share capital, and the delivery to him of a copy of the order and of a minute (approved by the court) showing, with respect to the share capital of the company as altered by the order, (i) the amount of the share capital, (ii) the number of shares into which it is to be divided, and the amount of each share, and (iii) the amount (if any) at the date of the registration deemed to be paid up on each share, must register the order and the minute: ibid., s. 138 (1). On the registration of the order and minute, and not before, the resolution for reducing share capital as confirmed by the order so registered takes effect: ibid., s. 138 (2). Notice of the registration must be published in such manner as the court may direct: ibid., s. 138 (3). The Registrar must give a certificate of the registration of the order and minute: ibid., s. 138 (4). His certificate is conclusive evidence that all the requirements of the Act with respect to the reduction of share capital have been complied with, and that the company's share capital is such as is stated in the minute: ibid., s. 138 (4). The minute, when registered, is deemed to be substituted for the corresponding part of the company's memorandum, and is valid and alterable as if it has been originally contained in it: ibid., s. 138 (5). (*See* MEMORANDUM OF ASSOCIATION).

Where the court makes an order confirming a reduction of a public company's capital which has the effect of bringing the nominal value of the company's allotted share capital below the authorised minimum, the Registrar must not register the order unless the court otherwise directs or the company is first re-registered as a private company: Companies Act 1985, s. 139 (1), (2). (*See* AUTHORISED MINIMUM: PUBLIC COMPANY; RE-REGISTRATION OF COMPANY). The court may authorise the company to be re-registered as a private company without its having passed a special resolution: Companies Act 1985, s. 139 (3). Where that authority is given, the court must specify in the order the alteration in the company's memorandum and articles to be made in connection with that re-registration: ibid., s. 139 (3).

Liability of members

Where a company's share capital is reduced a member of the company (past or present) is not liable in respect of any share to any call or contribution exceeding in amount the difference (if any) between the amount of the share as fixed by the minute and the amount paid on the share or the reduced amount (if any) which is deemed to have been paid on it, as the case may be: ibid., s. 140 (1). (*See* CALL; CONTRIBUTORY).

But if any creditor, entitled in respect of any debt or claim to object to the reduction of share capital, is, by reason of his ignorance of the proceedings for reduction, or of their nature and effect with respect to his claim, not entered in the list of creditors, and, after the reduction, the company is unable to pay the amount of his debt or claim, then every person who was a member of the company at the date of the registration of the order for reduction and minute, is liable to contribute for the payment of the debt or claim an amount not exceeding the amounts which he would have been liable to contribute if the company had commenced to be wound up on the day before that date: Companies Act 1985, s. 140 (3).

Further, if the company is wound up, the court, on the application of the creditor in question and proof of his ignorance, may (if it thinks fit) settle a list of persons liable to contribute, and make and enforce calls and orders on the contributories settled on the list, as if they were ordinary contributories in a winding up: ibid., s. 140 (4).

Nothing in the above provisions affects the rights of the contributories among themselves: ibid., s. 140 (5).

Penalty for concealing name of creditor etc.

If an officer of the company

(a) wilfully conceals the name of any creditor entitled to object to the reduction; or

(b) wilfully misrepresents the nature or amount of the debt or claim of any creditor; or

(c) aids, abets or is privy to any such concealment or misrepresentation,

he is liable on conviction on indictment to a fine, and on summary conviction to a fine not exceeding the statutory maximum: ibid., ss. 141, 730 and Sch. 24.

Register of directors and secretaries. Every company must keep at its registered office a register of its directors and secretaries: Companies Act 1985, s. 288 (1).

The register must contain the following particulars with respect to each director:—(a) in the case of an individual, his present Christian name and surname, any former Christian name or surname, his usual residential address, his nationality, his business occupation, particulars of any other directorships held by him, and in the case of a company subject to s. 293, the date of his birth; and (b) in the case of a corporation, its corporate name and registered or principal office: ibid., s. 289 (1).

The register must contain the following particulars with respect to the secretary or, where there are joint secretaries, with respect to each of them:—(a) in the case of an individual, his present Christian name and surname, any former Christian name or surname and his usual residential address; and (b) in the case of a corporation or a Scottish firm, its corporate or firm name and registered or principal office: ibid., s. 290 (1). But where all the partners in a firm are joint secretaries, the name and principal office of the firm may be stated instead of those particulars: ibid., s. 290 (2).

For the above purposes a shadow director is deemed a director and officer of the company: ibid., s. 288 (6). (*See* SHADOW DIRECTOR). The expression 'Christian name' includes a forename: ibid., s. 289 (2) (a). In the case of a peer or person usually known by a title different from his surname, the expression 'surname' means that title: ibid., s. 289 (2) (b). References to a former Christian name or surname do not include (i) in the case of a peer or a person usually known by a British title different from his surname, the name by which he was known previous to the adoption of or succession to that title; or (ii) in the case of any person, a former Christian name or surname where that name or surname was changed or disused before the person bearing the name attained the age of 18 years, or has been changed or disused for a period of not less than 20 years; or (iii) in the case of a married woman, the name or surname by which she was known previous to the marriage: ibid., s. 289 (2) (c).

The company must within 14 days from the occurrence of (a) any change among its directors or in its secretary, or (b) any change in the particulars contained in the register, send to the Registrar of Companies a notification in the prescribed form of the change and of the date on which it occurred: ibid., s. 288 (2). A notification of a person having become a director or secretary, or one of joint secretaries, of the company must contain a consent, signed by that person, to act in the relevant capacity: ibid., s. 288 (2).

The register must during business hours (subject to such reasonable restrictions as the company may by its articles or in general meeting impose, so that not less than 2 hours in each day be allowed for inspection) be open to the inspection of any member of the company without charge and of any other person on payment of 5p or such less sum as the company may prescribe, for each inspection: ibid., s. 288 (3).

If an inspection is refused or if default is made in complying with s. 288 (1) or (2), the company and every officer of the company who is in default are liable on summary conviction to a fine not exceeding one-fifth of the statutory maximum or on conviction after continued contravention, to a daily default fine not exceeding one-fiftieth of the statutory maximum: ibid., ss. 288 (4), 730 and Sch. 24.

In the case of a refusal, the court may by order compel an immediate inspection of the register: ibid., s. 288 (5).

The Registrar of Companies must cause to be published in the *Gazette* notice of the receipt by him of any notification of a change among the directors of a company: ibid., s. 711 (1) (c). The notice must state the name of the company, the description of the document and the date of receipt: ibid., s. 711 (1). A company is not entitled to rely against other persons on any change among the company's directors if the event had not been officially notified at the material time and is not shown by the company to have been known at that time to the person concerned, or if the material time fell on or before the 15th day after the date of official notification (or, where the 15th day was a non-business day, on or before the next day that was not), and it is shown that the person concerned was unavoidably prevented from knowing of the event at that time: ibid., s. 42 (1). 'Non-business day' means a Saturday or Sunday, Christmas Day, Good Friday and any other day which, is a bank holiday in the part of Great Britain where the company is registered: ibid., s. 42 (2) (b). (*See* BANK HOLIDAY).

Register of directors' shareholdings. (*See* DIRECTORS' SHAREHOLDINGS).

Register of disqualification orders. (*See* DISQUALIFICATION ORDER).

Register of members. A list of the members of the company.

Every company must keep a register of its members and enter in it (a) the names and addresses of the members, and in the case of a company having a share capital a statement of the shares held by each member, distinguishing each share by its number (so long as the share has a number) and, where the company has more than one class of issued shares, by its class, and of the amount paid or agreed to be considered as paid on the shares of each member; (b) the date at which each person was entered in the register as a member; and (c) the date at which any person ceased to be a member: Companies Act 1985, s. 352 (1), (2), (3) (a). But where the company has converted any of its shares into stock and given notice of the conversion to the Registrar of Companies, the register must show the amount and class of stock held by each member instead of the amount of shares and the particulars relating to shares specified above: ibid., s. 352 (3) (b). (*See* CONVERSION OF SHARES INTO STOCK).

A company's register of members must be kept at its registered office: Companies Act 1985, s. 353 (1). But if the making up of it is done at another office of the company, it may be kept there: ibid., s. 353 (1) (a). Further, if the company arranges with some other person for the making up of the register to be undertaken on its behalf by that other person, it may be kept at the office of the other at which the work is done: ibid., s. 353 (1) (b). But it must not be kept at a place outside England: ibid., s. 353 (1). Every company must send a notice in the prescribed form to the Registrar of Companies of the place where its register of members is kept, and of any change in that place: ibid., s. 353 (2). Where a company makes default in keeping a register of its members, or makes default for 14 days in sending the notice, the company and every officer who is in default are liable on summary conviction to a fine not exceeding one-fifth of the statutory maximum or, on conviction after continued contravention, to a daily default fine not exceeding one-fiftieth of the statutory maximum: ibid., ss. 353 (4), 730 and Sch. 24.

Every company having more than 50 members must, unless the register of members is in such form as to constitute in itself an index, keep an index of the names of the members of the company, and must within 14 days after the date on which any alteration is made in the register of members, make any necessary alteration in the index: ibid., s. 354 (1). The index must, in respect of each member, contain a sufficient indication to enable the account of that member in the register to be readily found: ibid., s. 354 (2). The index must be at all times kept in the same place as the register of members: ibid., s. 354 (3). If default is made by the company in complying with the above requirements, the company and every officer of the company who is in default are liable on summary conviction to a fine not exceeding one-fifth of the statutory maximum, or, on conviction after continued contravention, to a daily default fine not exceeding one-fiftieth of the statutory maximum: ibid., ss. 354 (4), 730 and Sch. 24.

On the issue of a share warrant the company must strike out of its register of members the name of the member then entered in it as holding the shares specified in the warrant as if he had ceased to be a member, and must enter in the register the following particulars:—(a) the fact of the issue of the warrant; (b) a statement of the shares included in the warrant, distinguishing each share by its number so long as the share has a number; and (c) the date of the issue of the warrant: ibid., s. 355 (1). The bearer of a share warrant is, subject to the company's articles, entitled, on surrendering it for cancellation, to have his name entered as a member in the register of members: ibid., s. 355 (2). The company is responsible for any loss incurred by any person by reason of the company entering in the register the name of the bearer of a share warrant in respect of the shares specified in it without the warrant being surrendered and cancelled: ibid., s. 355 (3). Until the warrant is surrendered, the particulars specified above are deemed to be the particulars required to be entered in the register of members, and, on the surrender, the date of the surrender must be entered: ibid., s. 355 (4). The bearer of a share warrant may, if the articles of the company so provide, be deemed a member of the company, either to the full extent or for any purposes defined in the articles: ibid., s. 355 (5). (*See* SHARE WARRANT).

The register, and index of the names, of the members of a company must during business hours (subject to such reasonable restrictions as the company in general meeting may impose, so that not less than 2 hours in each day is allowed for inspection) be open to the inspection of any member of the company without charge and of any other person on payment of 5p, or such less sum as the company may prescribe, for each inspection: ibid., s. 356 (1), (2), (4) (a). Any member or other person may require a copy of the register or any part of it on payment of 10p, or such less sum as the company may prescribe, for every 100 words or fractional part of 100 words required to be copied: ibid., s. 356 (4). The company must cause any copy so required by a person to be sent to him within 10 days beginning on the day next following that on which the requirement is received by the company: ibid., s. 356 (3). If any inspection is refused, or any copy is not sent within the proper period, the company and every officer who is in default are liable on summary conviction to a fine not exceeding one-fifth of the statutory maximum: ibid., ss. 356 (5), 730 and Sch. 24. In the case of such refusal or default the court may by order compel an immediate inspection of the register and index, or direct that the copies required be sent to the persons requiring them: ibid., s. 356 (6).

Where the register of members is kept at the office of some person other than the company, and by reason of any default of his the company fails to comply with s. 353 (2), s. 354 (3) or s. 356 or with any requirement of the Act as to the production of the register, that other person is liable to the same penalties as if he were an officer of the company who was in default: ibid., s. 357. The power of the court under s. 356 (6) extends to the making of orders against that other person: ibid., s. 357.

A company may, on giving notice by advertisement in a newspaper circulating in the district in which the company's registered office is situated, close the register of members for any time or times not exceeding in the whole 30 days in each year: ibid., s. 358.

If (a) the name of any person is, without sufficient cause, entered in or omitted from a company's register of members, or (b) default is made or unnecessary delay takes place in entering on the register the fact of any person having ceased to be a member, the person aggrieved or any member of the company, or the company, may apply to the court for rectification of the register: ibid., s. 359 (1). The court may either refuse the application or may order rectification of the register and payment by the company of any damages sustained by any party aggrieved: ibid., s. 359 (2).

Thus, applications may be made, e.g. (i) where a person has been induced by a misrepresentation to take shares (*Re Electrobes Co Ltd* [1906] WN 147), and (ii) to determine the right of a liquidator to place a person's name on the list of contributories (*Re Barangah Oil Refining Co, Arnot's Case* (1887) 36 Ch D 702).

On such an application the court may decide any question relating to the title of a person who is a party to the application to have his name entered in or omitted from the register, whether the question arises between members or alleged members on the one hand and the company on the other hand, and generally may decide any question necessary or expedient to be decided for rectification of the register: Companies Act 1985, s. 359 (3). In the case of a company required by the Act to send a list of its members to the Registrar of Companies, the court, when making an order for the rectification of the register, must by its order direct notice of the rectification to be given to the Registrar: ibid., s. 359 (4).

No notice of any trust, expressed, implied or constructive, must be entered on the register or is receivable by the Registrar of Companies: ibid., s. 360.

The register of members is *prima facie* evidence of any matters directed or authorised by the Act to be inserted in it: ibid., s. 118.

A company having a share capital whose objects include the transaction of business in any of the countries or territories specified in Part I of Sch. 14 to the Act may cause to be kept in any such country or territory in which it transacts business a branch register of members resident in that country or territory: ibid., s. 362 (1). Such a branch register is to be known as an 'overseas branch register': ibid., s. 362 (2). (*See* OVERSEAS BRANCH REGISTER).

Registered number of company. An official number given to the company.

The Registrar of Companies must allocate to every company a number known as 'the company's registered number': Companies Act 1985, s. 705 (1). He may, in addition, allocate to any company a letter which is then deemed for all purposes to be part of the registered number: ibid., s. 705 (1). The word 'company' includes (i) an oversea company, and (ii) any incorporated or unincorporated body to which any provision of the Act applies by virtue of s. 718: ibid., s. 705 (2).

Registered office. An office of the company to which all communications and notices may be addressed.

A company must at all times have a registered office: Companies Act 1985, s. 287 (1). The intended situation of the registered office on incorporation must be specified in the statement delivered prior to incorporation of the company: ibid., s. 10 (6). Notice in the prescribed form of any change in the situation of a company's registered office must be given within 14 days of the change to the Registrar of Companies, who must record the new situation: ibid., s. 287 (2). If default is made in complying with s. 287 (1) or s. 287 (2), the company and every officer of the company who is in default are liable on summary conviction to a fine not exceeding one-fifth of the statutory maximum or, on conviction after continued contravention, to a daily default fine not exceeding one-fiftieth of the statutory maximum: ibid., ss. 287 (3), 730 and Sch. 24.

The memorandum of every company must state whether its registered office is to be situate in England and Wales or Scotland: ibid., s. 2 (1) (b).

The Registrar of Companies must cause to be published in the *Gazette* notice of the receipt by him of any notice of a change in the situation of a company's registered office: ibid., s. 711 (1) (n). A company is not entitled to rely against other persons (as regards service of any document on the company) on any change in the situation of the registered office if the event had not been officially notified at the material time and is not shown by the company to have been known at that time to the person concerned, or if the material time fell on or before the 15th day after the date of official notification (or, where the 15th day was a non-business day, on or before the next day that was not), and it is shown that the person concerned was unavoidably prevented from knowing of the event at that time: ibid., s. 42 (1). 'Non-business day' means a Saturday or Sunday, Christmas Day, Good Friday and any other day which is a bank holiday in the part of Great Britain where the company is registered: ibid., s. 42 (2) (b). *See* BANK HOLIDAY.

Every company must have the address of its registered office mentioned in all business letters and order forms of the company: ibid., s. 351 (1) (b). If a company fails to comply with this sub-section, the company and every officer of the company who is in default are liable on summary conviction to a fine not exceeding one-fifth of the statutory maximum: ibid., ss. 351 (5) (a), 730 and Sch. 24.

Registered office clause. A clause in the memorandum of association stating whether the company's registered office is to be situate in England or Scotland, and thus fixing the nationality of the company. (*See* MEMORANDUM OF ASSOCIATION: REGISTERED OFFICE).

Registration of charges. The entry of the details of an incumbrance created over the property of a company

(a) in the register kept by the Registrar of Companies; or

(b) in the register kept by the company itself.

(a) *Registration with Registrar of Companies*

TYPES OF CHARGES TO BE REGISTERED: A charge of the type mentioned below created by the company so far as any security on the company's property or undertaking is conferred by it, is void as against the liquidator and any creditor of the company unless the prescribed particulars of the charge together with the instrument (if any) by which the charge is created or evidenced, are delivered to or received by the Registrar of Companies within 21 days after the date of its creation, but without prejudice to any contract or obligation for repayment of the money secured by it: Companies Act 1985, s. 395 (1), (2). When a charge becomes void, the money secured by it becomes immediately payable: ibid., s. 395 (2).

The charges concerned are (i) a charge for the purpose of securing any issue of debentures (*see* DEBENTURE); (ii) a charge on uncalled share capital of a company (*see* UNCALLED SHARE CAPITAL); (iii) a charge created or evidence by an instrument which, if executed by an individual, would require registration as a bill of sale; (iv) a charge on land (wherever situated) or any interest in land, but not including a charge for any rent or other periodical sum issuing out of the land; (v) a charge on book debts of the company; (vi) a floating charge on the company's undertaking or property (*see* FLOATING CHARGE); (vii) a charge on calls made but not paid (*see* CALL); (viii) a charge on a ship or aircraft, or any share in a ship; (ix) a charge on goodwill, on a patent or a licence under a patent, on a trademark or on a copyright or a licence under a copyright (*see* GOODWILL): Companies Act 1985, s. 396 (1).

When a company acquires property which is already subject to a charge, it must send to the Registrar of Companies particulars of the charge and a copy of the instrument creating it: ibid., s. 400 (1), (2).

Neither a vendor's lien (*London and Cheshire Insurance Co Ltd v Lapagreno Property Co Ltd* [1971] 1 All ER 766) nor a solicitor's lien (*Brunton v Electrical Engineering Corporation* [1892] 1 Ch 434) requires to be registered, for they arise by operation of law and are not charges 'created' by a company.

Where a series of debentures containing any charge to the benefit of which the debenture holders of that series are entitled *pari passu* is created by a company, it is sufficient if the following particulars in the prescribed form are delivered to or received by the Registrar of Companies

(a) the total amount secured by the whole series;

(b) the dates of the resolutions authorising the issue of the series and the date of the covering deed (if any) by which the security is created or defined;

(c) a general description of the property charged; and

(d) the names of the trustees (if any) for the debenture holders: ibid., s. 397 (1). (*See* DEBENTURE).

The deed containing the charge or, if there is no such deed, one of the debentures of the series must also be sent to the Registrar of Companies with the above particulars: Companies Act 1985, s. 397 (1).

DUTY OF COMPANY TO REGISTER CHARGES: It is a company's duty to send to the Registrar of Companies for registration the particulars of every charge created by the company and of the issues of debentures of a series requiring registration: ibid., s. 399 (1). But registration of any charge may be effected on the application of any person interested in it: ibid., s. 399 (1). Where registration is effected on the application of some person other than the company, he is entitled to recover from the company the amount of any fees properly paid by him to the Registrar of Companies on registration: ibid., s. 399 (2). If a company fails to comply with s. 399 (1), then, unless the registration has been effected on the application of some other person, the company and every officer of the company who is in default are liable on conviction on indictment to a fine, and on summary conviction to a fine not exceeding the statutory maximum, or, on conviction after continued contravention, to a daily default fine not exceeding one-tenth of the statutory maximum: ibid., ss. 399 (3), 730 and Sch. 24.

REGISTER OF CHARGES TO BE KEPT BY REGISTRAR OF COMPANIES: The Registrar of Companies must keep, with respect to each company, a register in the prescribed form of all the charges requiring registration: ibid., s. 401 (1). He must enter in the register

(a) in the case of a charge to the benefit of which the holders of a series of debentures are entitled:—

   (i) the total amount secured by the whole series;

   (ii) the dates of the resolutions authorising the issue of the series and the date of the covering deed, if any, by which the security is created or defined;

   (iii) a general description of the property charged; and

   (iv) the names of the trustees (if any) for the debenture holders. (*See* DEBENTURE).

(b) in the case of any other charge:—

   (i) if it is a charge created by the company, the date of its creation, and if the charge was on existing on property acquired by the company, the date of the acquisition of the property;

(ii) the amount secured by the charge;

(iii) short particulars of the property charged; and

(iv) the persons entitled to the charge: ibid., s. 401 (1).

The Registrar must give a certificate of the registration of any charge stating the amount secured by it: ibid., s. 401 (2). The certificate is conclusive that the requirements as to registration have been complied with: ibid., s. 401 (2).

Thus, the fact that the date has been wrongly stated on the charge and that the charge has been registered more than 21 days after its creation does not make it void as against the liquidator if the Registrar has given a certificate: *Re Eric Holmes Property Ltd* [1965] 2 All ER 333. Similarly, the certificate is conclusive evidence that the prescribed particulars of the charge have been delivered to him, and the charge will be valid even though the particulars are not accurate: *Re Mechanisations (Eaglescliffe) Ltd* [1964] 3 All ER 840. Again, where a mortgagee has mis-stated the date of the creation of the charge, the certificate is still conclusive: *Re C. L. Nye Ltd* [1970] 3 All ER 1061, CA.

The register is open to inspection by any person: Companies Act 1985, s. 401 (3).

RECTIFICATION OF REGISTER: The court, on being satisfied that the omission to register a charge within the time allowed or that the omission or mis-statement of any particular with respect to any charge was accidental or due to inadvertence or to some other sufficient cause, or is not of a nature to prejudice the position of creditors or shareholders or that on other grounds it is just and equitable to grant relief, may, on the application of the company or any person interested, and on such terms and conditions as seem to the court just and expedient, order that the time for registration shall be extended, or, as the case may be, that the omission or mis-statement shall be rectified: ibid., s. 404 (1), (2). See e.g. *Re Heathstar Properties Ltd (No. 2)* [1966] 1 All ER 1000.

(b) *Registration with company*

Every company must cause a copy of every instrument creating a charge requiring registration to be kept at its registered office: Companies Act 1985, s. 406 (1). In the case of a series of uniform debentures a copy of one debenture of the series is sufficient: ibid., s. 406 (2).

Every limited company must keep at its registered office a register of charges and enter in it all charges specifically affecting property of the company and all floating charges on the undertaking or any property of the company, giving in each case a short description of the property charged, the amount of the charge, and, except in the case of securities to bearer, the names of the persons entitled to it: ibid., s. 407 (1), (2). If an officer of the company knowingly and wilfully authorises or permits the omission of any entry to be made, he is liable on conviction on indictment to a fine, and on summary conviction to a fine not exceeding the statutory maximum: ibid., ss. 407 (3), 730 and Sch. 24.

The copies of instruments creating any charge requiring registration with the Registrar of Comanies and the company's register of charges must be open during business hours (but subject to such reasonable restrictions as the company in general meeting may impose so that not less than 2 hours in each day be allowed for inspection) to the inspection of any creditor or member of the company without fee: ibid., s. 408 (1). The register of charges must also be open to the inspection of any other person on payment of such fee, not exceeding 5p for each inspection as the company may prescribe: ibid., s. 408 (2). If inspection of the copies or register is refused, every officer of the company who is in default is liable on summary conviction to a fine not exceeding one-fifth of the statutory maximum or, on conviction after continued contravention, to a default fine not exceeding one-fiftieth of the statutory maximum: ibid., ss. 408 (3), 730 and Sch. 24. If any such refusal occurs, the court may by order compel an immediate inspection of the copies or register: ibid., s. 408 (4).

Registration of company. The process leading to the entry of a company in the index of companies kept by the Registrar of Companies and the issue by him of a certificate of incorporation. (*See* CERTIFICATE OF INCORPORATION).

The memorandum and the articles, if any, must be delivered to the Registrar of Companies, and he must retain and register them: Companies Act 1985, ss. 10 (1), 12 (2).

With the memorandum there must be delivered a statement in the prescribed form containing the names and particulars of
(a) the person who is or the persons who are to be the first director or directors of the company (see DIRECTOR); and
(b) the person who is, or the persons who are to be the first secretary or joint secretaries of the company (see SECRETARY): Companies Act 1985, s. 10 (2).

The Registrar must not register the memorandum unless he is satisfied that all the requirements of the Act in respect of registration and of matters precedent and incidental to it have been complied with: Companies Act 1985, s. 12 (1). A statutory declaration in the prescribed form by a solicitor engaged in the formation of a company, or by a person named as a director or secretary of the company in the statement mentioned above that the requirements have been complied with, must be delivered to the Registrar: ibid., s. 12 (3). The Registrar may accept such a declaration as sufficient evidence of compliance: ibid., s. 12 (3).

On the registration of a company's memorandum, the Registrar must issue a certificate of incorporation: ibid., s. 13 (1). (*See* CERTIFICATE OF INCORPORATION).

A public company may be re-registered as a private company and *vice versa.* A limited company may be re-registered as an unlimited company and *vice versa.* (*See* RE-REGISTRATION OF COMPANY).

Re-registration of company. The process of making an alteration in the entry of a company in the index of companies kept by the Registrar of Companies, such alteration being brought about by a change in the status of a company.

Private companies may be re-registered as public companies: Companies Act 1985, ss. 43–48. Public companies may be re-registered as private companies: ibid., ss. 53–55.

Limited companies may be re-registered as unlimited companies: ibid., ss. 49, 50. Unlimited companies may be re-registered as limited companies: ibid., ss. 51, 52.

Reserve, capital redemption. *See* CAPITAL REDEMPTION RESERVE.

Reserves, undistributable. *See* UNDISTRIBUTABLE RESERVES.

Resolution. A decision of (a) the members of the company; or (b) the board of directors. Resolutions may be (i) ordinary resolutions (*see* ORDINARY RESOLUTION); (ii) special resolutions (*see* SPECIAL RESOLUTION); and (iii) extraordinary resolution (*see* EXTRAORDINARY RESOLUTION).

In certain circumstances a resolution by the members may be required by them to be circulated by a company. (*See* CIRCULATION OF MEMBERS' RESOLUTIONS).

A copy of every special resolution and of every extraordinary resolution must, within 15 days of its being passed, be forwarded to the Registrar of Companies and must be recorded by him: Companies Act 1985, s. 380 (1). (*See* EXTRAORDINARY RESOLUTION; SPECIAL RESOLUTION).

Resolution, circulation of members'. *See* CIRCULATION OF MEMBERS' RESOLUTION.

Resolution, extraordinary. *See* EXTRAORDINARY RESOLUTION.

Resolution, ordinary. *See* ORDINARY RESOLUTION.

Resolution, special. *See* SPECIAL RESOLUTION.

Resolution for reducing share capital. *See* REDUCTION OF CAPITAL.

Resolution for voluntary winding up means a resolution under any of the provisions of the Companies Act 1985, s. 572 (1), which provides that a company may be wound up voluntarily

(a) when the period (if any) fixed for the duration of the company by

the articles expires, or the event (if any) occurs, on the occurrence
of which the articles provide that the company is to be dissolved,
and the company in general meeting has passed a resolution
requiring the company to be wound up voluntarily;

(b) if the company resolves by special resolution that the company be
wound up voluntarily;

(c) if the company resolves by extraordinary resolution to the effect
that it cannot by reason of its liabilities continue its business, and
that it is advisable to wind up: Companies Act 1985, s. 572 (2).
(*See* EXTRAORDINARY RESOLUTION; SPECIAL RESOLUTION).

Restoration to register. The re-insertion of the name of a company,
which has been struck off the register. (*See* STRIKING OFF REGISTER).

If a company or any member or creditor of it feels aggrieved by the
company having been struck off the register, the court on an
application made by the company or member or creditor before the
expiration of 20 years from publication in the *Gazette* of notice
that the company has been dissolved, may, if satisfied that the
company was at the time of the striking off carrying on business or in
operation, or otherwise that it is just that the company be restored to
the register, order the company's name to be restored: Companies Act
1985, s. 653 (1), (2).

On an office copy of the order being delivered to the Registrar of
Companies for registration, the company is deemed to have continued
in existence as if its name had not been struck off; and the court may by
the order give such directions and make such provisions as seem just
for placing the company and all other persons in the same position (as
nearly as may be) as if the name of the company had not been struck
off: ibid., s. 353 (2).

In order to qualify as a petitioner under the above provisions it must
be shown that at the date when the company was dissolved, he was a
member or creditor; anyone who purported to become a member or
creditor of the company afterwards, whether in ignorance or
otherwise of the dissolution of the company, is not a person so
qualified: *Re New Timbiqui Gold Mines Ltd* [1961] 1 All ER 865. A
'creditor' includes a person claiming damages under the Fatal
Accidents Act 1976: *Re Harvest Lane Motor Bodies Ltd* [1968] 2 All ER
1012. The word 'member' is construed as extending to the personal
representative of a deceased member although not on the register: *Re
Bayswater Trading Co Ltd* [1970] 1 All ER 608.

Where a company is restored to the register, the court has no
jurisdiction under s. 653 or any other section to impose a penalty other
than costs as a condition for the company's restoration to the register:
Re Moses and Cohen Ltd [1957] 3 All ER 232. The court has power to
order that, in the case of creditors whose claims were not statute-barred

at the date of the dissolution of the company, the period between then and the date of the restoration of its name to the register shall not be counted for the purpose of any statute of limitations: *Re Huntingdon Poultry Services Ltd* [1969] 1 All ER 328. The court is not empowered to make an order that it is 'to be without prejudice to any remedy which any creditor who became such on or after the date of dissolution might otherwise have against any person prior to the date of the order taking effect': *Re Lindsay Bowman Ltd* [1969] 3 All ER 601.

Retiring partner. A partner who leaves a partnership.

A partner who retires from a firm does not thereby cease to be liable for partnership debts or obligations incurred before his retirement: Partnership Act 1890, s. 17 (2). See *Court v Berlin* [1897] 2 QB 396, CA.

A retiring partner may be discharged from any existing liabilities by an agreement to that effect between himself and the members of the firm as newly constituted and the creditors, and this agreement may be either express or inferred as a fact from the course of dealing between the creditors and the firm as newly constituted: Partnership Act 1890, s. 17 (3).

Such a tripartite agreement is known as a 'novation'.

Where any member of a firm has ceased to be a partner, and the continuing partners carry on the business of the firm with its capital or assets without any final settlement of accounts as between the firm and the retiring partner, then, in the absence of any agreement to the contrary, the retiring partner is entitled at his option to such share of the profits made since the dissolution as the court may find to be attributable to the use of his share of the partnership assets, or to interest at the rate of 5 per cent per annum on the amount of his share of the partnership assets: Partnership Act 1890, s. 42 (1).

But where by the partnership contract an option is given to the continuing partners to purchase the interest of a retiring partner, and that option is duly exercised, the retiring partner is not entitled to any further or other share of profits: ibid., s. 42 (2). But if any partner assuming to act in exercise of the option does not in all material respects comply with its terms, he is liable to account to the retiring partner as above: ibid., s. 42 (2).

On the retirement of a partner, any partner may publicly notify it, and may require the other partner or partners to concur for that purpose in all necessary or proper acts, if any, which cannot be done without his or their concurrence: ibid., s. 37.

Return as to allotments. A return delivered to the Registrar of Companies showing what allotments of shares a company has made. (*See* ALLOTMENT).

When a company limited by shares or a company limited by

guarantee and having a share capital makes an allotment of its shares, the company must within 1 month thereafter deliver to the Registrar of Companies for registration

(a) a return of the allotments (in the prescribed form) stating the number and nominal amount of the shares comprised in the allotment, the names, addresses and descriptions of the allottees, and the amount (if any) paid or due and payable on each share, whether on account of the nominal value of the share or by way of premium; and

(b) in the case of shares allotted as fully or partly paid up otherwise than in cash, (i) a contract in writing constituting the title of the allottee to the allotment together with any contract of sale, or for services or other consideration in respect of which that allotment was made (such contracts being duly stamped) and (ii) a return stating the number and nominal amount of shares so allotted, the extent to which they are to be treated as paid up, and the consideration for which they have been allotted: Companies Act 1985, s. 88 (1), (2).

Where such a contract is not reduced to writing, the company must within 1 month after the allotment deliver to the Registrar of Companies for registration the prescribed particulars of the contract stamped with the same stamp duty as would have been payable if the contract had been reduced to writing: ibid., s. 88 (3).

If default is made in complying with the above provisions, every officer of the company who is in default is liable on conviction on indictment to a fine, and on summary conviction to a fine not exceeding the statutory maximum, or, on conviction after continued contravention, to a daily default fine not exceeding one-tenth of the statutory maximum: ibid., ss. 88 (5), 730 and Sch. 24. But in case of default in delivering to the Registrar of Companies within 1 month after the allotment any document required to be delivered, the company or any officer liable for the default may apply to the court for relief; and the court, if satisfied that the omission to deliver the document was accidental or due to inadvertence, or that it is just and equitable to grant relief, may make an order extending the time for the delivery of the document for such period as the court thinks proper: ibid., s. 88 (6).

Rights issue. A right given to a shareholder to subscribe for further shares in the company usually at a price lower than the market price of the existing shares, the number usually being in proportion to the shareholder's present shareholding e.g. a right to subscribe for 1 new share for every 5 which he holds.

Rotation of directors. An arrangement whereby a proportion of the directors retires each year.

Table A, art. 73 states: 'At the first annual general meeting all the directors shall retire from office, and at every subsequent annual general meeting one-third of the directors who are subject to retirement by rotation, or if their number is not 3 or a multiple of 3, the number nearest to one-third shall retire from office; but if there is only one director who is subject to retirement by rotation, he shall retire.'

Subject to the provisions of the Act, the directors to retire by rotation shall be those who have been longest in office since their last appointment or reappointment, but as between persons who became or were last reappointed directors on the same day those to retire shall (unless they otherwise agree among themselves) be determined by lot: Table A, art. 74.

If the company, at the meeting at which a director retires by rotation, does not fill the vacancy, the retiring director shall, if willing to act, be deemed to have been reappointed unless at the meeting it is resolved not to fill the vacancy or unless a resolution for the reappointment of the director is put to the meeting and lost: ibid., art. 75.

Where the articles provide that the number nearest but not exceeding one-third shall retire, and the number of directors is reduced to two, neither need retire: *Re Moseley and Sons Ltd* [1939] 2 all ER 791.

Royal British Bank v Turquand, Rule in. *See* RULE IN ROYAL BRITISH BANK V TURQUAND.

Rule in Foss v Harbottle. A rule that an individual shareholder cannot sue for a wrong done to the company: *Foss v Harbottle* (1843) 2 Hare 461. 'The Rule in *Foss v Harbottle* . . . comes to no more than this. First, the proper plaintiff in an action in respect of a wrong alleged to be done to a company . . . is *prima facie* the company . . . itself. Secondly, where the alleged wrong is a transaction which might be made binding on the company . . . and on all its members by a simple majority of the members, no individual member of the company is allowed to maintain an action in respect of that matter for the simple reason that if a mere majority of the members of the company . . . is in favour of what has been done, then *cadit quaestio*.': *Edwards v Halliwell* [1950] 2 All ER 1064 at 1066, CA (per Jenkins LJ). Thus, an individual shareholder could not bring an action against the directors, e.g. (i) for losses which had been incurred (*Foss v Harbottle*, supra); (ii) investing profits of the company in bank and other shares (*Burland v Earle* [1902] AC 83, PC); (iii) selling a mine owned by a company at an undervalue (*Pavlides v Jensen* [1956] 2 All ER 518).

The Rule has no application where the individual shareholder is suing to prevent an invasion of his own rights: *Edwards v Halliwell* (supra). 'It is implicit in the Rule [in *Foss v Harbottle*] that the matter relied on as constituting the cause of action should be a cause of action properly belonging to the whole body of corporators . . . as opposed to a cause of action which some individual member can assert in his own right': ibid., at 1067 (per Jenkins LJ). He is therefore entitled to have his vote recorded: *Pender v Lushington* (1877) 6 Ch D 70. He is entitled to say 'Whether I vote in the majority or minority, you shall record my vote, as that is a right of property belonging to my interest in the company, and if you refuse to record my vote, I will institute legal proceedings against you to compel you.': ibid., at 80 (per Jessel MR).

Exceptions to the rule
The Rule in *Foss v Harbottle* (supra) does not apply in the case of (i) any act which is illegal (*North-West Transportation Co v Beatty* (1887) 12 App Cas 589, PC) or *ultra vires* the company (*Edwards v Halliwell* (supra) at 1067 (per Jenkins LJ)); (ii) any act which is a fraud on a minority: *Menier v Hooper's Telegraph Works* (1874) 9 Ch App 350 (*see further*, ARTICLES OF ASSOCIATION); (iii) any act which needs a special resolution for it to be effective and such a resolution is not passed: *Cotter v National Union of Seamen* [1929] 2 Ch 58; (iv) any act committed by the directors intentionally or unintentionally, fraudulently or negligently, benefiting themselves at the expense of the company: *Daniels v Daniels* [1978] 2 All ER 89.

Rule in Royal British Bank v Turquand. A rule that so long as the act done is not inconsistent with the memorandum and the articles, a third party is not bound to inquire whether the directors have taken all necessary steps under them and have acted properly, e.g. where a company has power to issue bonds if authorised by a general resolution of the company, and the directors issue a bond to a third party, he is entitled to assume that such a resolution has in fact been passed: 'Parties dealing with the directors of these joint-stock companies are bound to read the deed or statute limiting the directors' authority, but they are not bound to do more. The plaintiffs, therefore, assuming them to have read this deed, would have found not a prohibition to borrow, but a permission to borrow. They have, in my opinion, a right to infer that the company which put forward their directors to issue a bond of this sort have had such a meeting and such a resolution passed as was requisite to authorise the directors in so doing': *Royal British Bank v Turquand* (1856) 25 LJQB 317 at 318 (per Jervis CJ).

The rule does not apply where (1) the person seeking to rely on it was not aware of the contents of the articles (*Rama Corporation Ltd v Proved Tin and General Investments Ltd* [1952] 1 All ER 554); (2) the person seeking to rely on it has notice of the irregularity (*Howard v Patent Ivory Manufacturing Co* (1888) 38 Ch D 156); (3) the document on which the person seeks to rely is a forgery (*Ruben v Great Fingall*

Consolidated [1906] AC 439, HL); and (4) where the person seeking to rely on it was put on inquiry, and the irregularity would have been discovered if he had made inquiries (*A. L. Underwood Ltd v Bank of Liverpool* [1924] 1 KB 775, CA).

S

Scheme of arrangement. A compromise or arrangement between a company and its creditors or between the company and its members.
Power to compromise with creditors and members
Where a compromise or arrangement is proposed between a company and its creditors, or any class of them, or between the company and its members, or any class of them, the court may, on the application of the company or of any creditor or member of it, or in the case of a company being wound up, of the liquidator, order a meeting of the creditors or class of creditors, or of the members of the company or class of members (as the case may be) to be summoned in such manner as the court directs: Companies Act 1985, s. 425 (1).

If a majority in number representing three-fourths in value of the creditors or class of creditors or members or class of members (as the case may be) present and voting either in person or by proxy at the meeting, agree to any compromise or arrangement, the compromise or arrangement, if sanctioned by the court, is binding on all the creditors or the class of creditors: ibid., s. 425 (2). The compromise is also binding on the members or class of members and also on the company, or in the case of a company in the course of being wound up, on the liquidator and contributories: ibid., s. 425 (2). (*See* CONTRIBUTORY).

The court's order has no effect unless an office copy of the order has been delivered to the Registrar of Companies for registration: Companies Act 1985, s. 425 (3). A copy of every order must be annexed to every copy of the company's memorandum of association issued after the order has been made: ibid., s. 425 (3). If a company makes default in complying with the above requirements, the company and every officer of the company who is in default are liable on summary conviction to a fine not exceeding one-fifth of the statutory maximum: ibid., ss. 425 (3), 730 and Sch. 24.

The term 'arrangement' includes a reorganisation of the company's share capital by the consolidation of shares of different classes or by the division of shares into different classes or by both of those methods: ibid., s. 425 (6). The term 'class' is confined to those persons whose rights are not so dissimilar as to make it impossible for them to consult together with a view to their common interest: *Sovereign Life Assurance*

Co v Dodd [1892] 2 QB 573 at 583, CA (per Bowen LJ), and at 580 (per Lord Esher MR).

The word 'compromise' implies some element of accommodation on each side and is not apt to describe a total surrender, and the word 'arrangement' implies some element of give and take: *Re NFU Development Trust Ltd* [1971] 1 All ER 135 at 139 (per Plowman J). A member whose rights are expropriated without any compensating advantage is not having his rights rearranged in any legitimate sense of the word: ibid.

Under the Companies Act 1985, s. 425, an arrangement can only be sanctioned if the question of fairness has first of all been submitted to the court. The court may sanction a scheme if the evidence is sufficient to show that it is a fair one, although all available information is not given because the company concerned is a banking company, and is therefore exempt under the Companies Act 1985, Sch. 4 from giving information in relation to its accounts: *Re NFU Development Trust Ltd* (supra).

Information as to compromises

When a meeting of creditors or any class of creditors or of members or any class of members is summoned, there must, with every notice summoning the meeting, be sent to a creditor or member a statement explaining the effect of the compromise or arrangement: Companies Act 1985, s. 426 (2).

In particular, the statement must state any material interests of the directors of the company (whether as directors or as members or as creditors of the company or otherwise) and the effect on them of the compromise or arrangement, in so far as it is different from the effect on the like interests of other persons: ibid., s. 426 (2).

In every notice summoning the meeting which is given by advertisement, there must be included such a statement as mentioned above or a notification of the place at which, and the manner in which, creditors or members entitled to attend the meeting may obtain copies of the statement: ibid., s. 426 (3).

Where the compromise or arrangement affects the rights of debenture holders of the company, the statement must give the like explanation as respects the trustees of any deed for securing the issue of the debentures as it is required to give as respects the company's directors: ibid., s. 426 (4). (*See* DEBENTURE; DEBENTURE TRUST DEED).

Where a notice given by advertisement includes a notification that copies of a statement explaining the effect of the compromise or arrangement proposed can be obtained by creditors or members entitled to attend the meeting, every such creditor or member, on making application in the manner indicated by the notice, must be furnished by the company free of charge with a copy of the statement: Companies Act 1985, s. 426 (5).

Where a company makes default in complying with any of the above requirements, the company and every officer of the company who is in default are liable on conviction on indictment to a fine, and on summary conviction to a fine not exceeding the statutory maximum: ibid., ss. 426 (6), 730 and Sch. 24.

It is the duty of any director of the company and of any trustee for its debenture holders to give notice to the company of such matters relating to himself as may be necessary for the purposes of s. 426: ibid., s. 426 (7). Any person who makes default in complying with this requirement is liable on summary conviction to a fine not exceeding one-fifth of the statutory maximum: ibid., ss. 426 (7), 730 and Sch. 24.

Facilitating reconstruction and amalgamation

Where an application is made to the court for the sanctioning of a proposed compromise or arrangement, and it is shown to the court that the compromise or arrangement has been proposed for the purposes of a scheme for the reconstruction of a company or the amalgamation of 2 or more companies, and that under the scheme the undertaking or the property of the transferor company is to be transferred to the transferee company, the court may make an order for

  (i) the transfer to the transferee company of the whole or any part of the undertaking and of the property or liabilities of any transferor company;

 (ii) the allotting or appropriation by the transferee company of any shares, debentures, policies or other like interests in that company which under the compromise or arrangement are to be allotted or appropriated by that company to or for any person;

(iii) the continuation by or against the transferee company of any legal proceedings pending by or against any transferor company;

 (iv) the dissolution, without winding up, of any transferor company;

  (v) the provision to be made for any persons who, within such time and in such manner as the court directs, dissent from the compromise or arrangement;

 (vi) such incidental, consequential and supplemental matters as are necessary to secure that the reconstruction or amalgamation are fully and effectively carried out: ibid., s. 427 (1), (2), (3).

Where an order provides for the transfer of property or liabilities, the property is transferred to and vests in and the liabilities are transferred to and become the liabilities of the transferee company: ibid., s. 427 (4). If the order so directs, the property vests freed from any charge which is by virtue of the compromise or arrangement to cease to have effect: ibid., s. 427 (4).

Where an order is made, every company in relation to which the order is made must cause an office copy of it to be delivered to the Registrar of Companies for registration within 7 days of its making: ibid., s. 427 (5). If default is made in complying with this requirement, the company and every officer of the company who is in default are liable on summary conviction to a fine not exceeding one-fifth of the statutory maximum or, on conviction after continued contravention, to a daily default fine not exceeding one-fiftieth of the statutory maximum: ibid., ss. 427 (6), 730 and Sch. 24.

Seal. Every company must have its name engraved in legible characters on its seal: Companies Act 1985, s. 350 (1).

Table A, art. 101 states: 'The seal shall only be used by the authority of the directors or of a committee of directors authorised by the directors. The directors may determine who shall sign any instrument to which the seal is affixed and unless otherwise so determined it shall be signed by a director and by the secretary or by a second director.'

Secretaries, register of. *See* REGISTER OF DIRECTORS AND SECRETARIES.

Secretary. An officer of a company dealing with the running of it from day to day and its general administration.

Every company must have a secretary and a sole director must not also be secretary: Companies Act 1985, s. 283 (1), (2). No company must have as secretary to the company a corporation the sole director of which is a sole director of the company: ibid., s. 283 (4).

It is the duty of the directors of a public company to take all reasonable steps to secure that the secretary (or each joint secretary) of the company is a person who appears to them to have the requisite knowledge and experience to discharge the functions of secretary of the company and who (a) on 22 December 1980 held the office of secretary or assistant or deputy secretary of the company; or (b) for at least 3 years of the 5 years immediately preceding his appointment as secretary held the office of secretary of a company other than a private company; or (c) is a member of any of the bodies specified below; or (d) is a barrister, advocate or solicitor called or admitted in any part of the United Kingdom; or (e) is a person who, by virtue of his holding or having held any other position or his being a member of any other body, appears to the directors to be capable of discharging those functions: ibid., s. 286 (1). The bodies referred to above are (a) the Institute of Chartered Accountants in England and Wales; (b) the Institute of Chartered Accountants of Scotland; (c) the Chartered Association of Certified Accountants; (d) the Institute of Chartered Accountants in Ireland; (c) the Institute of Chartered Secretaries and Administrators; (f) the Institute of Cost and Management Accountants; and (g) the Chartered Institute of Public Finance and Accountancy: ibid., s. 286 (2).

Anything required or authorised to be done by or to the secretary may, if the office is vacant or there is for any other reason no secretary capable of acting, be done by or to any assistant or deputy secretary, or if there is no assistant or deputy secretary capable of acting, by or to any officer of the company authorised generally or specially in that behalf by the directors: ibid., s. 283 (3). (*See* OFFICER). A provision requiring or authorising a thing to be done by or to a director and the secretary is not satisfied by its being done by or to the same person acting both as director and as, or in place of, the secretary: ibid., s. 284.

The secretary is usually appointed by the directors at a board meeting, and his powers and duties and salary are generally fixed by a written agreement. If not, they are determined by the terms of the resolution appointing him and by the articles.

He may be appointed by the directors for such term, at such remuneration and on such conditions as they may think fit, and any secretary so appointed may be removed by them: Table A, art. 99.

The secretary can act as agent to do such things as are delegated to him or are usually performed by a secretary, e.g. to sign contracts concerned with the administrative side of the business of a company, such as a contract ordering a car from a car hire firm: *Panorama Developments (Guildford) Ltd v Fidelis Furnishing Fabrics Ltd* [1971] 3 All ER 16, CA.

If he acts fraudulently in the course of his duties, he may expose the company to liability: *Lloyd v Grace, Smith & Co* [1912] AC 716. He is acting within the scope of his duties when he certifies a transfer, and if he does so fraudulently, the company is liable. (*See* CERTIFICATION OF TRANSFER).

He is not usually empowered to make contracts other than those of an administrative nature, and any representations made by him to induce persons to enter into contracts are not generally binding on the company: *Barnett v South London Tramways Co* (1887) 18 QBD 815.

He cannot without the authority of a resolution of the directors call a meeting of the company (*Re State of Wyoming Syndicate* [1901] 2 Ch 431), or alter the register of members (*Chida Mines v Anderson* (1905) 22 TLR 27). (*See* REGISTER OF MEMBERS). A director, who advances money to the company at the request of the secretary without the authority of the board of directors, cannot enforce the loan against the company: *Re Cleadon Trust Ltd* [1938] 4 All ER 518.

A company must include the name and address of the secretary in the register of directors and secretaries, and inform the Registrar of Companies of any change in its secretary: Companies Act 1985, s. 288 (2). (*See* REGISTER OF DIRECTORS AND SECRETARIES).

A secretary is an 'officer' of the company: Companies Act 1985, s. 744. He may incur penalties if he fails to comply with his duties concerning the annual return (ibid., s. 363 (7)) or the statement of affairs required in a compulsory winding up (ibid., s. 528 (7)). (*See* ANNUAL RETURN: STATEMENT OF AFFAIRS).

He is liable if he destroys or falsifies books or papers or makes false or fraudulent entries: Companies Act 1985, s. 627. He is also liable to proceedings for misfeasance: ibid., s. 631. (*See* MISFEASANCE).

Securities. In the Company Securities (Insider Dealing) Act 1985 means listed securities and, in the case of a company within the meaning of the Companies Act 1985 or a company registered under Chapter II of Part XXII of that Act or an unregistered company, the following securities (whether or not listed) that is to say, any shares, any debentures or any right to subscribe for, call for or make delivery of a share or debenture: Company Securities (Insider Dealing) Act 1985, s. 12 (a). (*See* LISTED SECURITIES).

Service contract of directors. *See* DIRECTOR'S SERVICE CONTRACT.

Services. In ss. 330 to 346 means anything other than goods or land: Companies Act 1985, s. 331 (8).

Settlement of list of contributories. *See* CONTRIBUTORY; LIQUIDATOR.

Shadow director. A person in accordance with whose directions or instructions the directors of a company are accustomed to act: Companies Act 1985, s. 741 (2). But a person is not deemed a shadow director by reason only that the directors act on advice given by him in a professional capacity: ibid., s. 741 (2).

Share. 'A share is the interest of a shareholder in the company, measured by a sum of money, for the purpose of liability in the first place, and of interest in the second, but also consisting of a series of mutual covenants entered into by all the shareholders *inter se* in accordance with [the Companies Act]. The contract contained in the articles of association is one of the original incidents of the share': *Borland's Trusteee v Steel Brothers & Co Ltd* [1901] 1 Ch 279 at 288.

'Share' means 'share in the share capital of the company and includes stock (except where a distinction between stock and shares is expressed or implied): Companies Act 1985, s. 744.

Types of share

Shares may be (i) ordinary shares (*see* ORDINARY SHARE); (ii) preference shares (*see* PREFERENCE SHARE) and (iii) deferred or founder's shares (*see* FOUNDER'S SHARE).

Shares may be issued as redeemable shares (*see* REDEEMABLE SHARES).

Table A, art. 2: 'Subject to the provisions of the Act and without prejudice to any rights attached to any existing shares, any share may be issued with such rights or restrictions as the company may by ordinary resolution determine.' (*See* ORDINARY RESOLUTION).

Table A, art. 3 states: 'Subject to the provisions of the Act, shares may be issued which are to be redeemed or are to be liable to be redeemed at the option of the company or the holder on such terms and in such manner as may be provided by the articles.'

Application and allotment

A person desirous of obtaining shares may apply for a certain number to be allotted to him. (*See* APPLICATION FOR SHARES; ALLOTMENT OF SHARES).

Register of members and share certificate

The names of shareholders are entered in a register specifying the number of shares which they hold (*see* REGISTER OF MEMBERS), and a share certificate in respect of his shares is issued to every member (*see* SHARE CERTIFICATE).

Transfer, transmission, mortgage, surrender and forfeiture of shares

Shares may be transferred (*see* TRANSFER OF SHARE) or transmitted to another person on the death or bankruptcy of a shareholder (*see* TRANSMISSION OF SHARE). A share may be mortgaged (*see* MORTGAGE OF SHARE). It may be surrendered (*see* SURRENDER OF SHARE) or forfeited (*see* FORFEITURE OF SHARE).

Calls and lien

The company may make a call on the members demanding payment of money due in respect of the amount remaining unpaid on their shares (*see* CALL). A company may have a lien on shares in respect of unpaid calls or unpaid debts due from a member (*see* LIEN ON SHARE).

Variation of shareholders' rights

If the rights of different classes of shareholders are fixed by the articles and not by the memorandum, they can be altered by special resolution.

If the rights are fixed by the memorandum, they can be altered where the memorandum provides for a special method of alteration: *Re Welsbach Incandescent Gas Light Co Ltd* [1904] 1 Ch 87, CA.

If the memorandum does not provide for or prohibits the alteration of the rights, they may be altered by a scheme of arrangement with the sanction of the court under the Companies Act 1985, s. 425: *Re Schweppes Ltd* [1914] 1 Ch 322, CA.

The rights of a class are not 'varied' merely by increasing the shares of another class even if the balance of voting power is thereby upset: *White v Bristol Aeroplane Co Ltd* [1953] 1 All ER 40, CA; *Re John Smith's Tadcaster Brewery Co Ltd* [1953] 1 All ER 518, CA. The cancellation of shares is not a 'variation' of the rights attached to them: *Re Saltdean Estate Co Ltd* [1968] 3 All ER 829.

Where the rights are varied by the requisite majority vote, the holders of not less than 15 per cent of the issued shares of the class affected may apply to the court to have the variation cancelled: Companies Act 1985, s. 127 (1), (2). The application must be made within 21 days after the date on which the consent of the specified proportion of the holders of the issued shares of the class was given or the resolution was passed: ibid., s. 127 (3). The application may be made on behalf of the shareholders entitled to make the application by such one or more of their number as they may appoint in writing for the purpose: ibid., s. 127 (3). The applicants must be persons who did not consent to or vote for the variation: ibid., s. 127 (2).

If an application is made, the variation has no effect unless and until it is confirmed by the court: ibid., s. 127 (2).

The court, after hearing the applicant and any other persons who apply to the court to be heard and appear to the court to be interested in the application, may, if satisfied, having regard to all the circumstances of the case, that the variation would unfairly prejudice the shareholders of the class represented by the applicant, disallow the variation and must, if not so satisfied, confirm it: ibid., s. 127 (4). The decision of the court on any such application is final: ibid., s. 127 (4).

Within 15 days after the making of an order by the court, the company must forward a copy of the order to the Registrar of Companies: ibid., s. 127 (5). If default is made in complying with this requirement, the company and every officer of the company who is in default are liable on summary conviction to a fine not exceeding one-fifth of the statutory maximum, or, on conviction after continued contravention, to a daily default fine not exceeding one-fiftieth of the statutory maximum: ibid., ss. 127 (5), 730 and Sch. 24.

Share, application for. *See* APPLICATION FOR SHARES.

Share, forfeiture of. *See* FORFEITURE OF SHARE.

Share, founder's. *See* FOUNDER'S SHARE.

Share, lien on. *See* LIEN ON SHARE.

Share, mortgage of. *See* MORTGAGE OF SHARE.

Share, ordinary. *See* ORDINARY SHARE.

Share, preference. *See* PREFERENCE SHARE.

Share, qualification. *See* QUALIFICATION SHARE.

Share, sub-division of. *See* SUB-DIVISION OF SHARES.

Share, surrender of. *See* SURRENDER OF SHARE.

Share, transfer of. *See* TRANSFER OF SHARE.

Share, transmission of. *See* TRANSMISSION OF SHARE.

Share certificate. A certificate specifying the number of shares held by a member.

A certificate under the common seal of the company or the seal kept by the company by virtue of s. 40 specifying any shares held by a member, is *prima facie* evidence of his title to the shares: Companies Act 1985, s. 186.

Duty to issue certificate

In general, every company must within 2 months after the allotment of any of its shares and within 2 months after the date on which any transfer of any shares is lodged with the company, complete and have ready for delivery the certificates of all shares allotted or transferred (unless the conditions of issue of the shares otherwise provide): ibid.,

s. 185 (1). The expression 'transfer' means a transfer duly stamped and otherwise valid, and does not include such a transfer as the company is for any reason entitled to refuse to register and does not register: ibid., s. 185 (2). (*See* ALLOTMENT OF SHARES; TRANSFER OF SHARES).

But s. 185 (1) does not apply to a company of which shares are allotted to a stock exchange nominee or with which a transfer is lodged for transferring any shares to a stock exchange nominee: Companies Act 1985, s. 185 (4).

If default is made in complying with s. 185 (1), the company and every officer who is in default are liable on summary conviction to a fine not exceeding one-fifth of the statutory maximum or, on conviction after continued contravention, to a daily default fine not exceeding one-fiftieth of the statutory maximum: ibid., ss. 185 (5), 730 and Sch. 24.

If a company on whom a notice has been served requiring the company to make good any default in complying with s. 185 (1) fails to make good the default within 10 days after the service of the notice, the court may, on the application of the person entitled to have the certificates delivered to him, make an order directing the company and any officer of it to make good the default within such time as may be specified in the order: ibid., s. 185 (6), (7). The order may provide that all costs of and incidental to the application are to be borne by the company or by any officer of the company responsible for the default: ibid., s. 185 (7).

Table A, art. 6 states: 'Every member, upon becoming the holder of any shares, shall be entitled without payment to one certificate for all the shares of each class held by him (and, upon transferring a part of his holding of shares of any class, to a certificate for the balance of such holding) or several certificates each for one or more of his shares upon payment for every certificate after the first of such reasonable sum as the directors may determine. Every certificate shall be sealed with the seal and shall specify the number, class and distinguishing numbers (if any) of the shares to which it relates and the amount or respective amounts paid up thereon. The company shall not be bound to issue more than one certificate for shares jointly held by several persons and delivery of a certificate to one joint holder, shall be a sufficient delivery to all of them.'

Loss of certificate

The articles usually provide that if a certificate is lost or destroyed, the company will supply a new one on satisfactory proof of the loss or destruction and on being indemnified by the applicant.

Table A, art. 7 states: 'If a share certificate is defaced, worn-out, lost or destroyed, it may be renewed on such terms (if any) as to evidence and indemnity and payment of the expenses reasonably incurred by the company in investigating evidence as the directors may determine but otherwise free of charge, and (in the case of defacement or wearing-out) on delivery up of the old certificate.'

Effect of certificate

The certificate does not certify anything as to the equitable interest in the shares: *Shropshire Union Railways and Canal Co v R* (1875) LR 7 HL 496.

The company may be estopped by the certificate from (i) disputing the title of the registered holder; or (ii) alleging that the amount stated as being paid on the shares has not been paid.

(i) ESTOPPEL AS TO TITLE: If a company authorises the issue of a certificate stating that a person is the registered holder of certain shares, it cannot afterwards allege that he is not entitled to those shares: *Dixon v Kennaway & Co* [1900] 1 Ch 833. But if an officer of the company, who has no authority to issue certificates, forges a certificate, there is no estoppel: *Ruben v Great Fingall Consolidated* [1906] AC 439 HL.

(ii) ESTOPPEL AS TO PAYMENT: If the certificate states that the shares are fully paid, the company cannot afterwards allege that they are not fully paid: *Bloomenthal v Ford* [1897] AC 156, HL. But the company is not estopped by such a statement in the certificate where a person knew that the shares were not fully paid for: *Re African Gold Concessions and Development Co, Markham and Darter's Case* [1899] 1 Ch 414, CA. The fact that the member's partner is also a director of the company does not amount to constructive notice that the shares are not fully paid: *Re Coasters Ltd* [1911] 1 Ch 86.

Share issued at a premium. *See* ISSUE AT A PREMIUM.

Share premium account. An account into which is paid a sum equal to the aggregate amount or value of the premiums on shares which are issued by a company at a premium: Companies Act 1985, s. 130 (1). (*See* ISSUE AT A PREMIUM). The share premium account may be applied by the company (i) in paying up unissued shares of the company to be allotted to members as fully paid bonus shares (*see* BONUS SHARE); (ii) in writing off the company's preliminary expenses; (iii) in writing off the expenses of, or the commission paid or discount allowed on, any issue of shares or debentures of the company (*see* UNDERWRITING COMMISSION); or (iv) in providing for the premium payable on redemption of any debentures of the company (*see* DEBENTURE): Companies Act 1985, s. 130 (2).

Share warrant. A warrant stating that its bearer is entitled to the shares specified in it: Companies Act 1985, s. 188 (1), (2). The shares may be transferred by delivery of the warrant: ibid., s. 188 (2). A company limited by shares, if so authorised by its articles, may, with respect to any fully paid up shares, issue under its common seal a share warrant and may provide (by coupons or otherwise) for the payment of the future dividends on the shares included in the warrant: ibid., s. 188 (1).

Shares, consolidation of. *See* CONSOLIDATION OF SHARES.

Sheriff includes any officer charged with the execution of a writ or other process: Companies Act 1985, s. 621 (4).

Show of hands. A method of voting in which the members raise their hands to vote in favour of or against a resolution. Each member present counts for one vote only, however many shares he may have.

It is immaterial that he holds proxies: *Ernest v Loma Gold Mines Ltd* [1897] 1 Ch 1.

Table A, art. 54 states: 'Subject to any rights or restrictions attached to any shares, on a show of hands every member who (being an individual) is present in person or (being a corporation) is present by a duly authorised representative, not being himself a member entitled to vote, shall have one vote . . .'.

Sleeping partner. A partner taking no active part in the administration of a firm. But as far as creditors are concerned, he is as much a partner and as responsible as such as if he took an equally active part in the administration with the partner or partners who ostensibly carry it on.

Special manager. A person appointed to manage the affairs of a company where the nature of the estate or business of the company or the interests of the creditors or contributories require this to be done.

Where the Official Receiver becomes the liquidator of a company, whether provisionally or otherwise, he may, if satisfied that the nature of the company's estate or business, or the interests of the creditors or contributories generally, require the appointment of a special manager of the estate or business other than himself, apply to the court: Companies Act 1985, s. 556 (1). The court may on such application appoint a special manager of the company's estate or business to act during such time as the court may direct with such powers (including any of the powers of a receiver or manager) as may be entrusted to him by the court: ibid., s. 556 (2). The special manager must give such security and account in such manner as the Secretary of State directs: ibid., s. 556 (3). He is to receive such remuneration as may be fixed by the court: ibid., s. 556 (3). (*See* MANAGER; RECEIVER).

Special notice. A notice of 28 days required to be given *to a company* of the intention to move certain resolutions: Companies Act 1985, s. 379. The company must then give notice of the resolution to the members (subject to some exceptions in cases of difficulty) at the same time and in the same manner as it gives notice of the meeting: ibid., s. 379.

This provision confers on the members the right to receive notice of any resolution of which 'special notice' is required. It does not confer on an individual member the right to compel the inclusion of a resolution in the agenda of a company meeting: *Pedley v Inland Waterways Association Ltd* [1977] 1 All ER 209.

The resolutions requiring 'special notice' are those (i) for removing a director (Companies Act 1985, s. 303 (2)); (ii) for authorising a director who has attained the age of 70 to act (ibid., s. 293 (5)); (iii) for appointing as auditor a person other than a retiring auditor (ibid., s. 388 (1) (a)); (iv) for filling a casual vacancy in the office of auditor (ibid., s. 388 (1) (b)); (v) for reappointing as auditor a retiring auditor who was appointed by the directors to fill a casual vacancy (ibid., s. 388 (1) (c)); and (vi) for removing an auditor before the expiration of his term of office (ibid., s. 388 (1) (d)).

Special resolution. A resolution passed by a majority of not less than three-fourths of such members as, being entitled so to do, vote in person or where proxies are allowed, by proxy, at a general meeting of which not less than 21 days' notice, specifying the intention to propose the resolution as a special resolution, has been duly given: Companies Act 1985, s. 378 (2). (*See* GENERAL MEETING; PROXY).

If it is so agreed by a majority in number of the members having the right to attend and vote at such a meeting, being a majority holding not less than 95 per cent in nominal value of the shares giving that right, or, in the case of a company not having a share capital, together representing not less than 95 per cent of the total voting rights at that meeting of all the members, a resolution may be proposed and passed as a special resolution at a meeting of which less than 21 days' notice has been given: ibid., s. 378 (3).

At any meeting at which a special resolution is submitted to be passed, a declaration of the chairman that the resolution is carried, is, unless a poll is demanded, conclusive evidence of the fact without proof of the number or proportion of the votes recorded in favour of or against the resolution: ibid., s. 378 (4).

In computing the majority on a poll demanded on the question that a special resolution has been passed, reference is to be had to the number of votes cast for and against the resolution: ibid., s. 378 (5).

Notice of a meeting is deemed duly given and the meeting duly held when the notice is given and the meeting held in the manner provided by the Act or the articles: ibid., s. 378 (6).

Special resolutions are required (i) to alter the articles of the company (ibid., s. 9 (1); (ii) to alter the objects of the company (ibid., s. 4); (iii) to change the name of the company (ibid., s. 28 (1)); and (iv) to reduce the capital of the company with the leave of the court (ibid., s. 135 (1).

A copy of every special resolution must within 15 days after it has been passed be forwarded to the Registrar of Companies and recorded by him: ibid., s. 380 (1). The copy must be either a printed copy or else a copy in some other form approved by him: ibid., s. 380 (1). If a company fails to comply with s. 380 (1), the company and every officer of the company who is in default are liable on summary conviction to a fine not exceeding one-fifth of the statutory maximum or, on conviction after continued contravention, to a daily default fine not exceeding one-fiftieth of the statutory maximum: ibid., ss. 380 (5), 730 and Sch. 24.

Where articles have been registered, a copy of every special resolution must be embodied in or annexed to every copy of the articles issued after the passing of the resolution: ibid., s. 380 (1). Where articles have not been registered, a printed copy of every special resolution must be forwarded to any member at his request on payment of 5p or such less sum as the company may direct: ibid., s. 380 (3). If a company fails to comply with s. 380 (2) or (3), the company and every officer of the company who is in default are liable on summary conviction to a fine not exceeding one-fifth of the statutory maximum for each occasion on which copies are issued or, as the case may be, requested: ibid., ss. 380 (6), 730 and Sch. 24.

Statement of affairs. A statement submitted to the Official Receiver in a winding up by the court showing the assets and liabilities of the company.

Where the court has made a winding up order or appointed a provisional liquidator, there must (unless the court otherwise orders) be made out and submitted to the Official Receiver a statement as to the affairs of the company in the prescribed form verified by affidavit: Companies Act 1985, s. 528 (1), (2). The statement must show the particulars of the company's assets, its debts and liabilities, the names, residences and occupations of its creditors, the securities held by them respectively, the dates when the securities were respectively given, and such further or other information as may be prescribed or as the Official Receiver may require: ibid., s. 528 (2). (*See* OFFICIAL RECEIVER; PROVISIONAL LIQUIDATOR; WINDING UP ORDER).

The statement must be submitted and verified by one or more of the persons who are at the relevant date the directors and by the person who at that date is the secretary of the company: Companies Act 1985, s. 528 (3). The 'relevant date' means in a case where a provisional liquidator is appointed, the date of his appointment, and, in a case where no such appointment is made, the date of the winding up order: ibid., s. 528 (5).

The statement may also be submitted by such of the following persons as the Official Receiver (subject to the direction of the court) may require to submit and verify the statement:

(a) persons who are or have been officers of the company;

(b) persons who have taken part in the formation of the company at any time within 1 year before the relevant date;

(c) persons who are in the employment of the company or have been in the employment of the company within a year before the relevant date, and are in the opinion of the Official Receiver capable of giving the information required; and

(d) persons who are or have been within that year date officers of or in the employment of a company which is, or within that year was, an officer of the company to which the statement relates: ibid., s. 528 (3), (4).

The statement must be submitted within 14 days from the relevant date, or within such extended time as the Official Receiver or the court may for special reasons appoint: ibid., s. 528 (6). A person making or concurring in making the statement and affidavit is allowed and must be paid by the Official ´Receiver or provisional liquidator, as the case may be, out of the company's assets such costs and expenses incurred in and about the preparation and making of the statement and affidavit as the Official Receiver may consider reasonable, subject to an appeal to the court: ibid., s.529 (1).

If a person, without reasonable excuse, makes default in complying with s. 528, he is liable on conviction on indictment to a fine, and on summary conviction to a fine not exceeding the statutory maximum or, on conviction after continued contravention, to a daily default fine not exceeding one-tenth of the statutory maximum: ibid., ss. 529 (7), 730 and Sch. 24.

A person stating himself in writing to be a creditor or contributory of the company is entitled by himself or by his agent at all reasonable hours, on payment of the prescribed fee, to inspect the statement which has been submitted and to a copy of it or extract from it: ibid., s. 529 (2). (*See* CONTRIBUTORY). A person untruthfully stating himself to be a creditor or contributory is guilty of a contempt of court, and, on the application of the liquidator or of the Official Receiver, punishable accordingly: ibid., s. 529 (3).

The statement may be used in evidence against any person making or concurring in making it: ibid., s. 529 (4).

For the procedure as to the submission of the statement of affairs, see Companies (Winding-up) Rules 1949, rr. 52–57.

Statutory maximum. The prescribed sum under the Magistrates' Courts Act 1980, s. 32: Companies Act 1985, Sch. 24.

Stock. The aggregate of full-paid shares which have been converted, portions of which aggregate may be transferred and split up into fractions of any amount without regard to the original nominal amount of the shares: *Morrice v Aylmer* (1875) LR 7 HL 717 at 724 (per Lord Hatherley).

Stock may be (i) *registered* i.e. a register of stockholders is kept and stock certificates are issued to them; or (ii) *unregistered* i.e. warrants are issued to the holders and are transferable on delivery.

233

A company limited by shares or a company limited by guarantee and having a share capital, if so authorised by its articles, may alter the conditions of its memorandum of association by converting all or any of its paid-up shares into stock and reconverting that stock into paid-up shares of any denomination: Companies Act 1985, s. 121 (1), (2) (c). If a company having a share capital has converted any shares into stock or reconverted stock into shares, it must, within one month after doing so, give notice in the prescribed form to the Registrar of Companies specifying the shares converted or the stock reconverted: ibid., s. 122 (1). If default is made in complying with this requirement, the company and every officer of the company who is in default are liable on summary conviction to a fine not exceeding one-fifth of the statutory maximum or, on conviction after continued contravention, to a daily default fine not exceeding one-fiftieth of the statutory maximum: ibid., ss. 122 (2), 730 and Sch. 24.

Stock certificate. A certificate showing that a stockholder is the owner of a specified amount of stock. (*See* STOCK).

Striking off register. The removal of a company's name from the register.

Where the Registrar of Companies has reasonable cause to believe that a company is not carrying on business or in operation, he may send to the company by post a letter inquiring whether the company is carrying on business or in operation: Companies Act 1985, s. 652 (1). If the Registrar does not within 1 month of sending the letter receive any answer to it, he must within 14 days after the expiration of that month send to the company by post a registered letter referring to the first letter, and stating that no answer to it has been received, and that if an answer is not received to the second letter within 1 month from its date, a notice will be published in the *Gazette* with a view to striking the company's name off the register: ibid., s. 652 (2).

If the Registrar either receives an answer to the effect that the company is not carrying on business or in operation, or does not within 1 month after sending the second letter receive any answer, he may publish in the *Gazette*, and send to the company by post, a notice that at the expiration of 3 months from the date of that notice the name of the company will, unless cause is shown to the contrary, be struck off the register and the company will be dissolved: ibid., s. 652 (3).

If, in any case where a company is being wound up, the Registrar has reasonable cause to believe that no liquidator is acting, or that the affairs of the company are fully wound up, and the returns required to be made by the liquidator have not been made for a period of 6 consecutive months, the Registrar must publish in the *Gazette* and send to the company or the liquidator (if any) a notice like the one referred to above: ibid., s. 652 (4). (*See* LIQUIDATOR).

At the expiration of the time mentioned in the notice the Registrar may, unless cause to the contrary is previously shown by the company, strike its name off the register, and must publish notice of it in the *Gazette*: Companies Act 1985, s. 652 (5). On the publication of that notice in the *Gazette* the company is dissolved: ibid., s. 652 (5). But the liability (if any) of every director, managing officer and member of the company continues, and may be enforced as if the company had not been dissolved: ibid., s. 652 (6) (a).

A notice to be sent to a liquidator may be addressed to him at his last known place of business: ibid., s. 652 (7). A letter or notice to be sent to a company may be addressed to the company at its registered office or, if no office has been registered, to the care of some officer of the company, or if there is no officer of the company whose name and address are known to the Registrar of Companies, may be sent to each of the persons who subscribed to the memorandum, addressed to him at the address mentioned in the memorandum: ibid., s. 652 (7). (*See* MEMORANDUM OF ASSOCIATION).

In certain circumstances the name of the company may be restored to the register. (*See* RESTORATION TO REGISTER).

Sub-division of shares. The division of shares of a certain nominal value into a larger number of shares of a smaller nominal value e.g. the division of a £1 share into four 25p shares. (Cf. CONSOLIDATION OF SHARES).

Subject to a marketing arrangement. Shares of a company are subject to a marketing arrangement on a recognised stock exchange if

(a) they are listed on that stock exchange; or

(b) the company has been accorded facilities for dealings in those shares to take place on that stock exchange without prior permission for individual transactions from the authority governing that stock exchange and without limit as to the time during which those facilities are to be available: Companies Act 1985, s. 163 (2).

Subscriber. (1) A person who signs the original memorandum of association and the articles of association. (*See* ARTICLES OF ASSOCIATION; MEMORANDUM OF ASSOCIATION; SUBSCRIBER OF MEMORANDUM). (2) A person who pays or agrees to pay a company in respect of shares or debentures offered to him by it. (*See* PROSPECTUS).

Subscriber of memorandum. A person who signs the memorandum of association. (*See* MEMORANDUM OF ASSOCIATION).

Any two or more persons associated for any lawful purpose may, by subscribing their names to a memorandum of association and otherwise complying with the requirements of the Act in respect of registration, form an incorporated company, with or without limited liability: Companies Act 1985, s. 1 (1). (*See* COMPANY LIMITED BY

GUARANTEE; COMPANY LIMITED BY SHARES; UNLIMITED COMPANY). The full name and description of each subscriber must be set out.

Any person may be a subscriber even if he is a minor (*Re Laxon & Co* [1892] 3 Ch 555) or a foreigner.

The signatures of the subscribers must be attested by a witness. But one witness to all the signatures is sufficient. (*See* ASSOCIATION CLAUSE).

The duties of the subscribers are (i) to pay for the shares for which they have subscribed; (ii) to sign the articles of association (*see* ARTICLES OF ASSOCIATION); (iii) to appoint the first directors (*see* DIRECTOR); and (iv) usually to act as such directors until they are appointed.

In the case of a company having a share capital no subscriber may take less than one share: Companies Act 1985, s. 2 (5) (b). There must be shown in the memorandum against the name of each subscriber the number of shares he takes: ibid., s. 2 (5) (c).

Subscription lists, time of opening of. *See* TIME OF OPENING OF SUBSCRIPTION LISTS.

Subsidiary company. A company controlled by another company.

A company is deemed to be a subsidiary of another if (but only if)
(a) that other
  (i) is a member of it and controls the composition of its board of directors; or
  (ii) holds more than half in nominal value of its equity share capital; or
(b) the first-mentioned company is a subsidiary of any company which is that other's subsidiary: Companies Act 1985, s. 736 (1).

'Equity share capital' means its issued share capital excluding any part of it which, neither as respects dividends nor as respects capital, carries any right to participate beyond a specified amount in a distribution: ibid., s. 744.

The composition of a company's board of directors is deemed to be controlled by another company if (but only if) that other company by the exercise of some power exercisable by it without the consent or concurrence of any other person can appoint or remove the holders of all or a majority of the directorships: ibid., s. 736 (2).

In determining whether one company is a subsidiary of another
(a) any shares held or power exercisable by that other in a fiduciary capacity must be treated as not held or exercisable by it;
(b) any shares held or power exercisable
  (i) by any person as a nominee for that other (except where that other is concerned only in a fiduciary capacity); or
  (ii) by, or by a nominee for, a subsidiary of the other (not being a subsidiary which is concerned only in a fiduciary capacity), must be treated as held or exercisable by the other;
(c) any shares held or power exercisable by any person by virtue of the

provisions of any debentures of the first-mentioned company or of a trust deed for securing any issue of such debentures must be disregarded;

(d) any shares held or power exercisable by, or by a nominee for, the other or its subsidiary must be treated as not held or exercisable by the other if the ordinary business of the other or its subsidiary (as the case may be) includes the lending of money and the shares are held or the power is exercisable by way of security only for the purposes of a transaction entered into in the course of that business: ibid., s. 736 (4).

Sub-underwriting agreement. *See* UNDERWRITING AGREEMENT.

Surrender of share. The yielding up of shares to the company by a member. The articles may give power to the directors to accept a surrender of shares. This relieves them of going through the formality of forfeiture if the member is willing to surrender the shares. (*See* FORFEITURE OF SHARES).

Validity

A surrender of shares which are not fully paid can be accepted only where a forfeiture would be justified: *Bellerby v Rowland and Marwood's SS Co Ltd* [1902] 2 Ch 14, CA. The same rule applies to fully paid shares which are surrendered for the purpose of being cancelled: ibid.

A surrender will be void if it is accepted for the purpose of relieving a member of his liabilities: *Re Companies Guardian Society, Lord Wallscourt's Case* (1899) 7 Mans 235.

But a shareholder may transfer his shares in trust for the company by way of gift, for this is not a surrender: *Cree v Somervail* (1879) 4 App Cas 648, HL; *Kirby v Wilkins* [1929] 2 Ch 444.

Fully paid shares can be surrendered without the leave of the court as long as the surrender does not involve a reduction of capital (*Re Denver Hotel Co* [1893] 1 Ch 495, CA) e.g. in exchange for other shares of the same nominal value (*Rowell v John Rowell & Sons Ltd* [1912] 2 Ch 609). (*See* REDUCTION OF CAPITAL).

T

Table A. The regulations for the management of a company limited by shares. (*See* COMPANY LIMITED BY SHARES).

Table B. The form of memorandum of association of a private company limited by shares. (*See* COMPANY LIMITED BY SHARES; MEMORANDUM OF ASSOCIATION).

Table C. The form of memorandum of association and articles of association of a company limited by guarantee, and not having a share capital. (*See* ARTICLES OF ASSOCIATION; COMPANY LIMITED BY GUARANTEE; MEMORANDUM OF ASSOCIATION).

Table D. The form of memorandum of association and articles of association of a company limited by guarantee and having a share capital. (*See* ARTICLES OF ASSOCIATION; COMPANY LIMITED BY GUARANTEE; MEMORANDUM OF ASSOCIATION).

Table E. The form of memorandum of association and articles of association of an unlimited company having a share capital. (*See* ARTICLES OF ASSOCIATION; MEMORANDUM OF ASSOCIATION; UNLIMITED COMPANY).

Table F. The form of memorandum of association of a public company limited by shares. (*See* MEMORANDUM OF ASSOCIATION; PUBLIC COMPANY).

Take over. A method of amalgamation of companies whereby one company (the 'transferee company') makes an offer (a 'take over bid') to purchase the shares of the members of another company (the 'transferor company').

If the holders of nine-tenths in value of the shares whose transfer is involved have approved the scheme involving the transfer of shares within 4 months of the making of the offer by the transferee company, the transferee company can serve notice in the prescribed manner on the dissentients within 2 months after the expiration of the 4 months' period that it desires to purchase their shares on the terms of the scheme: Companies Act 1985, s. 428 (1), (2). When such a notice is given, the transferee company (unless, on an application made by the dissentient shareholder within 1 month from the date on which the notice was given, the court thinks fit to order otherwise) is entitled and bound to acquire the shares: ibid., s. 428 (4).

238

In the calculation of the nine-tenths shares held by the transferee company or by a nominee or for the transferee company or its subsidiary are not counted: ibid., s. 428 (1).

If the offer made by the transferee company includes a right of an approving shareholder to sell his shares in the transferor company for shares in the transferee company, or, instead, to sell his shares at a specified price to a third party making the offer on behalf of the transferee company, the company is bound to make the necessary cash available to a dissenting shareholder where e.g. the right to sell to a third party is no longer available: *Re Carlton Holdings Ltd* [1971] 2 All ER 1082 at 1087 (per Brightman J).

Where the transferee company or its nominee or subsidiary holds more than one-tenth of the aggregate number of the shares affected, or any class of such shares, s. 428 does not apply unless the transferee company offers the same terms to all the holders of the shares affected, and the holders who approve the scheme are not less than three-fourths in number of the holders of those shares: Companies Act 1985 s. 428 (5). The date for caluclating the total number of shareholders on which the three-fourths majority is to be calculated is the date when the offer is made: *Re Simo Securities Ltd* [1971] 3 All ER 999 at 1009 (per Brightman J).

The notice which is required to be given to dissentients need only state that nine-tenths in value of the shareholders have accepted the offer. It need not state, where the acceptance by a three-fourths majority in number is necessary, that that majority has approved the scheme: ibid., at 1010 (per Brightman J).

Where the transferee company as a result of the scheme holds not less than nine-tenths in value of the shares of the transferor company, notice must be given by the transferee company to the holders of the remaining shares, and the holders may within 3 months from the giving of the notice require the transferee company to acquire their shares: Companies Act 1985, s. 429 (3). The transferee company is then bound to acquire the shares in question on the same terms as the shares of the approving shareholders were transferred or as the court thinks fit to order: ibid., s. 429 (4).

Dissenting shareholder

The expression 'dissenting shareholder' includes a shareholder who has not assented to the scheme, and any shareholder who has failed or refused to transfer his shares to the transferee company in accordance with the scheme: ibid., s. 428 (3).

A dissentient shareholder can apply to the court within 1 month after the notice is given by the transferee company that it wishes to acquire his shares: ibid., s. 428 (4).

The burden of showing that the scheme is unfair lies on the

applicant: *Re Press Caps Ltd* [1949] 1 All ER 1013; *Re Grierson, Oldham and Adams Ltd* [1967] 1 All ER 192 at 196 (per Plowman J). The market price on the Stock Exchange is cogent but not conclusive evidence of the true value of the shares: *Re Grierson, Oldham and Adams Ltd* (supra) at 197 (per Plowman J). The test of the fairness of the offer is not whether it is fair to the individual shareholder but whether it is fair to the body of shareholders as a whole: ibid., at 197 (per Plowman J). The fact that the applicant may be able to demonstrate that the scheme is open to criticism or is capable of improvement is not enough to discharge the burden of proof which lies on him: ibid., at 198 (per Plowman J). A scheme can be effective to bind the applicant without complying to the extent of 100 per cent with the highest possible standards of fairness, equity and reason: *Re Sussex Brick Co Ltd* [1960] 1 All ER 772n at 774n (per Vaisey J). It must be affirmatively established that, notwithstanding the view of the majority, the scheme is unfair, and that is a different thing from saying that the scheme is not a very fair or not a fair one; a scheme has to be shown affirmatively, patently, obviously and convincingly to be unfair: ibid., at 774n (per Vaisey J). The advantage accruing to the transferee company in obtaining control of the transferor company is not an element which ought to be taken into account as an additional item in computing the value of the shares: *Re Grierson, Oldham and Adams Ltd* (supra) at 200 (per Plowman J).

Duty of directors to their own shareholders
The directors of the transferor company have a duty to their own shareholders to be honest and not to mislead them. A minority can complain if it is being wrongfully subjected to the power of compulsory purchase by the transferee company as a result of a breach of duty on the part of the directors of the transferor company: *Gething v Kilner* [1972] 1 All ER 1166.

Compensation for loss of office
Where a director is to receive compensation for loss of office in the event of a successful take-over, particulars of the proposed payment must be included in or sent with the notice of the offer to the shareholders: Companies Act 1985, s. 314. (*See* COMPENSATION FOR LOSS OF OFFICE).

City Code
Where a take-over of a company listed on the Stock Exchange is concerned, it is necessary to comply with the City Code on Take-overs and Mergers. (*See* CITY CODE ON TAKEOVERS AND MERGERS).

Take over bid. *See* TAKE OVER.

Take-over offer for a company, means 'an offer made to all the holders (or all the holders other than the person making the offer and his nominees) of the shares in the company to acquire those shares or a specified proportion of them, or to all the holders (or all the holders other than the person making the offer and his nominees) of a particular class of those shares to acquire the shares of that class or a specified proportion of them.': Company Securities (Insider Dealing) Act 1985, s. 14.

Take-overs and Mergers, City Code on. *See* CITY CODE ON TAKE-OVERS AND MERGERS.

Take-overs and Mergers, Panel on. *See* CITY CODE ON TAKE-OVERS AND MERGERS.

Time of opening of subscription lists. The beginning of the third day after that on which a prospectus is first issued generally or at such later time (if any) as may be specified in the propsectus: Companies Act 1985, s. 82 (2). The reference to the day on which the prospectus is first issued generally is to the day on which it is first so issued as a newspaper advertisement: ibid., s. 82 (3). But if it is not so issued as a newspaper advertisement before the third day after that on which it is issued in any other manner, the reference is to the day on which it is first so issued in any manner: ibid., s. 82 (3).

Trading certificate. A certificate issued by the Registrar of Companies enabling a public company to commence business. (*See* PUBLIC COMPANY). The certificate is known as a 'trading certificate'.

A company registered as a public company on its original incorporation must not do business or exercise any borrowing powers unless the Registrar of Companies has issued it with a certificate or the company is re-registered as a private company: Companies Act 1985, s. 117 (1). (*See* PRIVATE COMPANY).

The Registrar must issue a company with a certificate if, on an application made to him by the company in the prescribed form, he is satisfied that the nominal value of the company's allotted share capital is not less than the authorised minimum, and a statutory declaration complying with the following requirements is delivered to him: Companies Act 1985, s. 117 (2). (*See* AUTHORISED MINIMUM: ALLOTMENT).

The statutory declaration must be in the prescribed form and signed by a director or secretary of the company and must:—

(a) state that the nominal value of the company's allotted share capital is not less than the authorised minimum;

(b) specify the amount paid up, at the time of the application, on the allotted share capital of the company;

(c) specify the amount, or estimated amount, of the company's preliminary expenses and the persons by whom any of those expenses have been paid or are payable; and

(d) specify any amount or benefit paid, given or intended to be paid or given to any promoter of the company, and the consideration for

241

the payment or benefit: Companies Act 1985, s. 117 (3). (*See* PROMOTER).

A share allotted in pursuance of an employees' share scheme must not be taken into account in determining the nominal value of the company's allotted share capital unless it is paid up at least as to one-quarter of the nominal value of the share and the whole of any premium on the share: Companies Act 1985, s. 117 (4). (*See* EMPLOYEES' SHARE SCHEME; PREMIUM).

The Registrar may accept a statutory declaration delivered to him as sufficient evidence of the matters stated in it: Companies Act 1985, s. 117 (5).

A certificate in respect of any company is conclusive evidence that the company is entitled to do business and exercise any borrowing powers: ibid., s. 117 (6).

If a company does business or exercises borrowing powers in contravention of the above provisions, the company and any officer of the company who is in default are liable on conviction on indictment to a fine, and on summary conviction to a fine not exceeding the statutory maximum: ibid., ss. 117 (7), 730 and Sch. 24.

The above provisions are without prejudice to the validity of any transaction entered into by a company: ibid., s. 117 (8). But if a company enters into a transaction in contravention of them, and fails to comply with its obligations in connection with them within 21 days from being called on to do so, the directors of the company are jointly and severally liable to indemnify the other party to the transaction in respect of any loss or damage suffered by him by reason of the company's failure to comply with those obligations: ibid., s. 117 (8).

Trading under misleading name. A person who is not a public company is guilty of an offence if he carries on any trade, profession or business under a name which includes, at its last part, the words 'public limited company': Companies Act 1985, s. 33 (1). A public company is guilty of an offence if, in circumstances in which the fact that it is a public company is likely to be material to any person, it uses a name which may reasonably be expected to give the impression that it is a private company: ibid., s. 33 (2). (*See* PUBLIC COMPANY).

Transaction or arrangement made for a person means a transaction or arrangement made for a person if (a) in the case of a loan or quasi-loan, it is made to him (*see* QUASI-LOAN); (b) in the case of a credit transaction, he is the person to whom goods or services are supplied, or land is sold or otherwise disposed of, under the transaction (*see* CREDIT TRANSACTION); (c) in the case of a guarantee or security, it is entered into or provided in connection with a loan or quasi-loan made to him or a credit transaction made for him (*see* GUARANTEE); (d) in the case of an arrangement within s. 330 (6) or (7), the transaction to which the arrangement relates was made for him; and (e) in the case of any other transaction or arrangement for the supply or transfer of, or of any interest in, goods, land or services, he is the person to whom the goods, land or services (or the interest) are supplied or transferred: Companies Act 1985, s. 331 (9).

Transfer, certification of. *See* CERTIFICATION OF TRANSFER.

Transfer, forged. *See* FORGED TRANSFER.

Transfer of share. The conveyance of a member's share to another person.

Form of transfer

The shares of a member are transferable in the manner provided by the articles: Companies Act 1985, s. 182 (1) (b). Notwithstanding anything in the articles, it is not lawful for a company to register a transfer unless a proper instrument of transfer has been delivered to the company: ibid., s. 183 (1).

A transfer need not be by deed unless the articles expressly require a deed.

Certain types of registered securities (i.e. transferable securities the holders of which are entered in a register) may be transferred by an instrument under hand in the forms set out in the schedule to the Act: Stock Transfer Act 1963, s. 1. 'Registered securities' include securities issued by any company except a company limited by guarantee or an unlimited company: ibid. s. 1 (4). (*See* COMPANY LIMITED BY GUARANTEE; UNLIMITED COMPANY).

In the case of these types of securities, the transfer needs to be executed by the transferor only: Stock Transfer Act 1963, s. 1 (1). The transfer must specify the particulars of the consideration, of the description and number or amount of the securities, and of the person by whom the transfer is to be made, and the full name and address of the transferee: ibid., s. 1 (1). The execution of a transfer need not be attested: ibid., s. 1 (2). Any instrument which would be effective to transfer securities apart from s. 1 of the Act is still valid: ibid., s. 1 (3). The Treasury is empowered to alter the forms set out in the Act and to substitute different ones: ibid., s. 3 (2).

Procedure

The transfer is executed by the transferor and handed to the transferee with the share certificate. The transferee executes the transfer where this is necessary, and sends it to the company for registration. The company then issues a certificate to the transferee.

The transfer must be brought before the directors within a reasonable time after it has been lodged: *Re Swaledale Cleaners Ltd* [1968] 3 All ER 619, CA.

Table A, art. 23 states: 'The instrument of transfer of a share may be in any usual form or in any other form which the directors may approve and shall be executed by or on behalf of the transferor and, unless the share is fully paid, by or on behalf of the transferee'.

Right to transfer shares

In general, every shareholder has a right to transfer his shares and the transfer will be valid even if made to a man of straw when the company is in difficulties: *Re Mexican and South American Co, Grisewood and Smith's Case, De Pass's Case* (1859) 4 De G & J 544; *Re Discoverers Finance Corporation Ltd, Lindlar's Case* [1910] 1 Ch 312, CA. But this right may be restricted by the articles and the directors may be given a power to refuse to register a transfer without assigning a reason.

Table A, art. 24 states: 'The directors may refuse to register the transfer of a share which is not fully paid to a person of whom they do not approve and they may refuse to register the transfer of a share on which the company has a lien. They may also refuse to register a transfer unless

(a) it is lodged at the office or at such other place as the directors may appoint and is accompanied by the certificate for the shares to which it relates and such other evidence as the directors may reasonably require to show the right of the transferor to make the transfer;

(b) it is in respect of only one class of shares; and

(c) it is in favour of not more than four transferees.'

The court will not interfere with the directors' discretion unless it can be shown that they did not act in good faith: *Re Smith and Fawcett Ltd* [1942] 1 All ER 524, CA.

The power given by the articles to veto a transfer of shares must be regarded as lost if there is unnecessary delay in placing the transfer before the board of directors: *Re Swaledale Cleaners Ltd* [1968] 3 All ER 619, CA.

Sometimes the articles provide that the other shareholders must be given the right of first refusal of the shares before they can be transferred to outsiders: *Clemens v Clemens Brothers Ltd* [1976] 2 All ER 268.

The articles may provide that a shareholder who is 'desirous of transferring' shares must inform the secretary of the company of the number which he desires to transfer and that he must sell them to any member who offers to buy them: *Lyle and Scott Ltd v Scott's Trustees* [1959] 2 All ER 661, HL.

An article stating that on the bankruptcy of any member his shares are to be sold to certain persons at a certain price is valid: *Borland's Trustee v Steel Brothers & Co Ltd* [1901] 1 Ch 279.

A right to refuse to register a transfer does not enable the company to object to a transmission of shares on the death of a member: *Moodie v W. and J. Shepherd (Bookbinders) Ltd* [1949] 2 All ER 1044. (*See* TRANSMISSION OF SHARE).

Specific performance of a contract to transfer shares may be decreed unless the directors, acting within their powers, refuse to register the transfer: *Birmingham v Sheridan, Re Waterloo Co (No. 4)* (1864) 33 Beav 660.

If a company refuses to register a transfer of any shares, the company must, within 2 months after the date on which the transfer was lodged with it, send to the transferee notice of the refusal: Companies Act 1985, s. 183 (5). If default is made in complying with this provision, the company and every officer of the company who is in default are liable on summary conviction to a fine not exceeding one-fifth of the statutory maximum, or, on conviction after continued contravention, to a daily default fine not exceeding one-fiftieth of the statutory maximum: ibid., ss. 183 (6), 730 and Sch. 24.

Void transfer

If a shareholder transfers his shares and the transfer turns out to be invalid, he remains liable for calls on the shares: *Re Patent Paper Manufacturing Co, Addison's Case* (1870) 5 Ch App 294. (*See* CALL).

In a winding up by the court, any transfer of shares made after the commencment of the winding up is void unless the court otherwise orders, void: Companies Act 1985, s. 522. (*See* COMMENCEMENT OF WINDING UP; PETITION FOR WINDING UP; WINDING UP BY THE COURT).

In a voluntary winding up, any transfer of shares made after the commencement of the winding up is, unless it is a transfer made to or with the sanction of the liquidator: Companies Act 1985, s. 576. (*See* COMMENCEMENT OF WINDING UP; LIQUIDATOR; VOLUNTARY WINDING UP).

Certification of transfer

Where a shareholder wishes to transfer only some of the shares represented by a share certificate, the transfer must be 'certificated' by the company pending the issue of a new certificate. (*See* CERTIFICATION OF TRANSFER).

Forged transfer

For the position where the transfer is forged, *see* FORGED TRANSFER.

Transmission of share. The vesting of a member's shares in another person by operation of law i.e. on the death or bankruptcy of the member.

(a) *On death*

On the death of the member, his shares vest in his personal representatives.

The production to a company of any document, which is by law sufficient evidence of probate of the will, or letters of administration of the estate, of a deceased person having been granted to some person, must be accepted by the company, notwithstanding anything in its articles, as sufficient evidence of the grant: Companies Act 1985, s. 187.

A transfer of the share of a deceased member of a company by his personal representative, although the personal representative is not himself a member of the company, is as valid as if he had been such a member at the time of the execution of the instrument of transfer: ibid., s. 183 (3). (*See* TRANSFER OF SHARE).

Subject to the provisions of the articles, the personal representatives are entitled to be put on the register of members if they so wish. (*See* REGISTER OF MEMBERS). Where by the articles a personal representative is entitled to be put on the register, the company cannot qualify the entry of the name on the register by showing that he holds the shares in a representative capacity: *Re T. H. Saunders & Co Ltd* [1908] 1 Ch 415.

If the personal representatives are placed on the register, they become personally liable for calls. (*See* CALL). In order that the company may get the benefit of this liability, the articles may contain a clause intended to induce or compel the personal representative to be registered within a certain time.

A notice of a call served at the registered address of a deceased shareholder is valid if the company has no notice of his death: *New Zealand Gold Extraction Co (Newberry-Vantin Process) v Peacock* [1894] 1 QB 622, CA. If the company has notice of his death, the notice should be served on his personal representative.

But the notice will be valid even where the company has notice of death, if the notice comes to the knowledge of the personal representatives: *James v Buena Ventura Nitrate Grounds Syndicate* [1896] 1 Ch 456, CA.

Table A, art. 29 states: 'If a member dies, the survivor or survivors where he was a joint holder, and his personal representatives where he was a sole holder or the only survivor of joint holders, shall be the only persons recognised by the company as having any title to his interest; but nothing herein contained shall release the estate of a deceased member from any liability in respect of any share which had been jointly held by him.'

'A person becoming entitled to a share in consequence of the death . . . of a member may, upon such evidence being produced as the directors may properly require, elect either to become the holder of the share or to have some person nominated by him registered as the transferee. If he elects to become the holder he shall give notice to the company to that effect. If he elects to have another person registered, he shall execute an instrument of transfer of the share to that person . . .': Table A, art. 30.

'A person becoming entitled to a share in consequence of the death
. . . of a member shall have the rights to which he would be entitled if
he were the holder of the share, except that he shall not, before being
registered as the holder of the share, be entitled in respect of it to attend
or vote at any meeting of the company or at any separate meeting of
the holders of any class of shares in the company': ibid., art. 31.

(b) *On bankruptcy*

On the bankruptcy of a member, his trustee in bankruptcy can sell and
transfer his shares, or may repudiate them if there is a liability in
respect of them.

If the shares are repudiated, the company can prove in the
bankruptcy for the amount remaining unpaid on them. If this is done,
and the company receives a payment in the bankruptcy from the
trustee, the company cannot sue the bankrupt for calls. But the shares
are not fully-paid shares, and are not entitled to rank as such if the
company goes into liquidation: *Re West Coast Gold Fields Ltd, Rowe's
Trustee's Claim* [1906] 1 Ch 1, CA.

Arts. 30 and 31 of Table A (supra) apply to a bankrupt member as
they do to one who has died, the trustee in bankruptcy being given the
same rights as a personal representative.

U

Ultra vires. Beyond the powers of. *See* ULTRA VIRES TRANSACTIONS.

Ultra vires transactions. Transactions by the company with another person which are (1) outside the powers given to the company by the memorandum of association (*see* MEMORANDUM OF ASSOCIATION), or (2) outside the powers of the directors given to them by the articles of association (*see* ARTICLES OF ASSOCIATION).

(a) *Transactions ultra vires the company*

(i) ENFORCEMENT BY THE COMPANY: If the transaction is *ultra vires* the company, it cannot be enforced by the company, and the company cannot make it valid even if every member purports to ratify it: *Ashbury Railway Carriage and Iron Co v Riche* (1875) LR 7 HL 653.

Even if the company alters its memorandum, the alteration cannot validate an *ultra vires* transaction which has already been entered into. (*See* OBJECTS CLAUSE).

Where the other party is sued on the transaction by the company, he is entitled to maintain by way of defence that the contract is *ultra vires* the company and void, and it makes no difference whether the contract is executory or whether the company has performed its part of the contract: *Bell Houses Ltd v City Wall Properties Ltd* [1965] 3 All ER 427 at 435, 436 (per Mocatta J).

(ii) ENFORCEMENT BY THE OTHER PARTY: (a) *Where the Companies Act 1985, s. 35 applies*

Even though the transaction between the company and the other party is *ultra vires* the company the other party can enforce it if the conditions set out in the Companies Act 1985, s. 35 apply.

The Act provides that in favour of a person dealing with a company in good faith, any transaction decided on by the directors is deemed to be one which it is within the capacity of the company to enter into, and the power of the directors to bind the company is deemed to be free of any limitation under the memorandum: Companies Act 1985, s. 35 (1). A party to a transaction so decided on is not bound to inquire as to the capacity of the company to enter into it or as to any such limitation on the powers of the directors, and is presumed to have acted in good faith unless the contrary is proved: ibid., s. 35 (2).

(b) *Where the Companies Act 1985, s. 35 does not apply*

The other party cannot enforce a transaction which is *ultra vires* the company, even though it has been ratified by the company.

Where a company borrows beyond its powers, the securities given by it are void and the lender cannot sue the company for the return of the loan.

But a person lending money to a company, which has power to borrow money for its business, need not inquire into the purpose for which it is to be used, and the loan will be valid as long as he does not know that the money was intended for an *ultra vires* purpose: *Re David Payne & Co Ltd* [1904] 2 Ch 608; *Re Introductions Ltd: Introductions Ltd v National Provincial Bank Ltd* [1969] 1 All ER 887, CA.

But if the money has not been spent, he may apply for an injunction to prevent the company from parting with it.

He may have an action against the directors for breach of warranty of authority: *Weeks v Propert* (1873) LR 8 CP 427; *Hely-Hutchinson v Brayhead Ltd* [1967] 3 All ER 98, CA.

If the money has been used to pay off debts which could have been enforced against the company, the lender may sue the company, being subrogated to the rights of the creditors who were paid off: *Neath Building Society v Luce* (1889) 43 Ch D 158; *Re Harris Calculating Machine Co* [1914] 1 Ch 920.

But this subrogation does not give the lender any priority which the original creditors may have had over the other creditors of the company: *Re Wrexham, Mold and Connah's Quay Railway Co* [1899] 1 Ch 440, CA.

(b) *Transactions ultra vires the directors*

(i) ENFORCEMENT BY THE COMPANY: Where the transaction is *ultra vires* the directors but within the powers of the company, any irregularity can be cured by the consent of all the shareholders and the company can then enforce the transaction: *Re Express Engineering Works Ltd* [1920] 1 Ch 466, CA. The assent of the shareholders may be given at different times or simultaneously: *Parker and Cooper Ltd v Reading* [1926] Ch 975 at 984 (per Astbury J). No formal meeting of the company need be called and no formal resolution need be passed: *Re Duomatic Ltd* [1969] 1 All ER 161.

(ii) ENFORCEMENT BY THE OTHER PARTY: (a) *Where the Companies Act 1985, s. 35 applies*

Where the transaction is *ultra vires* the directors but within the powers of the company, it can be enforced by the other party if the conditions imposed by the Companies Act 1985 apply.

The Act provides that in favour of a person dealing with a company in good faith, any transaction decided on by the directors is deemed to be one which it is within the capacity of the company to enter into, and the power of the directors to bind the company is deemed to be free of any limitation under the memorandum or articles of association: Companies Act 1985, s. 35 (1). A party to a transaction so decided on is not bound to inquire as to any such limitation on the powers of the directors and is presumed to have acted in good faith unless the contrary is proved: ibid., s. 35 (2).

(b) *Where the Act does not apply*

A person dealing with a company may hold it liable on a transaction where it is *ultra vires* the directors but within the powers of the company if

(i) the circumstances fall within the Rule in *Royal British Bank v Turquand*. (*See* RULE IN ROYAL BRITISH BANK V TURQUAND); or

(ii) the company has held out the director as having the necessary authority.

To enable him to hold the company liable it must be shown that

1. a representation that the director had authority to enter on behalf of the company into a contract of the kind sought to be enforced was made to him;

2. such representation was made by a person or persons who had actual authority to manage the business of the company either generally or in respect of those matters to which the contract relates;

3. he, in fact, relied on the representation;

4. under its memorandum or articles the company was not deprived of the capacity either to enter into a contract of the kind sought to be enforced or to delegate to a director authority to enter into a contract of that kind: *Freeman and Lockyer v Buckhurst Park Properties (Mangal) Ltd* [1964] 1 All ER 630 at 646, CA (per Diplock LJ); *Hely-Hutchinson v Brayhead Ltd* [1967] 3 All ER 98, CA.

Uncalled share capital. *See* CALLED-UP SHARE CAPITAL.

Underwriter. A person promising to take up shares in accordance with an underwriting agreement. (*See* UNDERWRITING AGREEMENT).

Underwriting agreement. An agreement under which, before a company issues shares to the public, a person undertakes, in consideration of a commission to take up the whole or a portion of such (if any) of the offered shares as may not be subscribed for by the public: *Re Licensed Victuallers' Mutual Trading Association, ex parte Audain* (1889) 42 Ch D 1. A similar agreement may be made for underwriting debentures. Sometimes an underwriter enters into a sub-underwriter agreement with other persons in order to relieve him of some or all of his liability in exchange for a commission. (*See* UNDERWRITING COMMISSION).

An underwriter, who gives an authority to apply for shares in his name, cannot withdraw the authority: *Re Hannan's Empress Gold Mining and Development Co, Carmichael's Case* [1896] 2 Ch 643. Nor can a sub-underwriter withdraw his authority: *Re Olympic Reinsurance Co* [1920] 2 Ch 341.

Underwriting commission. A commission paid to a person who agrees to take up the whole or a portion of the shares or debentures of a company offered to the public. (*See* UNDERWRITING AGREEMENT).

The company is entitled to pay underwriting commission to a person agreeing to underwrite an issue of shares if

(a) the payment of the commission is authorised by the articles;

(b) the commission does not exceed 10 per cent of the price at which the shares are issued or the amount or rate authorised by the articles, whichever is the less; and

(c) the amount or rate per cent of the commission
  (i) in the case of shares offered to the public for subscription, is disclosed in the prospectus; or
  (ii) in the case of shares not offered to the public for subscription, is disclosed in a statement in the prescribed form by every director of the company, and delivered (before the payment of the commission) to the Registrar of Companies for registration; and

(d) the number of shares which persons have agreed for a commission to subscribe absolute is disclosed: Companies Act 1985, s. 97 (1), (2), (3).

Nothing prevents a company from giving, as the consideration for underwriting shares, an option to take further shares at par: *Hilder v Dexter* [1902] AC 474.

Where shares have been issued at a premium, the share premium account may be applied in payment of commission on the issue of shares or debentures: Companies Act 1985, s. 130 (2). (*See* SHARE PREMIUM ACCOUNT).

The amount of commission paid within the 2 preceding years in respect of shares and debentures must be stated in every prospectus: Companies Act 1985, Sch. 3, Part I, para. 10. The total amount of sums paid by way of commission must be stated in the annual return: ibid., Sch. 15, para. 3. (*See* ANNUAL RETURN). The amount or rate of commission paid in respect of debentures must be included in the particulars of the debentures sent to the Registrar of Companies for registration: Companies Act 1985, s. 397 (2). (*See* REGISTRATION OF CHARGES).

Undistributable reserves means (a) the share premium account; (b) the capital redemption reserve; (c) the amount by which the company's accumulated, unrealised profits, so far as not previously utilised by any capitalisation of every description except a transfer of any profits of the company to its capital redemption reserve, exceed its accumulated, unrealised losses, so far as not previously written off in a reduction of capital duly made; and (iv) any other reserve which the company is prohibited from distributing by an enactment, other than one contained in Part VIII of the Act, or by its memorandum or articles: Companies Act 1985, s. 264 (3). (*See* CAPITAL REDEMPTION RESERVE; SHARE PREMIUM ACCOUNT).

Unfair prejudice to members. Conduct by act or omission on the part of a company which is unfair to some of its members.

A member of a company may apply to the court by petition for an order on the ground that the company's affairs are being or have been conducted in a manner which is unfairly prejudicial to the interests of some part of the members (including at least himself) or that any actual or proposed act or omission of the company is or would be so prejudicial: Companies Act 1985, s. 459 (1).

The word 'member' includes a person to whom shares in the company have been transferred (*see* TRANSFER OF SHARE) or transmitted by operation of law (*see* TRANSMISSION OF SHARE): Companies Act 1985, s. 459 (2).

If in the case of a company

(a) the Secretary of State has received an inspector's report or has exercised powers to inspect a company's books and papers (*see* INSPECTION AND INVESTIGATION OF COMPANY); and

(b) it appears to him that the affairs of the company are being or have been conducted in a manner which is unfairly prejudicial to the interests of some part of the members, or that any actual or proposed act or omission of the company is or would be so prejudicial,

he may himself (in addition to or instead of presenting a petition for the winding up of the company) apply to the court by petition for an order: ibid., s. 460 (1). (*See* PETITION FOR WINDING UP).

If the court is satisfied that a petition is well-founded, it may make such order as it thinks fit for giving relief in respect of the matters complained of: ibid., s. 461 (1).

An order may (*inter alia*)

(a) regulate the conduct of the company's affairs in the future;

(b) require the company to refrain from doing or continuing an act complained of by the petitioner or to do an act which the petitioner has complained it has omitted to do;

(c) authorise civil proceedings to be brought in the name and on behalf of the company by such person or persons and on such terms as the court may direct;

(d) provide for the purchase of the shares of any members of the company by other members or by the company itself and, in the case of a purchase by the company itself, the reduction of the company's capital accordingly: ibid., s. 461 (2). (*See* REDUCTION OF CAPITAL).

If an order requires the company not to make any, or any specified, alteration in the memorandum or articles, the company has no power without leave of the court to make any such alteration in breach of that requirement: Companies Act 1985, s. 461 (3).

An office copy of any order altering, or giving leave to alter, a company's memorandum or articles must, within 14 days of the making of the order or such longer period as the court may allow, be delivered by the company to the Registrar of Companies for registration: ibid., s. 461 (5). If a company makes default in complying with this requirement, the company and every officer of the company is in default are liable on summary conviction to a fine not exceeding one-fifth of the statutory maximum or, on conviction after continued contravention, to a daily default fine not exceeding one-fiftieth of the statutory maximum for every day until that copy is delivered: ibid., ss. 461 (3), 730 and Sch. 24.

Unlimited company. A company not having any limit on the liability of its members: Companies Act 1985, s. 1 (2) (c).

Unpublished price sensitive information means information in relation to any securities of a company which (a) relates to specific matters relating or of concern (directly or indirectly) to that company, i.e. is not of a general nature relating or of concern to that company; and (b) is not generally known to those persons who are accustomed or would be likely to deal in those securities but which would, if it were generally known to them, be likely materially to affect the price of those securities: Company Securities (Insider Dealing) Act 1985, s. 10.

Usual authority of partner. The authority of a partner to enter into transactions within the normal authority of a partner in the type of partnership concerned.

Every partner is an agent of the firm and his other partners for the purpose of the business of the partnership, and the acts of every partner who does any act for carrying on in the usual way business of the kind carried on by the firm of which he is a member bind the firm and his partners, unless the partner so acting has in fact no authority to act for the firm in the particular matter, and the person with whom he is dealing either knows that he has no authority, or does not know or believe him to be a partner: Partnership Act 1890, s. 5.

Trading partnerships

In the absence of express prohibition the usual authority of a partner in a trading partnership enables him (i) to pledge the partnership goods (*Ex parte Bonbonus* (1803) 8 Ves 540); (ii) to sell the partnership goods (*Dore v Wilkinson* (1817) 2 Stark 287); (iii) to buy goods on account of the firm (*Bond v Gibson* (1808) 1 Camp 185); (iv) to borrow money on account of the firm (*Lane v Williams* (1692) 2 Vern 277); (v) to engage employees for the firm (*Beckham v Drake* (1843) 11 M & W 315); (vi) to receive, and give receipts for debts due to the firm (*Porter v Taylor*

(1817) 6 M & S 156); (vii) to create an equitable mortgage of the firm's land or buildings by a deposit of title deeds (*Re Clough* (1885) 31 Ch D 324); (viii) to retain a solicitor to conduct an action for recovering debts due to the firm (*Court v Berlin* [1897] 2 QB 396); and (ix) to employ a solicitor to defend an action against the firm (*Tomlinson v Broadsmith* [1896] 1 QB 386).

Non-trading partnerships

In the case of a non-trading partnership (*see* NON-TRADING PARTNERSHIP) a partner cannot accept, make or issue negotiable instruments other than ordinary cheques nor borrow or pledge the partnership property: *Backhouse v Charlton* (1878) 8 Ch D 444. (*See* PARTNERSHIP PROPERTY).

Acts never within usual authority

In no case, whether the partnership is a trading partnership or a non-trading partnership, has a partner usual authority (i) to execute a deed (*Harrison v Jackson* (1797) 7 Term Rep 207) unless his authority is expressly conferred by deed (*Berkeley v Hardy* (1826) 5 B & C 335); (ii) to give a guarantee in the firm's name unless a trade custom to that effect is proved (*Brettel v Williams* (1849) 4 Exch 623); (iii) to submit a dispute to arbitration (*Adams v Bankart* (1835) 1 CM & R 681); (iv) to accept property in lieu of money in satisfaction of a debt due to the firm (*Niemann v Niemann* (1889) 43 Ch D 198); (v) to make his partners into partners with other persons in another business (*Hawksley v Outram* [1892] 3 Ch 359); or (vi) to authorise a third person to make use of the firm's name in legal or other proceedings (*Marsh v Josph* [1897] 1 Ch 213).

V

Value of a transaction or arrangement means (a) in the case of a loan, the principal of the loan; (b) in the case of a quasi-loan, the amount or maximum amount, which the person to whom the quasi-loan is made is liable to reimburse the creditor (*see* QUASI-LOAN); (c) in the case of a transaction or arrangement, other than a loan or quasi-loan or a transaction within paras. (d) or (e) below, the price which it is reasonable to expect could be obtained for the goods, land or services to which the transaction or arrangement relates if they had been supplied at the time the transaction or arrangement is entered into in the ordinary course of business and on the same terms (apart from price) as they have been supplied or are to be supplied under the transaction or arrangement in question; (d) in the case of a guarantee or security, the amount guaranteed or secured (*see* GUARANTEE); (e) in the case of an arrangement to which s. 340 (6) or (7) of the Companies Act 1985 applies, the value of the transaction to which the arrangement relates less any amount by which the liabilities under the arrangement or transaction of the person for whom the transaction was made have been reduced: Companies Act 1985), s. 340. (*See* TRANSACTION OR ARRANGEMENT MADE FOR A PERSON). For the purposes of the above provision the value of a transaction or arrangement which is not capable of being expressed as a specific sum of money (because the amount of any liability arising under the transaction is unascertainable, or for any other reason) is deemed, whether or not any liability under the transaction has been reduced, to exceed £50,000: Companies Act 1985, s. 340 (7).

Voluntary winding up. A winding up in which the company and its creditors are left to settle their affairs without coming to the court.

A voluntary winding up begins with the passing of a resolution that the company should be wound up. (*See* RESOLUTION FOR VOLUNTARY WINDING UP). The winding up is deemed to commence at the time of the passing of the resolution: Companies Act 1985, s. 574.

Consequences of voluntary winding up

In a voluntary winding up, the company is to cease to carry on business except so far as may be required for its beneficial winding up: ibid., s. 575 (1). But the corporate state and corporate powers of the company, notwithstanding anything to the contrary in its articles, continue until the company is dissolved: ibid., s. 575 (2).

Any transfer of shares, not being a transfer made to or with the sanction of the liquidator made after the commencement of the winding up, is void: ibid., s. 576.

Any alteration in the status of the members of the company made after the commencement of the winding up is also void: ibid., s. 576; *Castello's Case* (1869) LR 8 Eq 504.

Types of voluntary winding up

A voluntary winding up may be (1) a members' voluntary winding up if a 'declaration of solvency' has been made; and (2) a creditors' voluntary winding up where no such declaration has been made: Companies Act 1985, s. 578. (*See* CREDITORS' VOLUNTARY WINDING UP; DECLARATION OF SOLVENCY; MEMBERS' VOLUNTARY WINDING UP).

Compulsory order after resolution for voluntary winding up

The voluntary winding up does not bar the right of any creditor or contributory to have the company wound up by the court: Companies Act 1985, s. 605. (*See* CONTRIBUTORY; WINDING UP BY THE COURT). But in the case of an application by a contributory, the court must be satisfied that the rights of the contributories will be prejudiced by a voluntary winding up: Companies Act 1985, s. 605. See e.g. *Re National Company for Distribution of Electricity by Secondary Generators Ltd* [1902] 2 Ch 34, CA.

If some creditors support and others oppose a petition for the winding up of the company by the court, the court will consider the wishes of the majority: *Re Home Remedies Ltd* [1942] 2 All ER 552.

It is undesirable for a liquidator in a voluntary winding up to take steps which appear to be designed to secure support for himself and to be discouraging to creditors who take a contrary view e.g. by his indicating that the petition for a winding up by the court should be opposed. He ought not even to give the appearance of being one-sided: *Re Lubin, Rosen and Associates Ltd* [1973] 1 All ER 577 at 580 (per Megarry J).

Where, before the presentation of a petition for the winding up of a company by the court, a resolution has been passed by the company for voluntary winding up, the winding up of the company is deemed to have commenced at the time of the passing of the resolution: Companies Act 1985, s. 524 (1). Unless the court, on proof of fraud or mistake, directs otherwise, all proceedings taken in the voluntary winding up are deemed to have been validly taken: ibid., s. 524 (1).

Power to stay winding up

The liquidator or any contributory or creditor may apply for the voluntary winding up to be stayed, and the court may make an order staying the proceedings either altogether or for a limited time, on such terms and conditions as it thinks fit: ibid., s. 549 (1), as extended by ss. 596 and 602.

The court will, in normal circumstances, generally exercise its discretion to grant a stay only where the application shows that (i) each creditor has either been paid in full or satisfactory provision for him to be paid in full is to be made or he consented to the stay or is otherwise bound not to object to it; (ii) the liquidator's position is fully safeguarded, either by paying him the proper amount of his expenses or sufficiently securing payment; and (iii) each member either consents to the stay, or is otherwise bound not to object to it, or there is secured to him the right to receive all that he would have received if the winding up had proceeded to its conclusion: *Re Calgary and Edmonton Land Co Ltd* [1975] 1 All ER 1046 at 1051 (per Megarry J).

Appointment of liquidator

A liquidator must be appointed, his principal duties being to take the company's property into his custody, to pay the company's debts and to distribute the balance. (*See* LIQUIDATOR).

Dissolution of company

In due course, the company will be dissolved. (*See* DISSOLUTION OF COMPANY).

Vote. The right of a shareholder to express his decision for or against a proposed resolution. (*See* RESOLUTION).

In so far as the articles of the company do not make other provision, in the case of a company originally having a share capital, every member has one vote in respect of each share or each £10 of stock held by him, and in any other case, every member shall have one vote: Companies Act 1985, s. 370 (1), (6).

Unless otherwise provided by the articles, the person, who appears on the register as the holder of a share, is the only person entitled to vote in respect of it: *Wise v Lansdell* [1921] 1 Ch 420. A shareholder who is bankrupt can exercise the right to vote so long as his name remains on the register, but he must do so in accordance with the direction of his trustee in bankruptcy: *Morgan v Gray* [1953] 1 All ER 213.

A shareholder may be ordered by the court to vote in the manner indicated by some other person e.g. a mortgagee of shares: *Puddephat v Leith* [1916] 1 Ch 200. When a shareholder is voting for or against a resolution, he is voting as a person, owing no fiduciary duty to the company, who is exercising his own right of property to vote as he thinks fit; he does not cast his vote as an agent of the company: *Northern Counties Securities Ltd v Jackson and Steeple Ltd* [1974] 2 All ER 625 at 635 (per Walton J). But he is not entitled, as of right, to exercise his vote in any way he pleases, for such a right is 'subject to equitable considerations', e.g. where voting in a certain way would amount to oppression of another shareholder: *Clemens v Clemens Brothers Ltd* [1976] 2 All ER 268.

Subject to any rights or restrictions attached to any shares, on a show of hands every member who (being an individual) is present in person or (being a corporation) is present by a duly authorised representative, not being himself a member entitled to vote, shall have one vote and on a poll every member shall have one vote for every share of which he is the holder: Table A, art. 54. (*See* POLL; SHOW OF HANDS).

In the case of joint holders the vote of the senior who tenders a vote, whether in person or by proxy, shall be accepted to the exclusion of the votes of the other joint holders; and seniority shall be determined by the order in which the names of the holders stand in the register of members: Table A, art. 55.

A member in respect of whom an order has been made by any court having jurisdiction (whether in the United Kingdom or elsewhere) in matters concerning mental disorder may vote, whether on a show of hands or on a poll, by his receiver, and any such receiver may, on a poll, vote by proxy: ibid., art. 56.

No member shall vote at any general meeting or at any separate meeting of the holders of any class of shares in the company, either in person or by proxy, in respect of any share held by him unless all moneys presently payable by him in respect of that share have been paid: ibid., art. 57.

No objection shall be raised to the qualification of any voter except at the meeting, or adjourned meeting at which the vote objected to is tendered, and every vote not disallowed at the meeting shall be valid: ibid., art. 58. Any objection made in due time shall be referred to the chairman whose decision shall be final and conclusive: ibid., art. 58.

On a poll votes may be given either personally or by proxy: ibid., art. 59. A member may appoint more than one proxy to attend on the same occasion: ibid., art. 59.

W

Winding up. The process of the liquidation of the company.

The winding up of a company may be (a) by the court (*see* WINDING UP BY THE COURT); or (b) voluntary (*see* VOLUNTARY WINDING UP); or (c) subject to the supervision of the court (*see* WINDING UP SUBJECT TO SUPERVISION OF COURT): Companies Act 1985, s. 501 (1).

Winding up, commencement of. *See* COMMENCEMENT OF WINDING UP.

Winding up, voluntary. *See* VOLUNTARY WINDING UP.

Winding up by the court. A bringing to an end of the activities of a company by the court.

Jurisdiction of the court

A company may be wound up by the court if

(a) the company has by special resolution resolved that the company be wound up by the court (*See* SPECIAL RESOLUTION);

(b) being a public company which was registered as such on its original incorporation, the company has not been issued with a certificate under s. 117 and more than 1 year has expired since it was so registered (*See* CERTIFICATE AS TO POWER TO DO BUSINESS; PUBLIC COMPANY);

(c) the company does not commence its business within a year from its incorporation or suspends its business for a whole year;

(d) the number of members is reduced below 2;

(e) the company is unable to pay its debts;

(f) the court is of opinion that it is just and equitable that the company should be wound up: Companies Act 1985, s. 517 (1).

A company is deemed unable to pay its debts

(a) if a creditor (by assignment or otherwise) to whom the company is indebted in a sum exceeding £750 then due has served on the company, by leaving it at the company's registered office, a written demand requiring the company to pay the sum so due and the company has for 3 weeks thereafter neglected to pay the sum or to secure or compound for it to the reasonable satisfaction of the creditor; or

(b) if execution or other process issued on a judgment is returned unsatisfied in whole or in part; or

(c) if it is proved to the satisfaction of the court that the company is unable to pay its debts: ibid., s. 518 (1).

In determining whether a company is unable to pay its debts, the court must take into account the contingent and prospective liabilities of the company: ibid., s. 518 (1).

The words 'just and equitable' in s. 517 (1) must not be construed so as to include matters *ejusdem generis* as the preceding paragraphs of the section: *Ebrahimi v Westbourne Galleries Ltd* [1972] 2 All ER 492 at 496, HL (per Lord Wilberforce). The words enable the court to subject the exercise of legal rights to equitable considerations i.e. considerations of a personal character arising between one individual and another, which make it unjust or inequitable to insist on legal rights or to exercise them in a particular way: ibid., at 500 (per Lord Wilberforce).

The court's power to wind up a company on the 'just and equitable' ground has been exercised (i) where the whole object of the company is fraudulent: *Re T. E. Brinsmead & Sons* [1897] 1 Ch 406, CA; (ii) where the company is carrying on business at a loss: *Re Factage Parisien Ltd* (1865) 5 New Rep 227; (iii) where the substratum of the company has disappeared: *Re German Date Coffee Co* (1882) 20 Ch D 169, CA; (iv) where there is a deadlock between 2 members of the company, each of whom controls half the voting power: *Re Yenidje Tobacco Co Ltd* [1916] 2 Ch 426, CA; (v) where, in the case of a private company, one director treats the business of the company as his own: *Re Davis and Collett* [1935] Ch 693, (vi) where the company is a mere 'bubble': *Re Anglo Greek Steam Co* (1886) LR 2 Eq 1; (vii) where the company is insolvent: *Re Diamond Fuel Co* (1879) 13 Ch D 400; (viii) where the business of the company is being carried on for the benefit of the debenture holders: *Re Chic Ltd* [1905] 2 Ch 345 (*see* DEBENTURE); (ix) where a director of a private company, which was originally a partnership, is removed even though the removal is effected in accordance with the provisions of the articles: *Ebrahimi v Westbourne Galleries Ltd* (supra).

Petition for winding up

A petition for the winding up of the company by the court may be presented by a person entitled to do so. (*See* PETITION FOR WINDING UP).

Winding up order

When the petition has been heard, the court may make a winding up order. (*See* WINDING UP ORDER).

First meeting of creditors and contributories

The Official Receiver summons spearate meetings of the company's creditors and contributories to determine whether applications should be made to the court (a) to appoint a committee of inspection (*see* COMMITTEE OF INSPECTION); and (b) to appoint a liquidator in place of the Official Receiver: Companies Act 1985, s. 533 (3), 546 (1). (*See* LIQUIDATOR; OFFICIAL RECEIVER).

Liquidator

The liquidator is given various powers and has certain duties in the winding up of the company especially with regard to the payment of its debts. (*See* LIQUIDATOR).

Dissolution of the company

The liquidator may apply to the court for the dissolution of the company (*see* DISSOLUTION OF COMPANY), or the Registrar of Companies may strike the company off the register. (*See* STRIKING OFF REGISTER). In certain circumstances, the name of the company may be restored to the register. (*See* RESTORATION TO REGISTER).

Winding-up order. An order by the court bringing to an end the activities of the company.

On the making of a winding up order, a copy of the order must forthwith be forwarded by the company to the Registrar of Companies: Companies Act 1985, s. 525 (1).

When a winding up order has been made, no action or proceeding must be proceeded with or commenced against the company except by leave of the court and subject to·such terms as the court may impose: ibid., s. 525 (2). The term 'proceeding' includes an interpleader summons: *Eastern Holdings Establishment of Vaduz v Singer and Friedlander* [1967] 2 All ER 1192.

A defendant, when sued by a company, can, without the leave of the court, set up a cross-claim for liquidated or unliquidated damages: *Langley Construction (Brixham) Ltd v Wells* [1969] 2 All ER 46, CA. But he must obtain leave from the court if he counter-claims for an account and a declaration as to an amount in excess of the company's claim: ibid.

An order for winding up a company operates in favour of all the creditors and of all the contributories of the company as if made on the joint petition of a creditor and of a contributory: Companies Act 1985, s. 525 (4).

A winding up order operates as a discharge of the employees of the company: *Measures Brothers Ltd v Measures* [1910] 1 Ch 336, CA.

Submission of statement of affairs

When a winding up order has been made, a statement as to the affairs of the company in the prescribed form showing its assets, debts and liabilities must be submitted to the Official Receiver: Companies Act 1985, s. 528 (1). (*See* OFFICIAL RECEIVER; STATEMENT OF AFFAIRS).

Notification that company is in liquidation

Where a company is being wound up by the court, every invoice, order for goods or business letter issued by or on behalf of the company or the liquidator or a receiver or manager of the company's property must contain a statement that the company is being wound up: Companies Act 1985, s. 637 (1). If default is made in complying with this provision, the company, and any officer of the company, any liquidator, any receiver or manager who knowingly and wilfully authorises or permits the default are liable on summary conviction to a fine not exceeding one-fifth of the statutory maximum: ibid., ss. 637 (2), 730 and Sch. 24.

Power to stay winding up

The court may at any time after an order for winding up, on the application either of the liquidator or the Official Receiver or any creditor or contributory, and on proof to the satisfaction of the court that all proceedings in relation to the winding up ought to be stayed, make an order staying the proceedings, either altogether or for a limited time, on such terms and conditions as the court thinks fit: ibid., s. 549 (1). (*See* LIQUIDATOR; OFFICIAL RECEIVER). The court may, before making an order, require the Official Receiver to furnish to the court a report with respect to any facts or matters which are in his opinion relevant to the application: Companies Act 1985, s. 549 (2). A copy of every order staying the winding up must forthwith be forwarded by the company, or otherwise as may be prescribed, to the Registrar of Companies, who must enter it in his records relating to the company: ibid., s. 549 (3).

As a matter of practice, however, the court never grants a stay because as soon as a winding up order has been made, the Official Receiver has to ascertain (i) all the assets at the date of the order; (ii) the assets at the date of the presentation of the petition, and (iii) the liabilities of the company at the date of the order. If there was a stay of the order and there was an appeal, and the order was affirmed on appeal, the Official Receiver's ability to discover all these things would be very seriously hampered: *Re A and BC Chewing Gum Ltd* [1975] 1 All ER 1017 at 1029 (per Plowman J).

Rescission of winding up order

The inherent power of the court to revoke or vary a winding up order before it is drawn up is one which ought to be exercised with great caution: *Practice Note* [1971] 1 All ER 62. Although it is a matter of the court's discretion in each case, an application to rescind a winding up order will not normally be entertained by the court unless it is made within 3 or 4 days of the making of the order, and is supported by an affidavit of assets and liabilities: ibid. If an application is made later than this, the affidavit should also establish the exceptional circumstances relied on as justifying the application: ibid.

The application will be entertained only if it is made by a creditor, a contributory or the company jointly with a creditor or contributory: *Practice Note* [1971] 2 All ER 700. In the case of an unsuccessful application, the costs of the petitioning creditor and of supporting creditors will normally be ordered to be paid by the creditor or the contributory making or joining in the application, for otherwise, if the costs were made payable by the company, they would fall unfairly on the general body of the creditors: ibid.

Winding-up Rules. *See* COMPANIES (WINDING-UP) RULES 1949 (S.I. 1949 NO. 330).

Winding up subject to the supervision of the court. A voluntary winding up which is continued under the general control of the court. This type of winding up is rarely used.

When a company has passed a resolution for voluntary winding up (*see* RESOLUTION FOR VOLUNTARY WINDING UP), the court may make an order that the voluntary winding up shall continue but subject to such supervision of the court, and with such liberty for creditors, contributories, or others to apply to the court, and generally on such terms and conditions as the court thinks just: Companies Act 1985, s. 606.

A winding up subject to the supervision of the court is deemed for the purpose of the Companies Act 1985, s. 522 (avoidance of disposition of property) and s. 523 (avoidance of attachments), to be a winding up by the court: ibid., s. 608. (*See* PETITION FOR WINDING UP).

Where an order is made for a winding up subject to supervision, the court may by that or any subsequent order appoint an additional liquidator: Companies Act 1985, s. 609 (1). (*See* LIQUIDATOR). A liquidator so appointed has the same powers, is subject to the same obligations, and in all respects stands in the same position as if he had been duly appointed in a voluntary winding up: Companies Act 1985, s. 609 (2). The court may remove any liquidator so appointed by the court or continued under the supervision order, and fill any vacancy occasioned by the removal or by death or resignation: ibid., s. 609 (3).

Where an order is made for a winding up subject to supervision, the liquidator may (subject to any restrictions imposed by the court) exercise all his powers without the court's sanction or intervention, in the same manner as if the company were being wound up altogether voluntarily: ibid., s. 610 (1).

But the powers
  (i) to pay any classes of creditors in full,
  (ii) to make any compromise or arrangement with creditors; and
(iii) to compromise debts and claims
cannot be exercised by the liquidator except with the sanction of the court or, in a case where before the order the winding up was a creditors' voluntary winding up, with the sanction of the court or the committee of inspection, or (if there is no such committee) a meeting of the creditors: ibid., s. 610 (2). (*See* COMMITTEE OF INSPECTION;

CREDITORS' VOLUNTARY WINDING UP).

Certain sections of the Act do not apply in the case of a winding up subject to the supervision of the court: Companies Act 1985, s. 610 (3) Sch. 18.